The Cost of Voting in the American States

STUDIES IN GOVERNMENT
AND PUBLIC POLICY

The Cost of Voting in the American States

Michael J. Pomante II
Scot Schraufnagel
Quan Li

University Press of Kansas

Published by the University Press of Kansas (Lawrence, Kansas 66045), which was organized by the Kansas Board of Regents and is operated and funded by Emporia State University, Fort Hays State University, Kansas State University, Pittsburg State University, the University of Kansas, and Wichita State University.

The views expressed in this publication are those of the authors and do not necessarily reflect the views of their employers.

Library of Congress Cataloging-in-Publication Data
Names: Pomante, Michael J., II, 1982– author. | Schraufnagel, Scot, author.
  | Li, Quan, 1966– author.
Title: The cost of voting in the American states / Michael J. Pomante II,
  Scot Schraufnagel, and Quan Li.
Description: Lawrence : University Press of Kansas, 2023. | Series: Studies in government and
  public policy | Includes bibliographical references and index.
Identifiers: LCCN 2023016740 (print) | LCCN 2023016741 (ebook)
  ISBN 9780700635917 (cloth)   ISBN 9780700635924 (paperback)   ISBN 9780700635931 (ebook)
Subjects: LCSH: Voter registration—United States—States. | Voter suppression—United
  States—States. | Elections—United States—States—Statistics. | Political participation—
  Social aspects—United States—States. | Minorities—Political activity—United States—States.
  | Identification cards—Law and legislation—United States. | Election law—United States. |
  BISAC: POLITICAL SCIENCE / Political Process / Campaigns & Elections | SOCIAL
  SCIENCE / Discrimination
Classification: LCC KF4898 .P66 2023 (print) | LCC KF4898 (ebook) | DDC
  342.73/07—dc23/eng/20230523
LC record available at https://lccn.loc.gov/2023016740.
LC ebook record available at https://lccn.loc.gov/2023016741.

British Library Cataloguing-in-Publication Data is available.

Printed in the United States of America

10 9 8 7 6 5 4 3 2 1

The paper used in this publication is acid free and meets the minimum requirements of the American National Standard for Permanence of Paper for Printed Library Materials Z39.48–1992.

To my wife, Becky, for her continued support and encouragement.
Michael J. Pomante II

To my brother Jeff Schraufnagel
Scot Schraufnagel

To my wife, Jin, and daughter, Audrey
Quan Li

Contents

Introduction

The Fifteenth Amendment to the US Constitution, ratified in 1870, gave Black males in the United States the right to vote. Unfortunately, this caused many American state legislatures, especially in the South, to revise their election laws to prevent formerly enslaved people from voting and wielding any significant political power. As a result, the country entered a protracted period of racial discrimination in voting laws that went unaddressed until the 1960s. The first significant national government effort to address the issue came with the Civil Rights Act of 1964. The law explicitly prohibits voter discrimination based on race, ethnicity, religion, color, and sex. Yet the language of the 1964 law was sufficiently vague to allow those intent on disenfranchising people of color to find ways to work around the decree. Finally, to close some loopholes, Congress passed, and President Lyndon B. Johnson signed, the Voting Rights Act (VRA) of 1965.

The VRA tightened the legal language and addressed the most prominent forms of discrimination that had defined voting practices since the 1870s. For example, the act's section 2 succinctly prohibits all states and local governments from imposing any voting law that results in discrimination against racial and language minorities.[1] Specifically, this section of the 1965 act focuses on the effect of election laws on particular subgroups, regardless of the law's stated intent. Due to the increase of new state laws, which appear to have discriminatory effects, this book also focuses on how state laws influence the electoral participation of certain groups, regardless of whether the laws ostensibly serve some other purpose. As was the case in 1965, our concern is with the consequences of state election law.

Sections 4 and 5 of the 1965 law specified that those electoral jurisdictions with a history of voter discrimination needed to obtain preclearance from the national government before changing their election policies and practices. Section 4(b) laid out a coverage formula that identified the specific states and electoral districts with a history of discriminatory voting practices. The law stated that any state or electoral jurisdiction that used a "test or device" to restrict the opportunity to register to vote would require preclearance for changes to any policy. Moreover, the law held that jurisdictions where less than half of eligible citizens registered to vote, or less than half of eligible citizens voted in the 1964 presidential contest, were restricting the right to vote. Election jurisdictions that met the criteria in section 4(b) would need approval from the federal government before changing their election laws. An explanation of the pre-clearance process appeared in section 5 of the act; the US Attorney General's office and the US District Court for the District of Columbia were tasked with determining if any proposed new law was potentially discriminatory.

The initial formula identified Alabama, Alaska, Georgia, Louisiana, Mississippi, South Carolina, and Virginia as states with questionable election laws and practices. In addition, the formula identified electoral districts in Arizona, Hawaii, Idaho, and North Carolina. These states and districts needed preclearance due to past electoral performance. Reapplication of the coverage formula occurred in 1968 and 1972, which updated the list of states and electoral districts needing preclearance. Notably, the act's original provisions expired in 1970, five years after passage. However, in 1975 President Gerald Ford signed a law that extended the coverage formula for seven years. Then, in 1982, Congress and President Ronald Reagan extended the timeframe, this time adding twenty-five years. In 2006 another twenty-five-year extension passed Congress by a vote of 390 to 33 in the House of Representatives and 98 to 0 in the Senate. President George W. Bush signed the legislation extending the coverage formula during his second term in office, with overwhelming bipartisan support. However, in April 2010 Shelby County, Alabama, filed suit, arguing that the formula used to identify states with discriminatory election practices was outdated. Despite losing their case in the US District Court for the District of Columbia and the US Court of Appeals for the District of Columbia Circuit, the county challenged the legality of the coverage formula in front of the US Supreme Court.

In a five to four decision, delivered in June 2013, the US Supreme Court in *Shelby County v. Holder* ruled that section 4 of the VRA of 1965 had become dated. The court held that Congress would need to refresh the law and enact a new coverage formula to maintain the preclearance provision. The position of a slim majority of the court was that Congress needed to decide anew what jurisdictions would need to obtain preclearance if they wished to keep the practice in place. Since the Supreme Court ruling, no president, or legislative leader, has had sufficient influence or resolve to reformulate the law.

Specifically, the majority Supreme Court opinion argued that section 4 of the VRA was outdated because the country elected its first Black president in 2008. With Obama's election and reelection in 2012, the court majority believed that the United States had reached a postracial moment and that preclearance was no longer necessary. However, Ruth Bader Ginsburg's dissenting opinion noted that "throwing out preclearance when it has worked and is continuing to stop discriminatory changes is like throwing away your umbrella in a rainstorm because you are not getting wet."[2]

Notably, within twenty-four hours of the Supreme Court ruling in 2013, Texas, which had needed preclearance, announced it would implement a photo identification requirement at polling locations. A law to that effect had passed the state's legislature in 2011, but the existing preclearance provision had prevented the state from implementing the new law.[3] Two other former preclearance states, Mississippi and Alabama, also began to enforce photo ID laws previously precluded by the VRA (Lopez 2014). The publicly stated motivation of state legislators was the prevention of voter fraud. Yet, there has been little evidence of fraud (Minnite 2010; Levitt 2014). Moreover, scholars have long argued that the "costs" of voting (Downs 1957) prevent many eligible voters from participating in elections. And one wonders how many voters can afford the higher costs of committing voter fraud (Alvarez et al. 2008). Near the end of this book, in chapter 7, we look for and do not find any evidence that more accessible voting increases voter fraud in the contemporary United States.

Beyond changes to voter ID laws, post-*Holder* states began to introduce and pass other laws in the name of election security. The true motives behind increased restrictions are difficult to determine. Yet, comments by a Republican Party official preceding the 2016 presidential election point to potentially partisan and racial motives. In October 2013 Don Yelton, a North Carolina Republican Executive Committee member, boasted about the state's new voter identification law on a late-night talk show. He noted, "If it [voter ID] hurts a bunch of lazy Blacks, so be it." He continued, "the law is going to kick the Democrats in the butt."[4] We provide other "open mic" comments by Republican lawmakers justifying voting restrictions in chapter 4, when we wrestle with explaining state variation in the cost of voting. The comments, at minimum, mark clear attempts to gain partisan advantage.

Overall, there is a seemingly sensible resolution to the impulse by state legislators to gain electoral advantage by regularly remaking state election laws.[5]

A reasonable solution would be minimal national standards for voter inclusion or access to the ballot box. However, any bipartisan determination to produce standards is seemingly lacking in the third decade of the twenty-first century. Arguably, before the federal government can produce national standards, scholars and practitioners must appreciate that election policies have consequences. Concerns related to voter turnout are most obvious. Yet, there are broader worries regarding the quality of representation and subsequent public policies. Therefore, after establishing and attempting to understand cross-state variation in the cost of voting, this book attempts to better understand the consequences of election restrictions.

A leading premise of this volume is that providing citizens a voice in government through voting is an essential part of quality governance, as it establishes regime and system legitimacy. Moreover, when elections occur without incident, this bodes well for democratic authenticity and political stability. In other words, an engaged and peaceful voting process is consistent with competent democracy, adept governance, and a more politically secure society. These contentions are well-regarded truisms of classic democratic theory, ideas that have existed since the earliest recorded experiences with democracy, over twenty-four hundred years ago in Athens (Dahl 2006, 191).

Further, when eligible voters can easily exercise the franchise in consequential elections, this should lead to greater citizen worth and greater acceptance of government action. Again, these are important assumptions that encourage the research contained in this book. Although threats to governing legitimacy have long existed, recent attacks on electoral fairness led by a losing presidential candidate after the 2020 election make this inquiry more urgent. When something other than votes determines an election outcome, citizen participation in elections becomes farcical, which becomes a prescription for protest, unrest, and even regime upheaval. When or how this can occur warrants serious attention. However, any investigation must be fact-based and not the product of the imagination of a losing candidate or the fantasies of unfounded conspiracy theories held by the losing candidate's supporters.

For many years, people have studied the stability of democratic governance (Dahl 1971; Stillman 1974; Lowenthal 1976), with considerable focus placed on the "democratizing" process (Murphy 1999; Fails and Pierce 2010). Historically, many have considered the United States a standard-bearer for democratic institution-building and governing legitimacy. The presumption is that political institutions in the United States are valid and enjoy widespread citizen approval. Yet, what are we to make of periods of unrest like those the country experienced in 2020 and 2021? Many recall mass demonstrations and rioting throughout the country in the summer of 2020 and the turmoil in Washington, DC, and state capitols on January 6, 2021.

While there was significant unrest throughout 2020 and early 2021, not all the protests and riots were the result of alleged election conspiracies. However, the individuals involved in these events were certainly questioning the legitimacy of governing institutions. For example, during the summer of 2020, protesters railed against discriminatory police brutality practices. And then in early 2021, individuals who believed the presidential election had been stolen attacked the Capitol. Notably, the two protest waves, which took place within a roughly six-month window, were organized by citizens from opposite ends of the ideological spectrum. Today, both the Left and the Right in the United States are questioning government legitimacy. In the case of protests over police brutality, one can assume these citizens also had little faith that they could address their concerns at the ballot box in the next election cycle.

There are many questions about the quality of elections in democracies, and these concerns regularly prompt scholarly investigations. In the United States, we wonder if the political system is vulnerable to systematic political unrest in the same manner as it routinely occurs in newer democracies. Moreover, is the United States still the standard-bearer of a competent electoral process? More specifically, what threats to electoral legitimacy exist in the United States? Is election fraud a genuine concern? Alternatively, is electoral exclusion or barriers to voting the principal matter? To be sure, in the contemporary United States, when citizens question government legitimacy, the potential for unease and unrest is genuine. We witnessed this in 2020 and 2021. However, we wonder to what extent electoral exclusion fuels these protests. For example, there was a relatively high voter turnout in the 2020 presidential election. Yet approximately 34 percent of eligible voters did not cast a ballot and had no say in election outcomes that year.

Our concerns for political stability in the United States predate 2020 and the attempted insurrection. Indeed, this work began long ago, and the more recent developments only prove a point we have tried to make for some time. Political instability in the United States is a genuine concern. Recent events have only created an unanticipated urgency for our work. We have long imagined the United States was not so different from other countries in terms of the potential for regime instability. The basis for democracy, ruled by competing factions, is wrought with potential disruption. Indeed, the Founding Fathers, designers of much of the current regime, worried about the same. Things spiraling out of control on January 6, 2021, should not have come as a surprise.

Notably, scholars have been expressing concerns over increasing political party polarization, especially regarding the possibility that this leads to political unrest (Hare and Poole 2014). Too often, the polarization of political elites and their followers creates an "us versus them" mentality. This worldview is consistent with base tribalism or other divisions based on religion or class (Whitt et al. 2021). Under an intense party polarization scenario, losing is unacceptable and winning at any cost becomes acceptable (Arbatli and Rosenberg 2021). Concern for the collective, or the greater good, is secondary or perhaps lost entirely. In these instances, if political operatives do not consider elections capable of producing meaningful change, then wildly diverging worldviews have the potential to add fuel to smoldering anxieties.

Until recently, many assumed the United States, a leader in democratic institution building, was less vulnerable than other countries to electoral chaos and broad concerns for regime stability. Unfortunately, recent events suggest this may not be the case. For the first time in US history, we had a losing presidential candidate blatantly, unabashedly, and consistently questioning the legitimacy of the electoral process. Political observers recognize such actions as commonplace worldwide in authoritarian or pseudo-democratic regimes. These regimes often toy with democratic institution-building and free elections but keep a steady eye on the outcome of elections to ensure the governing party remains in power.

In the United States, from a historical perspective, we must consider the unrest associated with the 2020 election ironic. There certainly have been much closer presidential contests than the Trump versus Biden race. The elections of 1824, 1876, 1888, 2000, and 2016 come to mind. In each instance, the losing presidential candidate received more popular votes than the Electoral College winner. In 1876 and 2000, the losing candidates, Governor Samuel J. Tilden and Vice President Al Gore, won the popular vote. Election irregularities in the state of Florida were primarily responsible for each of them losing the Electoral College contest. Yet ultimately Tilden and Gore conceded. Historically, in presidential contests, leadership and discretion have won out. The candidate losing the election eventually accepted the outcome, allowing for a peaceful transition of the people and political party in power. Recent events, however, suggest this may no longer be the case in the United States.

Scholars have long recognized that meaningful electoral participation is a core tenet of competent democratic governance (Dahl 1971; Powell 1982). William Riker, for his part, argues that "the essential democratic institution is the ballot box" and that therein lies government accountability (1965, 25).[6] Accordingly, concern for the ability of citizens to effect change through elections has been at the forefront for reformers, academics, and concerned individuals who value political equality, justice, fairness, and stability. Indeed, many readily recognize that citizen efficacy, or the feeling that one can change things, is essential to civil harmony in societies worldwide (Ekman 2009; on this phenomenon in Russia, see Henry 2012).

Furthermore, scholars note that when citizens lack political efficacy, it can lead to the belief that the system does not work for them (Bowler and Donovan 2002; Chamberlain 2012). For example, suppose people no longer consider voting a viable option for promoting meaningful political change. In that case, attacks on political institutions like those recently in the United States will likely continue in subsequent election cycles. If, on the other hand, citizens feel elections give them a meaningful voice and a peaceable and effective role in governance, there ought to be less potential for political unrest. To examine how open states are to meaningful citizen efficacy this volume focuses on the *cost of voting*.

By "cost," we mean the time, energy, and hassle required to vote. We suggest that when the costs are higher, this exacerbates the problems associated with electoral illegitimacy. We fully appreciate that the difficulties of establishing democratic authenticity are considerable and that our work is taking on only one aspect of broader concerns. Yet, scholars often tackle significant problems in a piecemeal fashion. Therefore, we must content ourselves with addressing one piece of the puzzle. Nevertheless, we believe our work on electoral-institutional inclusion, integrity, and legitimacy is an important place to start.

Our immediate concern is with the cost of voting. It seems particularly important that everyone who wishes to vote has a reasonably easy time doing so. On the contrary, if state legislatures go out of their way to make voting more difficult, this seems like a prescription for lower voter turnout, less citizen efficacy, and increased political unrest. We hold that politicians who seek to restrict voting for partisan advantage engage in troubling actions. Efforts to curtail meaningful competition via the demobilization of eligible voters run counter to all the basic prescriptions of classic democratic theory. Moreover, the appearance of partisan manipulation is likely as damning as success in electoral scheming. Specifically, suppose one party has altered election laws that allow them to win elections systematically; citizens will likely lose confidence in the legitimacy of elections. On the other hand, the alternation of the political party in control would likely increase electoral legitimacy and citizen satisfaction.

Book Overview

In chapter 1, we provide a short history of some major controversies surrounding voting rights in the United States. We do this to provide the reader with context for our more contemporary concerns. Historically, the motivation for many voting restrictions has been nativist sentiments (Bentele and O'Brien 2013), often accompanied by the perception of a racial threat (Behrens, Uggen, and Manza 2003). Those in dominant social positions have worried that minority groups threaten the status quo arrangements, which work to their advantage. We must consider the possibility that these sentiments motivate many current efforts to restrict voting.

In the end, it is difficult to prove racial motives or intent. However, we look for discriminatory outcomes and test whether variation in the cost of voting has implications for the demobilization of specific subpopulations. In other words, we seek to learn whether voting restrictions disproportionately disadvantage certain groups. Upfront, we can easily recognize that states particularly harm the undereducated when they make the voting processes more complicated. Moreover, if we can suppose that certain minority subpopulations are more likely to be undereducated, there is the possibility of a link between voting restrictions and minority group demobilization, regardless of an overt racial motive.

Having provided the historical backdrop for electoral exclusion, we measure state electoral-institutional climates since 1996 and discuss the implications of the uncovered variation. We began our analysis in 1996 for two primary reasons. First, 1996 was the first presidential election after the passage of the National Voter Registration Act of 1993, which established some important present-day national standards. Second, beginning with 1996 assures the availability of reliable data. We focus our study on the seven presidential election cycles from 1996 to 2020, exploring variations in the relative cost of voting in the American states. Our comprehensive measurement strategy produces state-specific values that are reliable, defensible, and that others see as reasonable.

Chapter 2 lays out the specifics of our approach to measuring the cost of voting across the fifty states. Specifically, the chapter chronicles the many state laws affecting the time and energy required to get and stay registered to vote and cast a ballot on Election Day. In 1996, we started with six distinct issue areas. As states changed election laws, this grew to nine issue areas that now comprise the 2020 Cost of Voting Index (COVI). In the 2020 version, five categories tap voter registration laws, and four issue areas address the actual casting of ballots. Changing our measurement strategy by growing the relevant issues areas is necessary to produce a comprehensive picture of the cost of voting over time. It seems state legislators have not tired of finding new ways to make voting either more accessible or more difficult. The advantages of a consistent or static measurement strategy notwithstanding, we opt for trying to capture the contemporary electoral climate in each state in each presidential election year.

Chapter 3 displays the COVI values. We are confident we have obtained reasonable and reliable scores for each American state over roughly twenty-five years. We display raw values, indicating where voting is more restricted, along with the relative state rank. Movement in state ranks is particularly enlightening because they allow us to trace where, when, and how states have made voting more accessible. Notably, state ranks move in a manner consistent with the intuition of political observers. To check the validity of our measurement strategies, we look to see if specific changes in state law correspond with changes in state rank. We discuss these legal modifications and the corresponding deviations in state rank. Finally, the chapter looks closely at movement in rank for a sample of states. It breaks the fifty states into quintiles, distinguishing the class of states that make voting the easiest or most difficult.

Chapter 4 tests the relationship between partisan control of the state legislative process and voter restrictions. We initially imagined that the Republican Party's sway over state legislatures would lead to higher COVI values and state ranks throughout our study. However, Republican control alone does not explain higher COVI values until the most recent election cycles (2016 and 2020). Yet, when we interact Republican influence over the state legislative process with the size of state Black populations and growing state Hispanic populations, we find more restrictive electoral climates going back to 1996. These findings suggest that the motivation behind some state law changes may not be generous. Specifically, some laws appear to have had punitive intentions, such as creating obstacles to voting for minority populations.

Chapter 5 turns to voter turnout to check if there is a disproportionate demobilization of individuals representing minority groups when the variable cost of voting is higher. In this instance, we find that more restrictive voting laws particularly affect Hispanics. We also learn that states where the Black population has grown the fastest in recent years see lower reported voter turnout when COVI values are higher. Still more, we find that restrictive voting laws disproportionately prevent the undereducated from voting. Last, we learn that minorities and the undereducated are significantly less likely to vote when they do not own their own home. The latter finding, we suggest, occurs because nonhomeowners are more mobile and must reregister to vote more often than homeowners.

In chapter 6, we learn that Black and Hispanic citizens are less likely to run for and hold public office in states with a more restrictive electoral climate. We also find that when COVI values are higher, and individuals representing these groups do run for public office, they are more likely, on average, to receive less electoral support. In addition, these minority representatives are more likely to lose electoral contests under more restrictive voting scenarios. This trend suggests that higher voting costs have real-world and immediate implications for demographic representation in elected office. In auxiliary analyses, we find less representation of Black and Hispanic residents, as well as women, in state legislatures with a higher COVI value.

Chapter 7 tackles the first Big Lie that Republican state lawmakers have used to justify more restrictions since 2020. Specifically, we check to see if voter fraud is more rampant in states that make voting easier. Conversely, we check to see if restrictive voting practices reduce the occurrences of fraud. To explore the issue of voter fraud, we use data from the Heritage Foundation, which has worked to uncover all instances of fraud. In the end, we do not find a relationship between reported fraud and lower COVI values. Put differently, when states change rank and make voting relatively more or less restricted, there is no corresponding change in the number of fraud cases identified by the Heritage Foundation.

Chapter 8 dives into the second Big Lie that Republican and Democratic Party operatives have accepted, specifically, that more accessible voting benefits the Democratic Party and more restrictive voting helps the Republican Party. To address this topic, we investigated the 2020 election and found that President Donald Trump did better in 2020 than in 2016 when voting was easier. In other words, Trump performed worse in 2020 when states maintained a more restrictive election posture.

Lastly, in the conclusion, we summarize the lessons from this exploration of state election laws. Ultimately, we suggest a new coverage formula that Congress could use to refresh the preclearance requirements in the Voting Rights Act of 1965. Using this new approach to decide which states need federal oversight, we find that several previous preclearance states are unlikely to need oversight because they have made progress in making voting more accessible. However, we find that some previous preclearance states, and some new states, would benefit from federal oversight of their election law changes due to seemingly unjustified efforts to make voting more burdensome.

Putting COVI to work to address questions related to competent and legitimate elections, we uncover some troubling insights. Many of the findings give us cause for concern. Traditionally underrepresented groups, such as those without a high school diploma and renters, are discouraged from voting when the cost of voting is higher. This trend, in turn, aggravates the underrepresentation of Black and Hispanic voters, who are more likely to be undereducated and not own their homes. Moreover, the targeted demobilization of minority citizens remains a genuine concern. Finally, our findings indicate the possibility of civil rights abuses similar to those that have occurred throughout US history.

Suppose the maintenance and modification of state election laws effectively discriminate. In that case, this is consistent with the racial threat arguments academics, and others, have been making (King and Wheelock 2007; Enos 2016). Scholars propose that "racialization occurs when Whites use their disproportionate power to implement state control over minorities and, in the face of a growing minority population, encourage more rigorous, racialized practices to protect their existing power and privileges" (Dollar 2014, 1). Specifically, Blalock

(1967) identifies three forms of racial threat—economic, political, and symbolic. Of the three, we are most interested in political threats. Blalock (1967) explains that a political threat emerges when Whites begin to fear the loss of political power. Although our research stops short of unequivocal proof of racist attempts to undermine equitable minority political participation, we have uncovered considerable evidence demonstrating the racist effects of more restrictive state election laws.

When we look for evidence that restricted voting prevents voter fraud, we find none. If electoral fraud were pervasive, one might reasonably justify more voting restrictions. However, the failure to find a relationship between the ease of voting and voter fraud leads one to conclude that there is little to defend the state's failure to adopt policies that make voting more accessible.

Perhaps most surprisingly, we failed to uncover systematic partisan advantage when states were more restrictive during the 2020 election cycle. In the current era, one might imagine Republican Party operatives have some insights that cause them to limit voting strategically to gain electoral benefits. We hold this as a real possibility. Historically, the Democratic Party effectively used voting restrictions to promote electoral success in the southern states for much of the post–Civil War era and into the second half of the twentieth century. Yet, in the contemporary period, Republican Party efforts to restrict voting failed to provide President Donald Trump an electoral boost in the 2020 election. In fact, the party did reasonably better than expected in the 2020 elections when states made voting easier in response to the global pandemic. In all, we look for and cannot find evidence that, across the board, the cost of voting correlates with either fraud or partisan advantage.

As noted, political instability born of electoral illegitimacy motivates this critical examination of each state's electoral-institutional climate. We know that voter turnout in the American states varies considerably throughout history and in the modern era. We imagine that state election laws are part of the explanation (Springer 2012). We recognize and appreciate that citizens in some states embrace a more participatory political ethos or culture (Lieske 2012). Yet, we envision that state election laws also have important implications. Moreover, we hold that higher voter turnout suggests a more competent electoral process. We argue that the failure to include people in the governing process has implications for quality democracy, regime stability, and socioeconomic prosperity.

1: A Brief History of Voting Restrictions in the United States

The 1876 presidential electoral contest between Republican Rutherford B. Hayes of Ohio and Democrat Samuel Tilden of New York was one of the closest in American history. An agreement settled the hotly contested election in Hayes's favor after he promised Democratic members of Congress to withdraw federal troops from Southern states (Brooks and Starks 2019, 69). There had been soldiers representing the newly re-United States in the former Confederate States of America since the South signed the cease-fire to end the Civil War in 1865.

The removal of federal troops from the South ended an era commonly referred to as Reconstruction (1865–1877). Policies and practices intended to rebuild infrastructure in the South and revive the southern economy defined the roughly twelve-year post–Civil War period. At the same time, an auxiliary motive of Reconstruction was to protect the voting rights of newly freed African American citizens. During the Reconstruction era, formerly enslaved people gained full citizenship and some ran for and won public office. Beginning with the 1866 midterm elections and ending with the withdrawal of federal troops in 1877, about two thousand Black leaders won and held seats in state and local government offices. Most of the electoral success was in South Carolina and Louisiana. Also, sixteen Black men served in the US Congress during Reconstruction.[1]

Unfortunately, post-Reconstruction, things changed.[2] Once the troops were gone, state legislatures in the South, dominated by white Democrats, scrambled to pass laws limiting formerly enslaved peoples' voting and citizenship rights (Logan 1997). Many of the laws, such as poll taxes, literacy tests, and grandfather clauses, worked to negate the rights of Black voters on criteria other than race. While southern legislators wrote these laws in such a way as to avoid suspect classifications, such as race, it was clear that the intention was to disenfranchise formerly enslaved individuals. As a result, the country entered a new period commonly referred to as Jim Crow and characterized by discriminatory voting practices. The term "Jim Crow" originates from a minstrel show character played by a white actor in blackface, which mocked and ridiculed individuals enslaved in the pre–Civil War era.

The discriminatory practices put in place by the Democratic Party during the Jim Crow era intended to undo the effects of the Thirteenth, Fourteenth, and Fifteenth Amendments to the US Constitution. The amendments, collectively known as the Civil War Amendments, were adopted between 1865 and 1870 and attempted to codify civil liberties and civil rights for Black citizens. Specifically, the Thirteenth Amendment forbade slavery; the Fourteenth Amendment gave formerly enslaved people equal protection under the law; and the Fifteenth Amendment enfranchised formerly enslaved men. Indeed, the amendments attempted to establish equal rights for all citizens of the United States. Notably, the Fifteenth Amendment explicitly addresses voting and equal access to the ballot box. Unfortunately, the former Confederate States' white population did not welcome the amendment's passage, as many believed Black citizens were not worthy of equal footing and should not have the right to participate in the political process.

Moreover, the Thirteenth Amendment still left open the possibility of slavery: one of the amendment's clauses forbids slavery "except as a Punishment for crime whereof the party shall have been duly convicted." White southern politicians used the clause's language to justify a new "legal" form of slavery to reestablish and maintain a coerced labor force. Notably, in the twenty-first century, scholars are still wrestling with the implications of the Thirteenth Amendment and how it forces prisoners to work for nothing or minimal wages (Gilmore 2000; Browne 2007; Smith and Hattery 2008). One commonly drawn conclusion is that the Thirteenth Amendment did not go far enough to end slavery in the United States. While the Thirteenth Amendment freed enslaved individuals, the Fourteenth Amendment sought to limit the political power of those who took part in the insurrection against the United States, many of whom were former enslavers.

Specifically, a clause in the Fourteenth Amendment prevented people who participated in "insurrection or rebellion" from holding public office. This clause allowed Republican Party members from the North to win many elected offices in the southern states, ushering in the era of "carpetbaggers." The derogatory term refers to a Republican from the North filling a carpetbag, or suitcase, with belongings, moving to the South, taking up residence, and running for public office in southern electoral districts. Within this context, the Democratic Party of the South fought back, for example through the passage of Black Codes, or state laws requiring formerly enslaved people to sign yearly labor contracts. If someone refused to sign such a contract, they broke the law and risked arrest and jail time (Bass 2001, 160; Worger 2004). As felons, they would subsequently lose their voting privileges, limiting support for Republican candidates from the North.

With the withdrawal of federal troops in 1876–1877, the Democratic Party found ways to regain control of state and local governments in the South. Moreover, and unfortunately, their tactics often involved violence and intimidation, including deploying paramilitary groups such as the White League and the Red Shirts. These groups and tactics intimidated Northern Republican legislators, scaring many out of office (Adamson 1983; Prince 2012). Furthermore, these same groups would use lynching and other violent means to discourage Black males from participating in elections.

Scholars have documented this historical narrative, which is not controversial (Bentele and O'Brien 2013). Less understood, however, is whether this style of systematic racism still exists in the United States. For example, are Southern states still more likely to make voting more difficult? If so, is it their intention to discriminate against Black or other minority voters? We address the first question head-on. Specifically, in chapters 2 and 3, we check if southern states, on average, maintain a more restrictive electoral-institutional climate than other states. However, the question of intent is trickier to tackle, but we look for evidence in chapters 4, 5, and 6.

Before we initiate these investigations, we think it essential to provide the historical context of efforts to discourage voting. Our hope is that the historical context clarifies the considerable precedent for existing discriminatory voting practices. This foundation alone is not evidence of discriminatory intent in the contemporary context but makes the possibility more plausible as it is the case that certain states, more than others, have gone out of their way historically to restrict voting to discourage certain groups from voting.

Jim Crow: 150+ Years of Voter Suppression

In the 1870s, the Democratic Party took back control of state legislatures in the South; these legislatures then began to pass laws restricting Black citizens' rights using criteria other than race. The laws were varied and far-reaching, including specific efforts to restrict voting. For example, they included poll taxes that required eligible citizens to pay a fee to vote.[3] Individuals could not participate if they could not afford the tax. For example, in 1917, in Jefferson Parish, Louisiana, voters were required to pay a tax of one dollar at the polling location on Election Day. In 2020 dollars this amounts to about twenty dollars. Unfortunately, the legacy of slavery had produced a Black underclass in the South, and the tax was not affordable to most Black citizens.

Moreover, Black citizens were often subject to literacy tests, which required voters to read and know specific things about government operations and the US Constitution. For example, as recently as 1965, an Alabama literacy test required test takers to know the swearing-in date for elected US senators.[4] Often, a group of white individuals in a back room at the polling site determined who passed a literacy test, deciding whether the test taker would be able to vote. There were many notable instances when those grading the test deemed Black citizens ineligible to vote even when they obtained a perfect score. At the same time, the test graders often provided allowances to white voters who could not pass the test. One justification used was a "grandfather clause," legal stipulations that allowed individuals to vote if they had ancestors who voted before the Civil War. This law created a convenient loophole for white voters unable to pass the literacy test but did nothing for Black citizens whose ancestors could not vote before the war.

Notably, in 1915 two unanimous Supreme Court decisions, *Guinn v. United States* and *Myers v. Anderson*, ruled that grandfather clauses were unconstitutional because they discriminated based on race. Still, once the court deemed grandfather clauses unacceptable, states created new laws to disenfranchise Black voters. For example, Oklahoma attempted to circumvent the *Guinn* ruling by implementing a new registration process. Specifically, the new law automatically registered all citizens who had voted in the 1914 election while requiring all others to register within a twelve-day window or else be barred from the franchise. The law was challenged in 1934 by I. W. Lane, a Black man whose attempt to register to vote was denied because he had been an Oklahoma resident since 1908 and had failed to register during the law's prescribed twelve-day period that started in late April 1916. Initially, the trial court and the court of appeals ruled against Lane, deeming that the law was not discriminatory because it applied to all citizens regardless of race. Yet, Lane appealed, and the Supreme Court heard the case in 1939. In the *Lane v. Wilson* decision, the

Supreme Court ruled that the Oklahoma registration law was illegal because it was a substitute for the grandfather clause they had previously ruled unconstitutional. Yet, the court's consistent rulings on grandfather clauses did little to prevent states from administering other discriminatory practices, such as literacy tests and poll taxes. Astonishingly, these laws were in place even after the passage of the Civil Rights Act of 1964. Some southern states maintained literacy tests until the 1970 amendments to the Voting Rights Act of 1965.

Importantly, the Civil Rights Act of 1964 established voting as a constitutional right guaranteed to all citizens. Accordingly, Jim Crow laws, or attempts to systematically prevent a subpopulation of citizens from voting, began to have implications for constitutionally protected civil rights. Specifically, the courts began questioning the constitutionality of laws that discriminated against specific groups defined by race, ethnicity, color, religion, or gender. Around the same time, age and disability came to be accepted as legally protected categories. There is no mistaking that the Civil Rights Act of 1964, and subsequent laws, firmly establish that voting discrimination based on any of the covered classifications is unconstitutional. As a result, it remains essential to consider whether attempts to restrict voting in the twenty-first century systematically prevent voting by people representing protected categories, consistent with the abuse of individually guaranteed civil rights.

Throughout the extended period of discriminatory voting practices, there had been little political will, or public resolve, to do anything about it. Of course, the formerly enslaved population, not allowed to vote, had no chance to replace the people in power in a manner that might promote change. In the third decade of the twenty-first century, political efforts to prevent specific populations from voting may be gaining traction in some states. Unfortunately, many assume that since the United States elected its first Black president in 2008, the country no longer restricts access to the ballot box based on race. These operatives argue that the issue of systematic racism in state voting policies is no longer relevant. Research reported in this book tests this proposition.

National Voting Standards

Some have argued that establishing national voting standards violates the US Constitution's elections clause, the primary authoritative source addressing US House and Senate elections. The clause reads, "The Times, Places and Manner of holding Elections for Senators and Representatives shall be prescribed in each State by the Legislature thereof." However, the clause does not stop there. It continues, "but the Congress may at any time by Law make or alter such Regulations." The reference to "Congress" makes it very plain that the national government can play a role in establishing election procedures and administration.[5] Importantly, even though the elections clause makes states primarily responsible for administering elections, it vests ultimate power in the US Congress. In summer 1787, in Philadelphia, Pennsylvania, when writing the US Constitution, the Framers were concerned that states might establish unfair election practices that would undermine the national government. Therefore, they empowered the national legislature to do something about it.

Indeed, on many occasions, the US Congress has exercised its power to "make or alter" rules concerning elections. Some of these laws lie at the heart of the modern electoral process. For example, constitutional law dictates voting rights for women and eighteen-year-olds. Moreover, federal statutes establish a single national Election Day and mandate that states with multiple members in the House of Representatives distribute themselves into congressional districts of equal population size.[6] In addition, the Constitution specifically bans poll taxes, and the previously mentioned legislation in the 1960s clearly addressed national standards for voting.[7]

Moreover, the National Voter Registration Act of 1993 (NVRA) is an excellent example of federal government involvement in election practice and policy. Signed by President Bill Clinton early in his time in office, the NVRA, often referred to as the Motor Voter bill, sought to help citizens get and stay registered to vote by creating national standards for voter registration processes. For instance, the law requires all states to accept registration applications by mail. Other aspects of the law required states to allow citizens to register to vote at state offices providing public assistance, specifically mentioning state Department of Motor Vehicles facilities as appropriate locations. Alternatively, states could adopt same-day voter registration, allowing voters to register to vote on Election Day. In all, the NVRA makes voter registration less costly and more accessible.

The main goal of the NVRA was to increase voter registration, with a concomitant increase in voter turnout. While the legislation created new national standards, making registering to vote less burdensome, some states attempted to limit its effectiveness. For example, the national government sued the state of Pennsylvania for its lackadaisical implementation of the law.[8] Other states, such as Rhode Island, Maine, New Jersey, South Dakota, Utah, and Washington, failed to report any registrations at state agencies listed in the NVRA. Likewise, other states implemented altered registration applications, which made them more difficult for voters to fill out and led the courts to intercede (Crocker 2013).[9]

Critically, before the passage of the NVRA, states would often eliminate registered voters from their voting rolls if they had not cast a ballot after a specified time. This purging of voter rolls due to failure to vote is addressed and explicitly forbidden by the NVRA. However, in a 5–4 decision in 2018, the US Supreme Court ruled in *Husted, Ohio Secretary of State v. A. Philip Randolph Institute et al.* that states can strike registered voters from registration rolls if they fail to return a mailed address confirmation form and do not vote for the subsequent four years.

Unfortunately, states have adopted innovative registration roll manipulations, or purges, which vary in frequency across the country. For instance, some states, remove voters from registration rolls with duplicate names more aggressively than others. While they do so as part of the voter list maintenance required by the NVRA, the timing and aggressiveness of these practices have caused the national government to take note of possible illegality. As a result, as of 2022, the federal government has filed fifteen different lawsuits against states and/or electoral districts for potential violations of the NVRA's purging practices.[10]

Provisions of the NVRA went into effect in most states on January 1, 1995. After this date, there were few changes to state election policies for a time. Most states made only minimal changes between 1995 and the election of President Barack Obama in 2008. Changes in the roughly twelve-year period tended to make voting more convenient across all fifty states. However, after 2008 things changed. Legislatures in Republican-leaning states began to adopt restrictive electoral-institutional policies. Interestingly, other states countered with laws intended to make voting more accessible, such as expanding early voting opportunities and eliminating voter registration deadlines. Consequently, the relative gap in voting restrictiveness between states began to grow after 2008.

One of the many tactics that helped President Obama win in 2008 was a Get Out the Vote (GOTV) effort. His campaign expended considerable resources to get eligible citizens registered to vote and later cast a ballot. With the possible intention of limiting the future success of Democratic Party candidates in GOTV campaigns, some Republican-controlled state governments passed legislation restricting voter registration drives. Before 2008 few states paid much attention to voter registration efforts by political parties and interest groups. After 2008 this changed. Specifically, we see five distinct policies adopted by states, all publicly justified by the intent to prevent voter registration fraud.

One type of new law required those wanting to participate in registration drives to obtain permission from the state. Another required individuals and groups to take an actual state certification class before conducting a voter registration drive. Still another type required organizations engaging in voter registration drives to register with the state, obtain and submit specific forms, and provide detailed information about their organization. A fourth provided some sort of specific punishment for breaking existing rules regarding a group's voter registration efforts. Lastly, two states (New Hampshire and Wyoming) went out of their way to outlaw or ban voter registration drives outright.

In addition to registration drive restrictions, post-2008 some states began to pass new voter ID laws or modify enforcement practices. While such efforts have garnered significant media attention since 2008, voter ID laws had been in place in numerous states long before President Obama's electoral success. Still, we witnessed stricter enforcement in the aftermath of Obama's victory. In states with strict enforcement, election officials must provide potential voters with a provisional ballot if the voter does not have the appropriate identification. The officials do not count the ballot unless the voter returns with the proper identification in a specific timeframe. If the voter fails to produce the appropriate ID, the provisional ballot is "spoiled," or not counted.

By themselves, voter ID laws are not discriminatory. Simply increasing the "cost" of voting does not by itself constitute prejudice in voting practice. However, in certain circumstances, there is cause for concern. For example, the US Supreme Court found North Carolina's strict voter ID law, passed before the 2016 election, unconstitutional. Specifically, the court learned that, while drafting the legislation, Republican state legislators gathered evidence regarding which forms of identification specific subpopulations were most likely to hold. These legislators then designed the law in such a way as to accept the types of ID most often carried by their supporters, while at the same time outlawing other forms of identification held by voters who typically supported Democratic Party candidates.[11]

In another case, Republican legislators and a Republican governor in Wisconsin passed legislation establishing a new voter ID requirement. Part of the language in the law stipulated that a college identification card was not an acceptable form of voter identification. Arguably, the motivation was the assumption that younger, college-educated voters were more inclined to support Democratic Party candidates. Other aspects of the Wisconsin legislation conflicted with the Twenty-Fourth Amendment to the Constitution, which outlaws the poll tax. Specifically, the new law required potential voters to present a state-issued photo ID to vote, which is not free. In response, the courts forced the state to begin providing state-issued IDs free of charge upon request if the state was going to require the ID as a condition for voting eligibility.[12] Subsequently, the media conglomerate Reuters learned that state government officials discouraged employees from volunteering information about free IDs.[13] In addition, the journalists found that the state failed to guarantee the delivery of the ID by Election Day, even when the individual requested the ID before the state-mandated deadline.

Still more, Wisconsin began requiring individuals to provide original birth certificates or passports as a basis for voter registration. The state was again creating a situation where citizens must obtain costly documents to be eligible to vote. Collectively, the issues in Wisconsin resulted in legal challenges that temporarily blocked the new voter ID law.[14] The stop was in place for the 2012 election, won by President Barack Obama. The incumbent president garnered 52.83 percent of the popular vote in the state compared to 45.89 percent for Governor Mitt Romney, the Republican Party candidate. After the state legislature made adjustments, the Supreme Court upheld the constitutionality of the Wisconsin ID law, and the provision was in force for the 2016 presidential election cycle. In the popular press, some have argued that the new law contributed to Donald Trump narrowly winning the state's popular vote in 2016, 47.22 percent to Hillary Clinton's 46.45 percent.[15]

Shelby County v. Holder

The Supreme Court case *Shelby County v. Holder* (2013) warrants additional discussion, as this ruling set an important legal precedent for current state election laws and recent efforts to restrict voting further. In effect, the court's decision removed an existing national government standard. Specifically,

Shelby County, Alabama, sued US Attorney General Eric Holder in 2011, arguing that section 4(b) and section 5 of the Voting Rights Act of 1965 were unconstitutional. The US District Court for the District of Columbia first heard the case. The judge, in this instance, ruled in favor of the national government, indicating that the 2006 reauthorization sufficiently justified the preclearance requirements using the original formula. Before heading to the Supreme Court, the US Court of Appeals for the District of Columbia Circuit affirmed the lower court ruling that preclearance was allowable based on the previous formula. However, at the next level, the Supreme Court ruled that the formula was outdated based on the narrowest possible majority, a five-to-four decision. Correspondingly, today, no state or district is required to receive preclearance from the national government to change their election laws, with the result that state legislatures have significant leeway in making voting more costly.

The effects of removing preclearance were swift and evident during the 2016 presidential election cycle. That year, seven southern states (Alabama, Arizona, Louisiana, Mississippi, North Carolina, South Carolina, and Texas) appreciably reduced the number of polling locations in their state.[16] For our purposes, we suggest that fewer polling locations make voting more costly. While researchers find evidence that a reduction in polling locations in North Carolina did not create a partisan advantage or prevent minorities from voting (Shepherd et al. 2021), there has been less attention paid to whether reductions in other states might have served strategic political purposes. Moreover, it is hard to test the effect of polling location reductions because, without preclearance, the precise shuffling of locations is tricky to determine. As a result, political observers only became aware of many of the moves after considerable time has passed. Moreover, creating vote centers to offset some reductions complicates testing for racial or partisan motives. In any event, we hold that the passage of these laws in the immediate aftermath of the Shelby County decision points to a decline in electoral standards and possible disreputable political motives.

Ultimately, we wish to debunk any claim that majority party-state legislators are entirely free from improper motives and only wish to promote the public good when they change state election laws. Unfortunately, various and unnecessary voting restrictions still exist and are being created anew. Even if the measures have become more nuanced and difficult to trace, it is the case that many old efforts to restrict voting, such as registration deadlines, still exist because some states refuse to update their election laws. In other words, some states have failed to take advantage of new secure technologies to make voting easier for citizens. For example, same-day voter registration software is readily available, cost-effective, and creates more accurate registration rolls than the old paper processes (Maluk et al. 2015). In another outdated practice, many states still restrict voting for citizens with a felony conviction. The initial intention of these laws was to prevent formerly enslaved people from voting during the Jim Crow era. Unfortunately, the prohibition is still widely used in the twenty-first century, with thirty states in 2020 maintaining some restriction on voting by those with a felony conviction.

With the historical backdrop in place and considerable contemporary evidence of electoral mischief to consider, we now move forward with testing. We focus on developing a statistical measure of the relative cost of voting in the fifty American states. With a numerical indicator in hand, the federal system in the United States provides robust opportunities to look for systematic evidence of partisan motives and discriminatory outcomes. The significant variability in election law across the fifty states provides a laboratory for our investigation. Any difference we uncover in voter turnout (chapter 5) or minority representation (chapter 6) cannot be the product of the many things the fifty states do the same or have in common. We now turn to measuring the "cost" of voting.

2: The Changing Nature of State Election Law

Some readers may be surprised to learn how election laws can make voting either more difficult or hassle-free. This chapter walks through all the different state election laws we have identified that alter the relative cost of voting in the American states. By "cost," we mean the time and effort required to vote.[1] We then use these laws to create a Cost of Voting Index (COVI) score for each state in each presidential election year from 1996 through 2020. Notably, state legislatures continue to revise state election laws.

The Brennan Center for Justice indicates that nineteen states passed thirty-four new laws restricting voting in 2021.[2] In some instances, states have created wholly new categories of restrictive election policy. One new consideration, post-2020, is a law prohibiting food and water distribution to potential voters in voting lines. Doing so arguably increases the cost of voting for some potential voters, especially if the line is long. On the other hand, recent moves in certain states have further streamlined and automated the voter registration process, making voting less costly. When collecting data on state election laws over the seven presidential election cycles, it was imperative to interpret each new law as either increasing or decreasing the time, energy, and hassle associated with voting.

Upfront, it is important to recognize that voting in the United States is a two-stage process, one that is different from what takes place in many democracies around the world. Many countries have a truly automatic voter registration (AVR) process in place. Generally, a national electoral commission or agency administers the automated registration process. In these countries, all citizens and other eligible voters simply show up at the polls if they wish to vote. In the United States, registering to vote represents only the first voting stage, while casting a ballot completes the process. Consequently, states have two opportunities to alter the relative cost of voting. Our analysis distinguishes laws affecting the voter registration process from those that address balloting. Both broad categories hold great potential for altering the ease or difficulty of voting.

This chapter takes the reader through different issue areas involved in the construction of the COVI, some that deal with voter registration and others that address casting a ballot. There were six issue areas in 1996, three related to registration and three dealing specifically with balloting. The number of issue areas grew to nine by 2020, five having to do with voter registration and four with balloting. We explain each issue area and provide examples of state laws that fit the category and subsequently discuss index construction specifics.

With each of the seven iterations of the COVI (1996–2020), we incorporated some new considerations. We did not limit ourselves to the same variables each time we updated the index during this period. Consequently, the raw values are not comparable over time. State legislators are creative and develop new laws or sets of laws, making a static approach to index construction impractical. However, we can make comparisons over time by considering state ranks. What we would gain by consistency in measurement using the same set of variables would come at the price of completeness. Throughout the different versions of the COVI, we have always erred on the side of providing a comprehensive look and sacrificed the value of a fixed comparison over time. Our use of subindices, identified as issue areas, is consistent over the seven different editions of the COVI, as is the use of the principal component analysis (PCA) to produce index values.[3] We score all included variables with each version so that a larger number indicates greater cost.[4]

The First Stage: Voter Registration

In examining the many different state policies that address voter registration, we must note that every state except North Dakota requires citizens to register to vote before casting a ballot. In the forty-nine remaining states, citizens who do not register are not eligible to vote on or before Election Day. Previous research has found that an individual's registration status is the most significant predictor of whether they turn out to vote (Erikson 1981; Piven and Cloward 1988; Squire, Wolfinger, and Glass 1987; Wolfinger, Glass, and Squire 1990). Moreover, previous research, and work reported in this volume, finds that lower-educated and lower-income citizens are less likely to vote. Scholars note that registration policies are an essential explanation for the socioeconomic differences between voters and nonvoters (Cunningham 1991, 372).[5] While requirements such as poll taxes and literacy tests are now banned, some scholars argue that remote registration and complicated registration forms are "*de facto* income and literacy tests" (Piven and Cloward 1989, 584–585). Therefore, we must consider the large variety of state voter registration laws to accurately determine the cost of voting in each state.

The Second Stage: Casting a Ballot

The second stage of voting in the United States involves casting a ballot. Beginning in 1845, this took place on a single day, the Tuesday following the first Monday in November. However, in the 1970s, some states began adopting policies that allowed for no-excuse absentee voting. (Absentee voting with an excuse emerged as early as the Civil War era). Today, early voting sites and absentee voting processes vary considerably across the American states, with some still maintaining a single-day rule. In 2020 twenty-three states still had not adopted any early voting options other than a cumbersome absentee voting process that requires a state-sanctioned excuse. States with more generous early voting options have effectively reduced voting costs for eligible citizens. In addition, by 2020 vote-by-mail processes in five states meant even more variability in terms of casting a ballot on some day other than the prescribed Tuesday in November.

It is common for people to confuse the terms "early voting," "absentee voting," and "vote-by-mail." When we use the phrase "early voting," we refer to state laws that allow registered voters to travel to a temporary or part-time voting site to cast a ballot in person sometime before Election Day. In 2020 twenty-seven states permitted this. However, in these states, there is still considerable variability in the number of early voting days. When we talk about "absentee voting," we refer to state laws that allow registered voters to vote through the mail or in person ahead of Election Day if the eligible voter has requested a ballot, in advance, by filling out a designated form. Some states have made absentee voting processes much more accessible than others, by allowing voters to go to an election administration office in person, fill out the absentee voting form, and cast their ballot in a single visit. We should note that this type of in-person absentee voting looks a lot like early voting. However, the difference is that with the absentee voting process, states typically require potential voters to travel to a government facility during regular business hours. This stipulation differs from "early voting," wherein election officials set up early voting sites around an electoral jurisdiction, usually a county. Sometimes, local election administrators even use sports stadiums or large public facilities to avoid crowding and make the process particularly convenient.

When we use the term "vote-by-mail," we refer to the states where election officials automatically send all registered voters a ballot (until 2020, this included Oregon, Utah, Colorado, Hawaii, and Washington). In these states, voters return the ballot through the mail or drop it off at a predetermined location, sometimes referred to as a ballot drop box. This process differs from even the most progressive absentee voting law because all potential voters automatically receive a ballot through the mail. In the 2020 election, four other states—California, Nevada, New Jersey, and Vermont—adopted a statewide vote-by-mail process in response to the COVID-19 pandemic. By 2022, California, Nevada, and Vermont had passed laws to make vote-by-mail the new state standard even as the pandemic recedes.

One can quickly recognize that there is quite a bit of variation in state balloting procedures. Even vote-by-mail is not the same in the few states that allow this practice. Oregon and Washington, for instance, have done away with polling stations on Election Day. The other vote-by-mail states in the 2020 presidential election (Colorado, Hawaii, and Utah) kept the option of voting at a polling station. In developing the COVI, we attempt to account for as many interstate variations in balloting procedures as possible and the different types of vote-by-mail practices. Importantly, the COVI scores combine both voting stages in the United States.[6]

Constructing the Cost of Voting Indices

THE 1996 COVI

We began with 1996, partly because of data limitations but importantly because it was the first presidential election cycle after President Bill Clinton signed the NVRA into law. To recall, the 1993 statute significantly changed national election law, mandating each state to establish specific voter registration processes, among other considerations. For instance, since 1994 all states have been required to allow voter registration by mail and at state Department of Motor Vehicle facilities.[7] The change in law was sufficiently far-reaching to

Table 2.1. Original Policies Included in the Cost of Voting Index: 1996

Issue area (measurement)	Cost of voting consideration
No. 1—Registration deadlines (ratio variable)	No. of days prior to election voter must be registered to vote
No. 2—Registration restrictions (5-item additive index; 0–4)	Same-day voter registration not allowed for all elections
	Same-day voter registration not located at polling station
	Felons not allowed to register while incarcerated
	Felons not allowed to register after incarceration
No. 3—Preregistration laws (6-item ordered scale)	0: 16-year-olds allowed to preregister
	1: 17-year-olds allowed to preregister
	2: 17.5-year-olds allowed to register
	3: Allowed to register 90 days prior to 18th b-day
	4: Allowed to register 60 days prior to 18th b-day
	5: No state preregistration policy
No. 4—Voting inconveniences (5-item additive index; 0–4)	No early voting
	Excuse required for absentee voting
	No in-person absentee voting
	No state Election Day holiday
No. 5—Voter ID laws (5-item ordered scale)	0: No ID required to cast a ballot, only signature
	1: Nonphoto ID required, not strictly enforced
	2: Photo ID required, not strictly enforced
	3: Nonphoto ID, strictly enforced
	4: Photo ID, strictly enforced
No. 6—Poll hours (ratio variable)	Minimum and maximum number of poll hours (values averaged and reversed)

Source: Michael Pomante, Scot Schraufnagel, and Quan Li

compromise any interstate comparison pre-1993 and post-1993. The 1996 index consists of twenty-one unique considerations, or laws, grouped into six issue areas. The first three deal with voter registration practices, and the latter three relate to casting a ballot. Table 2.1 displays the considerations included in the original COVI.[8]

Issue Area No. 1: Registration Deadlines

The number of days before an election an individual must register to vote is of considerable importance. Research on registration deadlines has come to a consensus that the further out the closing date for registration for an upcoming election the lower the voter turnout (Brians and Grofman 2001, 171; Fournier et al. 2004; Gimpel, Dyck, and Shaw 2004; Gopoian and Hadjiharalambous 1994; Vonnahme 2011). Conversely, states with no registration deadline or allowing people to register on Election Day have higher voter turnout levels (Leighley and Nagler 2014).[9] Figure 2.1 shows the mean, median, and mode number of days before the General Election that one must register to vote if they wish to cast a ballot in the seven presidential election cycles from 1996 through 2020.[10]

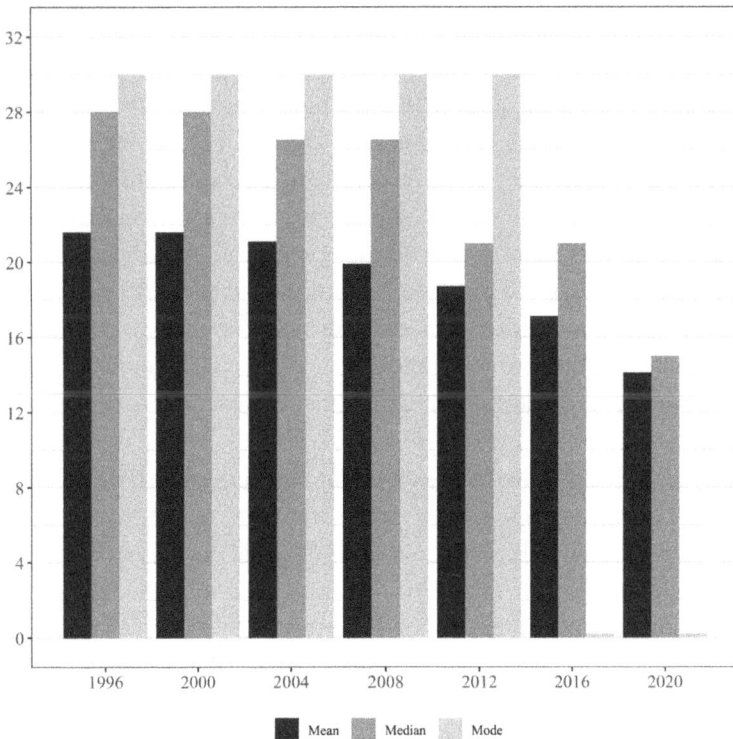

Figure 2.1. The average number of days before an election voters needed to register to vote: 1996–2020

Source: Michael Pomante, Scot Schraufnagel, and Quan Li

In the figure, we can note that by 2016 the modal number of days was zero, indicating the most common policy in recent election cycles is same-day or Election Day registration (EDR). In other words, these states, like North Dakota, do not have a preelection registration requirement. The most common practice before 2016 (1996–2012) was a thirty-day deadline. In 1996 the mean registration deadline or number of days before an election a citizen needed to complete the registration process was 21.5 days. Over time, this average value goes down, although the mean stayed around twenty-one days until 2008, when it dropped below twenty days for the first time. In 2020 the mean number of days was just over fourteen days. Essentially, the drop occurs because states pass and implement same-day or EDR laws.[11]

Issue Area No. 2: Registration Restrictions

We give EDR additional weight in index construction by making it the first item in our registration restriction additive subindex.[12] Presumably, the goal of EDR is to combine both stages of the voting process (registering to vote and casting a ballot) into a single stop. Research suggests that making voting a one-step process increases voter participation rates (Alvarez, Ansolabehere, and Wilson 2002, 17). Yet not all state EDR policies are the same. Specifically, some states burden citizens more by not allowing registration at the actual polling location. In these states, the prospective voter may register the same day they vote but must travel to a different location, usually a county government office. This variation, or additional step, arguably increases the cost of voting and the consideration becomes the second item in the registration restriction additive subindex.[13]

The third and fourth items in our initial registration restriction subindex include laws regarding felon voter registration and eligibility, respectively. Many believe (inaccurately) that once an individual is guilty of a felony, they lose their right to vote indefinitely in the United States. However, it is the case that those states that previously banned incarcerated felons from registering to vote stand alone among the democracies of the world (Manza and Uggen 2004, 491). No other developed democracy has this sort of punitive voting provision. As noted, felon-voting bans began in the South in response to the passage of the Fifteenth Amendment, which gave Black males the right to vote (1870). At the time, white southern lawmakers sought different ways to disenfranchise this new potential voting bloc. Felony restrictions were part of the effort.

Considerable legal maneuvering in this regard occurred throughout the Jim Crow era. Behrens, Uggen, and Manza (2003) find that states with a greater percentage of Black inhabitants instituted the most stringent felon voting restrictions. Indeed, it was common to strip voting rights permanently from anyone with a felony conviction. Many of these state laws remained untouched until 1996, when legislators began to revisit the question.[14] Despite changes, research shows that in 2020 states still prohibited about 5.2 million Americans from voting because of a felony conviction (Uggen et al. 2020).

Our first consideration in this respect distinguishes whether a state allows people convicted of a felony to register to vote while incarcerated. In 1996, Maine, Massachusetts, Utah, and Vermont allowed citizens in prison an opportunity to register to vote and cast a ballot. However, in 1998 the Utah State Legislature passed legislation denying the right. In 2000, in Massachusetts, a citizen referendum approved a new law that banned incarcerated citizens from registering to vote. From the 2004 election cycle forward, Maine and Vermont remain the only states allowing felons to register to vote while incarcerated.[15] One might wonder why this is the case with these two states in particular. As noted, states began taking away felon rights in the Jim Crow era, policies aimed specifically at preventing Black citizens from voting. The overwhelming number of prisoners in Maine and Vermont has always been white, making this outcome perhaps less surprising.

Although only two states presently allow felons to register to vote while incarcerated, there has been more variation in the number of states that allow felons to register to vote once released from jail. In these instances, citizens who have done their time can register and vote, and this consideration becomes the fourth and last item in the original registration restriction issue area. Still, the adoption of this law has been slow to gain traction. Ten states allowed non-incarcerated felons to vote in 1996, with one additional state joining in 2004 and two more in 2008. This number stayed constant until the 2020 presidential election cycle. Then, between 2016 and 2020, seven additional states allowed nonincarcerated felons to register to vote.

Issue Area No. 3: Preregistration Laws
Newly eligible voters, or young adults, have consistently been the least likely to vote. Scholars alternatively attribute lower voter turnout of young eligible voters to their lack of political knowledge (Wattenberg 2012; Rankin 2013; Delli

and Keeter 1991; Galston 2004) and their greater mobility (Highton 2000; Squire Wolfinger and Glass 1987). Still others note that potential young voters lack a civic engagement mindset (Valenzuela, Park, and Kee 2009; Andolina et al. 2003) and distrust politicians (Niemi and Klinger 2012), and that older political candidates fail to appeal to younger voters (Pomante and Schraufnagel 2015; Pomante 2017). Considering these clarifications for lower youth voter turnout, we appreciate that these explanations double as reasons for the failure of this subpopulation to register to vote.

Given the many different explanations for lower youth voter turnout, one can certainly imagine this group is easily "demobilized" when the costs of voting are higher (Juelich and Coll 2020). True, some state legislatures have explored ways to address the problem and engage young citizens in the political process. One method states have adopted is preregistration laws that allow eligible young Americans to register to vote before their eighteenth birthday. The laws typically combine the preregistration process with a state mandate to discuss the importance of voting in civics classes in public high schools. As it turns out, many potential young voters do not realize they need to register before becoming eligible to vote. Still more are unsure how to register, where to register, or if there is a registration deadline. Preregistration attempts to reduce the costs of answering these questions.

In some states, sixteen-year-olds preregister to vote, making them eligible to vote when they turn eighteen. In these states, registration often occurs in high schools or the Department of Motor Vehicle offices when young individuals obtain their first driver's license. In 1996, five states had some preregistration program, and Hawaii became the first state to allow citizens as young as sixteen to register to vote. Since 1996 twenty additional states have passed and implemented a preregistration program. Of course, not all laws are alike. We initially note five variations based on the time an individual may register before their first eligible election. (See table 2.1).[16] We suggest any preregistration policy that gives potential young voters more time to register lowers the costs of voting. We assume a failure to adopt a preregistration policy indicates that the state legislature is less concerned about making voter registration easy for younger citizens.[17] Research finds that states offering preregistration have witnessed a measurable increase in youth voter turnout (McDonald 2009; McDonald and Thornburg 2010; Cherry 2011; Holbein and Hillygus 2016).

Issue Area No. 4: Voting Inconveniences

The fourth issue area begins our exploration of the second stage of voting. Specifically, the category taps a variety of state laws that alter the convenience of casting a ballot.[18] Notably, the voting inconvenience subindex had grown to thirteen items by 2020. A rise in available data explains some increase in the number of index items. However, in other instances, state legislators have created new laws for us to consider. The first item in this issue area is early voting, which was rare in 1996. Only nine states had electoral districts setting up early voting sites as recently as 1996. As noted, for our purposes, early voting is distinct from absentee voting, with the latter requiring a potential voter to complete a ballot request form. Since 1996, many more states have adopted early voting sites. Indeed, scholars find that the steep increase in the implementation of early voting policies has changed how candidates run their campaigns (Gronke, Galanes-Rosenbaum, and Miller 2007; Giammo and Brox 2010). By 2020 twenty-seven states mandated local electoral jurisdictions to designate early voting times and locations.

Our second item in the 1996 inconvenience scale deals with absentee voting laws, which have been around in the United States since the Civil War era. However, most states adopted absentee voting laws between 1911 and 1938 (Fortier 2006, 7–10). Again, not all laws are equal, and we make two initial distinctions. First, we consider whether states require citizens to provide an appropriate "excuse" for voting absentee. Indeed, all the first absentee voting laws required a state-sanctioned excuse, usually addressing health concerns or an inability to travel to a polling location on Election Day. Over time, states began adjusting what they considered an acceptable excuse until some states just stopped requiring one altogether. Scholars find that less restrictive absentee voting laws have increased voter turnout when combined with party mobilization efforts (Oliver 1996; Biggers and Hammer 2015). Others note, however, that any increase in turnout is short-lived (Giammo and Brox 2010). In 1996 only twenty-one states required an excuse to vote absentee, a value that dropped to sixteen states by 2020.

Third, we consider whether a state allows in-person absentee voting, which allows individuals to go to a government-designated location sometime before Election Day to cast their absentee ballot. This process alleviates the inconvenience of a two-staged mail process—first requesting the ballot by mail and then submitting it via the post office. Indeed, county officials acknowledge that this allowance is popular among voters because it allows them to cast a ballot near work or while running errands (Fullmer 2021, 32). While previous research has shown that early voting makes voting more accessible, contemporary researchers argue that voter turnout's effects vary by locality (Walker, Herron, and Smith 2019). Still, others found that when a state reduces the number of early voting days, this decreases the participation rate of those least likely to vote (Herron and Smith 2014). The number of states that allow in-person absentee voting grew from twelve in 1996 to forty-three by 2020.[19]

The final inconvenience item, used since 1996, measures whether a state considers Election Day a state holiday. Unfortunately, these state laws are unique, because of the variability in who gets the day off. Therefore, we opt for a single-simple consideration. Namely, does the state government close state buildings on Election Day?[20] Previous research on voting as a holiday found that only a bare majority of Americans support this policy (Alvarez et al. 2011). However, despite minimal public support, scholars predict that implementing this policy increases voter turnout in the United States, specifically among those who claim they are "too busy with work, family," or "don't have enough time," or "forget to vote" (Bradfield and Johnson 2017, 25). Overall, making Election Day a state holiday has not gained significant traction in the period studied. Over the seven election cycles, the number of states with this sort of policy has ranged from just ten to thirteen.[21]

Issue Area No. 5: Voter ID Laws
Over the last two decades, more states have begun to require additional forms of identification to cast a ballot. It is important to note that all states, including North Dakota, which does not require voter registration, require voters to identify themselves at the polls. The default form of identification has been a voter's signature, which must match the signature on the registration roll. We assume stricter scrutiny of a voter's identification, requiring something more than a matching signature, increases the cost of voting. Unfortunately, there is no consensus in the literature on the effect ID requirements have on voter turnout. Some researchers find that laws that require additional ID disproportionately discourage voter participation among minorities (Hajnal, Kuk, and Lijevardi 2018; Kuk, Hajnal, and Lajevardi 2022), the elderly, women, the disabled, and those who speak a minority language (Sobel and Smith 2009;

Hajnal, Kuk, and Lajevardi 2017). However, others (Grimmer et al. 2018) suggest that data constraints limit cohesive conclusions on the subject matter. Still others suggest that current studies cannot parse out the effects because not enough time has passed since the implementation of strict photo ID laws (Valentino and Neuber 2017).

As is the norm with election laws, state ID policies vary. Moreover, in this case, enforcement also differs significantly. Fortunately, we can borrow a coding scheme from the National Council of State Legislatures (NCSL) to aid the reliability of our coding process.[22] Specifically, the NCSL establishes "strict" and "not strict" enforcement of identification laws. Moreover, the group distinguishes a state-issued photo ID requirement from other forms of ID, such as a library card, student ID, or utility bill. In their coding, states with a "strict" voter ID law mandate that the voter produces, on the spot, the required identification at the polling location. As noted earlier, states typically give voters a provisional ballot if they cannot produce the appropriate ID.[23] However, the damage is likely already done. That is, the potential voter is more likely to stay home if they know there is an ID requirement.

The uptick in states adopting voter ID laws began shortly after the 2008 election. Scholars find that the adoption of identification laws is primarily a function of Republican control of state legislatures (Rocha and Matsubayashi 2014). Figure 2.2 reports the number of states that have adopted each level of restriction in each presidential election cycle from 1996 to 2020. In the first year, forty-one of fifty states did not require any identification to cast a ballot other than a signature. The nine states that required identification administered a "non-strict" policy. During this time, states with ID laws often allowed voters to cast a ballot if a poll worker vouched for them or signed an affidavit that they were who they said they were. Georgia and Indiana were the first states in 2008 to implement a strict photo ID requirement. Stricter enforcement of voter identification laws does not begin, in earnest, until after the 2008 election cycle. By 2012 the number of states with strict photo ID (lightest gray bar) increased to four, which grew to seven by 2016, and dropped back to six in 2020. Specifically, the Virginia legislature passed a new law early in 2020 that removed strict enforcement of a photo ID.[24]

Notice the jump in figure 2.2 from six states to ten states with either form of a strict enforcement policy between 2012 and 2016. This increase takes place after the *Shelby County v. Holder* Supreme Court decision. The states that felt

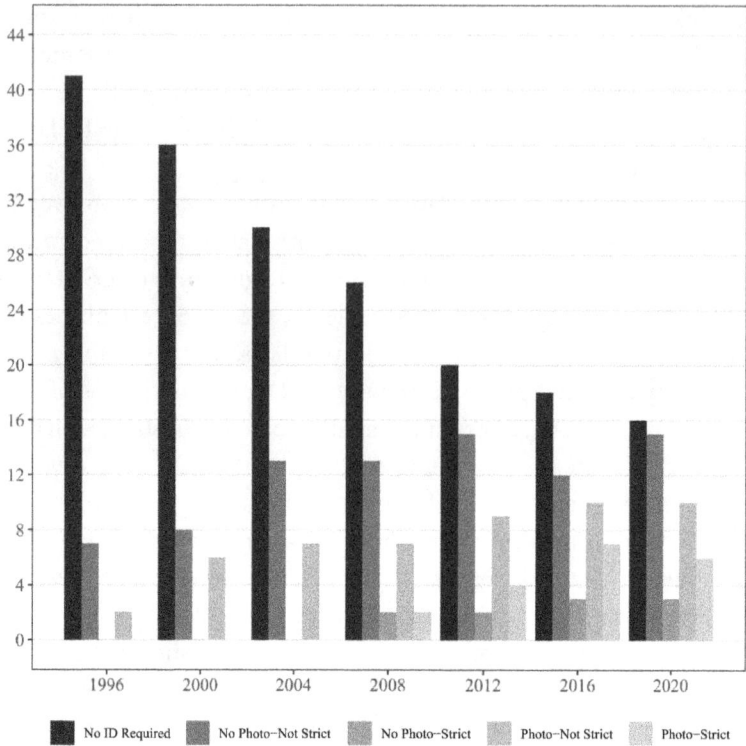

Figure 2.2. The frequency of different state voter identification laws: 1996–2020

Source: Michael Pomante, Scot Schraufnagel, and Quan Li

voter ID required stricter scrutiny were Missouri, North Dakota, Virginia, and Wisconsin. Notably, when these new policies passed, the Republican Party controlled the state legislative process in all four states. Yet, we must point out that, during the time studied, a few states with strict enforcement of an ID law were under Democratic legislative control—namely, Hawaii and Rhode Island. No states adopted new strict photo identification policies between 2016 and 2020. However, we suspect this issue area continues to witness considerable cross-state variation. Conceivably, unfounded claims of election fraud in the 2020 election might lead more states to adopt strict policies for the 2024 presidential election cycle.

Issue Area No. 6: Poll Hours

The hours polling locations are open vary across the United States. Indeed, several states allow electoral districts within the state to determine their polling hours, provided they fall within a broader state guideline. Polling hours are critical to those who intend to vote in person on Election Day. Scholars find that polling stations open for fewer hours increase the costs associated with voting, especially for hourly wage earners (Eisner 2004, 122; Patterson 2002). Others find that more restrictive poll hours lower voter turnout (Wolfinger, Highton, and Mullin 2005; Garmann 2017). For example, the state of New York, since 1996, has mandated polling locations be open for a minimum of fifteen hours, representing the highest value in 1996. To measure the restrictiveness of each state's poll hours, we use the average between the minimum and the maximum number of hours when state law allows some variation in the time that polls must be open.

The average number of hours varies from nine to fifteen during the period studied. However, beginning in 2000 Oregon implemented vote-by-mail and voters in the state could drop off a ballot at specific locations on Election Day up until eight in the evening. Therefore, starting that year, we count these "polling locations" as being open from midnight to 8:00 p.m., or twenty hours on Election Day.[25]

Having discussed the original items that make up the 1996 COVI, we now elaborate on changes made with each new execution of the COVI from 2000 through 2020.

CHANGES FOR THE 2000 COVI

Notably, there is only one change for the 2000 COVI. Specifically, we add a single consideration to Issue Area No. 4, the voting inconvenience additive scale. The 2000 presidential contest was the first to witness a statewide vote-by-mail process. The state of Oregon implemented universal vote-by-mail in 1998. However, 2000 was the first presidential election in which all Oregonians received their ballots by mail. Once registered voters received their ballot, they simply had to complete it and turn it in by Election Day for their vote to count. In Oregon, citizens can mail the completed ballot with a postmark on or before Election Day or drop the ballot off at a predetermined location.

After Oregon, four other states (Colorado, Washington, Utah, and Hawaii) adopted vote-by-mail policies before 2020.[26] Since 2020 three additional states (California, Nevada, and Vermont) have adopted the process. Early research has uncovered significantly higher voter turnout in vote-by-mail elections (Karp and Banducci 2000).[27] Importantly, we distinguish between voting by mail and even the most progressive absentee voting policies. Arguably, vote-by-mail reduces the burden, or costs, for the voter because the eligible voter is not required to request a ballot, either in person or via mail. Instead, the election administrators simply mail a ballot to them.

CHANGES FOR THE 2004 COVI

The 2004 COVI includes three additional registration restrictions. Two restrictions result from new state laws, and we add the third because of the enhanced availability of reliable data. In 2004 we account for online voter registration and a ban on registration drives. The third consideration taps state laws that address mental competency for voter registration. We add these three policies to Issue Area No. 2—the registration restriction additive subindex.

Online Voter Registration
Arizona was the first state to adopt voter registration via the internet. Throughout the time studied, some states have taken advantage of new technologies to reduce the monetary costs of election administration. States implementing online voter registration (OVR) report saving taxpayer money while creating more accurate voter rolls (Pew 2014, 1). Accordingly, scholars note that support for adopting OVR has often been bipartisan (Hicks, McKee, and Smith, 2016). In addition, when states adopt OVR, they see an increase in voter turnout (Yu 2019). Increases in the ease of voting and cost savings have made this a widespread and popular reform. Figure 2.3 shows the considerable growth in the adoption of OVR since 2004.

Arizona had an online registration website up and running during the 2004 presidential election cycle. Washington was the second state to adopt OVR and had a system in place for the 2008 presidential election. Following the 2008 election, the number of states creating an OVR process increased significantly. As of 2020 forty states have passed legislation allowing voters to register to vote online. We score North Dakota "0" on this consideration because the state does not require voter registration. Still, in 2020 nine states failed to take advantage

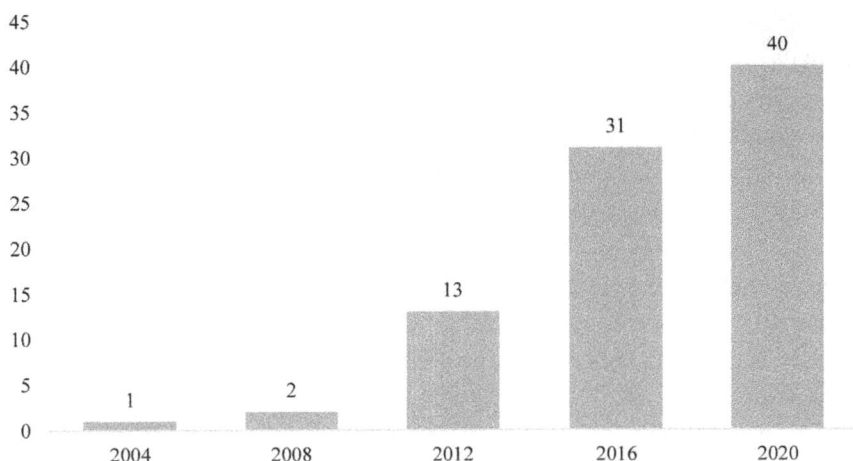

Figure 2.3. Number of states with online voter registration: 2004–2020

Source: Michael Pomante, Scot Schraufnagel, and Quan Li

of the cost savings associated with OVR (PEW 2014): Arkansas, Maine, Mississippi, Montana, New Hampshire, Oklahoma, South Dakota, Texas, and Wyoming.

Ban on Registration Drives

With the passage of the NVRA in 1993, registration drives became a popular tool used by political parties and interest groups to bolster voter turnout of individuals judged to likely cast votes in their favor. Specifically, the passage of the 1993 law, which allowed voter registration by mail and required registration forms at specific government locations, made registration drives more viable. In 2004 Wyoming became the first state to ban the practice of registration drives by organized interests, and New Hampshire followed suit shortly thereafter. Notably, restricting registration drives became more popular after the successful 2008 presidential campaign of Barak Obama, which used registration drives effectively to grow voter turnout. Therefore, in 2004, we treated the ban instituted by Wyoming as a new item in the registration restriction subindex. However, other state laws related to third-party voter registration drives following the 2008 election cause us to create a new stand-alone issue area for the 2012 COVI.[28]

Mental Competency

Mental competency laws for voting have a long history (Hamer and Finlayson 2015). The nature of the restrictions varies significantly by state. Often, legislative language is challenging to interpret (Bazelon Center for Mental Health Law 2016). To identify individuals who lack mental competency, legislators have used terms such as "idiots," "insane persons," and "non compos mentis" in legislation. However, these terms fail to identify the citizens not permitted to register to vote (Appelbaum 2000, 849). Moreover, many policies do not designate who is responsible for deciding who is mentally incompetent (Okwerkwu et al. 2018). Some states leave the question unanswered, while others require a court to determine incapacity. Still others prevent anyone "under guardianship" from registering to vote.[29]

One might imagine that these laws do not affect many people and are unnecessary in COVI construction. Yet, as best as possible, we intend to capture each state's electoral–institutional climate. We suggest these laws help identify which states operate with a more inclusive mindset. Presumably, state legislatures that pass laws restricting specific individuals from registering to vote are states with a more restrictive posture. We opt for a simple measure that scores any state with language identifying a mental competency disability "1" and other states "0" and add this item to the registration restriction additive subindex. Despite these laws being around for some time, we do not consider mental competency until 2004 because of an inability to obtain second-party verification of the laws before that year. In 2004 thirty-seven states had some sort of statute regarding mental competency. By 2020 only seventeen states were maintaining this type of law.

Changes for the 2008 COVI

For the 2008 COVI, we add four new considerations to Issue Area No. 4—the voting inconveniences additive scale. New policies include the allowance of permanent absentee voter status, the use of vote centers, time off from work to cast a ballot, and paid time off from work to vote. The absentee voting consideration and the vote centers are, principally, new laws. We include the time off from work considerations because reliable data becomes available for this period.

Permanent Absentee Voter Status

In 2008 California became the first state to permit registered voters to ask for and receive permanent absentee voter status. The permanent condition allows voters to receive an absentee ballot by mail for every election, assuming they do not move and that there is no other change to their registration status.[30] Notably, there are variations to permanent absentee voting laws. For example, while some states allow all eligible voters to take advantage of this option, other states require an excuse, such as a disability or an age consideration.[31]

Following the lead of California, five additional states (Arizona, Hawaii, Montana, New Jersey, and Utah) implemented permanent absentee voter laws for the 2012 presidential election.[32] Interestingly, California, Hawaii, and Utah subsequently passed vote-by-mail, negating the need to request permanent absentee voter status. Another early adopter, New Jersey, implemented a vote-by-mail process in response to the COVID-19 pandemic in 2020. It is not difficult to imagine that a permanent absentee voting process is a precursor to vote-by-mail. The administration of these policies would be similar, with the latter simply expanding the delivery of ballots to all registered voters. In 2020, when we include the vote-by-mail states, nineteen states afforded their citizens a simple, low-cost permanent absentee voting option.

Vote Centers

Since 2008 states have begun establishing "vote centers" that allow people to cast a ballot at some central location in the state or an electoral jurisdiction, regardless of which precinct they reside. In effect, vote centers allow eligible voters the convenience of an additional place to cast their ballot. In states with voting centers, a potential voter away from their hometown or neighborhood has another way to cast a legal ballot. By 2008 Colorado and North Dakota adopted statewide use of vote centers, and by 2020, fifteen additional states had followed suit. By 2020 Iowa had not adopted the policy statewide, so we do not include it in our count.[33] With the relative newness of vote centers, researchers have not yet determined their independent effect on voter turnout. Yet, we hold that the availability of an additional voting location logically decreases the cost of voting. Moreover, vote centers, we suggest, are indicative of a state trying to establish a more inclusive electoral climate. However, there is one caveat to consider. In Texas, the state adopted vote centers but also closed many precinct sites. Since 2012, we have scored Texas "0," indicating it had vote centers. However, beginning in 2016 we also scored Texas as a more restrictive state for reducing the number of polling locations following the *Shelby v. Holder* decision.

Time Off from Work to Vote: Unpaid and Paid

The third and fourth new considerations for 2008 involve state laws that mandate employers give at least some of their employees time off from work to vote.[34] We also distinguish whether the state law requires employers to pay their workers for the time they take off to vote. One can relate these legal considerations to the Election Day holiday law, which was part of the original COVI. However, these new considerations relate to more than just government workers. Now, some states include private-sector employees. Variations of these laws have been around for a considerable time (Gradwohl 1951); however, uneven state reporting and enforcement of the laws prevent us from including the considerations before 2008. The number of states with time off laws stayed constant, at thirty-one, from 2008 to 2020. However, the number of states providing paid time off grew from twenty-two to twenty-four between 2008 and 2012 when Arizona and Kansas began to give this benefit to private-sector employees.[35]

CHANGES FOR THE 2012 COVI

Following the election of the first Black president in 2008, many states began to adopt voting restrictions. For example, Kansas increased the deadline (Issue Area No. 1) for voters to register to vote from fifteen days to twenty-one and moved to strict enforcement of a photo ID law (Issue Area No. 5). Tennessee also adopted a new strict photo ID law. Other states passed and implemented restrictions on voter registration drives. Some mandated a state training course, while others required groups to file specific paperwork to conduct a voter registration drive. In response to these developments, we added registration drive restrictions as a new issue area (Issue Area No. 7) when calculating state COVI values in 2012.

Additionally, we add one more consideration to the registration restriction additive index (Issue Area No. 2). This new concern measures whether states have same-day voter registration for all elected offices. The number of policies in the registration restriction subindex stays constant at seven. We add the new consideration but remove bans on registration drives, as this now becomes part of the new Issue Area No. 7, which deals more comprehensively with registration drive restrictions.

Issue Area No. 7: Registration Drive Restrictions

Registration drive restrictions have not yet received significant scholarly scrutiny. However, the Brennan Center for Justice has been paying attention. The group notes, "More than half of the states [now] have some laws governing community-based voter registration drives."[36] The first laws restricting voter registration drives, in one fashion or another, without an outright ban, passed shortly after the election of Barack Obama and were in force for the 2010 midterm elections. As a result, new voter registrations dropped to 17 percent compared to the 2006 midterm election (Kasdan 2012, 3). We argue that this finding suggests that policies restricting registration drives increase the cost of voting by increasing the effort citizens must spend to register and become eligible to vote.

With the help of the Brennan Center, we identify four unique registration drive restrictions. We add the outright ban of registration drives, which occurs in New Hampshire and Wyoming, to obtain a five-item additive subindex. The first consideration is whether registration drive participants must be "certified" by the state before conducting a drive. The certification process looks different across the states, but we count any certification law the same. Second, in addition to being certified, some states mandate that registration drive participants take a training course sponsored by the state. Third, some states have passed a law requiring all groups wishing to conduct a public registration drive to submit documentation about the organization before receiving approval. Generally, these latter laws require a report submitted to the state summarizing group activities. Lastly, states began to penalize individuals and groups for violations of certification deadlines or other registration drive rules.

Notably, in 2012, only Texas had all four restrictions in place.[37] Several states, such as New Jersey, New York, and North Carolina, have had no restrictions throughout the period studied.[38] However, Colorado and New Mexico, two states that have leaned Democratic in recent presidential elections, have some of the most restrictive laws in the new issue area. Considering the unique considerations that make up the subindex, the most common state law is some sort of punishment for mishandling registration forms as part of a registration drive. Since we began tracking restrictions in 2012, twenty-seven states have specified a specific punishment for the mishandling of registration forms.[39]

Election Day Registration, but Not All Elections

The 1996 COVI and all subsequent versions have considered whether a state has EDR. In 2012 Rhode Island joined the states that allow EDR, but only for presidential elections. Indeed, eligible citizens who take advantage of EDR in Rhode Island can only cast a ballot for president and no other races. If Rhode

Islanders want to vote in races down the ballot, they must register thirty days before the election. We create a new consideration that measures whether citizens can use EDR to vote for all offices because of Rhode Island's policy deviation. When we adopted this consideration, we imagined other states might follow suit with a similar arrangement. Alaska is the only other state to pass a law like Rhode Island's. However, Alaska's citizens cannot take advantage of this new law until the 2024 presidential election.[40]

CHANGES FOR THE 2016 COVI

For the 2016 COVI, we add one item to the registration restriction scale (Issue Area No. 2). In 2016 Connecticut, Georgia, and Oregon became the first states to try making voter registration more "automatic."[41] We also added two items to the voting inconvenience subindex (Issue Area No. 4), growing this issue area to eleven unique considerations. The first new "inconvenience" taps states that have begun reducing their number of polling locations, arguably making voting less convenient for some potential voters. The second inconvenience measures whether vote-by-mail states also provide an opportunity to vote on Election Day at designated polling locations.

Automatic Voter Registration

Automatic voter registration (AVR) occurs when state governments place individuals on voter rolls and the process requires no personal initiative on the part of the eligible voter. This process is routine in many democracies around the world. In the United States, states began experimenting with different forms of an "automatic" process in 2015. The term "automatic" is in quotes because no state has yet to adopt a universal automated voter registration process, as in many advanced democracies worldwide.[42] The new consideration materialized in this country when California, Connecticut, Georgia, Oregon, and Vermont passed legislation that caused citizens to register to vote when interacting with the state's DMV and/or other state agencies. However, California and Vermont did not implement the law in time to register citizens for the 2016 election. Therefore, we scored only Connecticut, Georgia, and Oregon "0" on this consideration in 2016.

By 2020 nineteen states had some sort of automated voter registration process; with the 2020 COVI, this becomes a new issue area (Issue Area No. 8).[43] Many observers see AVR as a bipartisan policy option because of its promise of improving both "access" and "integrity" to voting processes (Mann, Gronke, and Adona 2020, 2). Democrats believe AVR increases access to voting by making it less time-consuming to get and stay registered to vote (Griffin et al. 2017; Weiser 2016). At the same time, Republicans view it as an attempt to improve election integrity. Specifically, Republicans prefer this law because it removes local election officials from the registration process, with the state taking over the administration of voter registration.[44]

Reductions in the Number of Polling Locations
States can also modify the time and energy citizens must spend to cast a ballot by adjusting the number of polling locations available. Until recently, the trend had been for states to adopt more polling sites, but that has changed since 2012. We can tie states' ability to decrease polling location numbers to the 2013 US Supreme Court case *Shelby County v. Holder*. Principally, the Supreme Court ruling removed the need for federal preclearance for states with a history of racial discrimination in voting practices.

Between the *Shelby County* ruling in 2013 and 2016, seven states reduced the number of polling locations measurably. All seven states (Alabama, Arizona, Louisiana, Mississippi, North Carolina, South Carolina, and Texas) were among the nine that required preclearance before 2013, although only parts of North Carolina required preclearance. A nonprofit organization, CivilRights.org, found that many of the closures occurred in regions of these states with larger-than-average Black or Hispanic populations.[45] By 2020 the number of states reducing the number of polling locations climbed to forty. Some of this change is attributable to creating vote centers or centralized voting facilities. However, the closures in states with a history of discriminatory election practices are concerning. One can easily imagine that when an election administrator moves a polling location this increases the time or hassle required to vote because the voter must find the new polling location.

Vote-By-Mail States—No In-Person Option
By 2016 three states were sending all registered voters an official ballot by mail: Colorado, Oregon, and Washington. Of these states, only Colorado continued to make available an in-person polling option on Election Day. We hold that voting by mail is, on average, much less costly, but we also know that potential voters can lose track of the ballot they receive in the mail. Arguably, an

in-person voting option on Election Day reduces the time and effort associated with locating a lost ballot or requesting a new one. We argue that voting is the least costly in Colorado because of the extra voting opportunity, which includes vote-by-mail and in-person at a polling location. It is essential to point out that even though Oregon and Washington have done away with polling locations, both states maintain secure drop-off locations. By 2020 two additional states (Hawaii and Utah) had fully developed a vote-by-mail process. Both join Colorado in maintaining an in-person polling option on Election Day.

CHANGES FOR THE 2020 COVI

The most significant changes to calculating the COVI values occurred between 2016 and 2020. First, we add one more item to the registration restriction additive subindex (Issue Area No. 2), namely the relative ease of OVR. The registration restriction scale stays at eight unique considerations because we move the AVR item out of the issue area. We also add two new considerations to the voting inconvenience additive subindex (Issue Area No. 4), which increases the total number of items to thirteen. Specifically, we add an item that taps whether states have some other absentee voting restriction beyond the need for a state-sanctioned excuse. We also begin to count states that have reduced polling locations by more than 50 percent in some electoral districts within the state.

Beyond our changes to the additive subindices, we include two new issue areas. The first one (Issue Area No. 8) is an ordered scale that taps the type of AVR law states have adopted. The reader may recall that three states had a law for the 2016 presidential election cycle. By 2020 sixteen more states had implemented some type of AVR law. We also create a new issue area (Issue Area No. 9) to capture the recent expansion of early voting options. In this instance, we are now counting the number of days of early voting (values reversed). Table 2.2 lists all the different considerations used to create the 2020 COVI.

Online Voter Registration Deadline Greater than the Median

Our first new consideration for 2020 involves OVR. In 2020 a comfortable majority of states (forty states) allowed voter registration via the internet. Yet, we find considerable variability in the deadline to register to vote online. We imagine that if all states adopt OVR in the future, the deadlines will still vary, and this may become an important stand-alone consideration. For 2020 we

Table 2.2. Policies Included in the Cost of Voting Index: 2020

Issue area (measurement)	Cost of voting consideration
No. 1—Registration deadlines (ratio variable)	No. of days prior to election voter must be registered to vote
No. 2—Registration restrictions (9-item additive subindex; 0–8)	Same-day voter registration not allowed for all elections
	Same-day voter registration not located at polling station
	Felons not allowed to register while incarcerated
	Felons not allowed to register after incarceration
	No online voter registration
	Mental competency required for voter registration
	No same-day registration for all elections
	Online voter registration deadline > median number of days
No. 3—Preregistration laws (6-item ordered scale)	0: 16-year-olds allowed to preregister
	1: 17-year-olds allowed to preregister
	2: 17.5-year-olds allowed to register
	3: Allowed to register 90 days prior to 18th b-day
	4: Allowed to register 60 days prior to 18th b-day
	5: No state preregistration policy
No. 4—Voting inconveniences (14-item additive subidex; 0–13)	No early voting
	Excuse required for absentee voting
	No in-person absentee voting
	No state Election Day holiday
	No vote-by-mail
	No permanent absentee voting status
	No vote centers
	No time off from work
	No time off from work with pay
	Measurable reduction in the number of polling locations
	Vote-by-mail state with no in-person voting option
	Absentee voting restriction in addition to state excuse
	Reduction in polling locations > 50% some parts of state
No. 5—Voter ID laws (5-item ordered scale)	0: No ID required to cast a ballot, only signature
	1: Nonphoto ID required, not strictly enforced
	2: Photo ID required, not strictly enforced
	3: Nonphoto ID, strictly enforced
	4: Photo ID, strictly enforced

continued

Table 2.2. *continued*

Issue area (measurement)	Cost of voting consideration
No. 6—Poll hours (ratio variable)	Minimum and maximum number of poll hours (values averaged and reversed)
No. 7—Registration drive restrictions (5-item additive scale; 0–4)	Group certification required State-mandated training course required Groups must provide documentation of drive specifics State penalty for the mishandling of registration forms Ban on registration drives
No. 8—Automatic voter registration (4-item ordered scale)	0: No automatic registration law 1: Automatic registration, DMV only 2: Automatic registration, DMV + other state agencies 3: Automatic registration, not asked if you want to optout
No. 9: Early voting days (ratio variable)	Number of days early voting is held (values reversed)

Source: Michael Pomante, Scot Schraufnagel, and Quan Li

consider if a state has an OVR deadline greater than the median number of days. In some states, the deadline for OVR is the same as the deadline for in-person and mail registration; however, other states have notable differences.[46] Moreover, there is another important distinction. All states have in-person and mail registration options, but not all states allow voter registration via the internet. The consideration becomes part of the registration restriction subindex (Issue Area No. 2), and specifically, we score states with a deadline longer than the median value and states without OVR "1." We score states below the median number of days, a shorter deadline "0."[47]

Absentee Voting Restrictions

The voting inconvenience subindex is our next concern (Issue Area No. 4). In addition to the need for a state-sanctioned excuse, some states have other absentee voting restrictions. More complete and accessible record-keeping in 2020 allows us to broaden our measurement of voting inconveniences and begin counting different types of absentee voting restrictions. The types of policies we include vary, and we do not try to weigh the relative restrictiveness of each unique law. Nineteen of the fifty states in 2020 had some additional restrictions on absentee voting. The laws often involve an age consideration or whether the potential voter had previously voted in a specific electoral jurisdiction. For example, some states limited absentee voting to senior citizens, and other states did not allow first-time voters the opportunity to vote absentee. We count these limiting policies as more costly because they burden some individuals more than others.[48]

Reduction in Polling Locations Greater than 50 Percent
Staying with Issue Area No. 4, the voting inconvenience subindex, we began tracking a new consideration related to reducing polling locations. We argue that removing polling locations increases the cost of voting because of the trouble of finding a new polling place and the possibility of long lines at the remaining polling stations. Specifically, Texas, Arizona, and Georgia have aggressively closed polling locations since the *Shelby County v. Holder* ruling. Each of these states has reduced the number of polling locations by more than half (50 percent) in some election jurisdictions. We hold that it is necessary to consider that some states have been especially egregious in limiting polling locations. It is difficult to project whether this practice continues or disappears as an item of concern. The dynamic nature of voting processes in the American states requires continuous observation.

Issue Area No. 8: Automatic Voter Registration
By 2020 nineteen states had some form of AVR law. These AVR policies are much less time-consuming than state policies that require eligible voters to take a personal initiative to stay registered to vote. Specifically, there are two types of AVR implemented in the United States: Front-End AVR and Back-End AVR. The distinction between the two types is significant. For example, Alaska and Oregon implemented Back-End AVR, wherein state employees do not ask people if they want to opt out of registering to vote. Instead, they register the eligible individual and then send a postcard to the eligible voter, who must take the initiative to return the card if they wish to stay off the voter rolls. We consider this "less costly" because these states are more proactive in getting and keeping people registered to vote, indicative of a more inclusive state electoral institutional climate. On the other hand, Front-End AVR allows citizens to opt out at the point of the interaction with a state agency when the state worker asks if the eligible individual wishes to be registered. We also account in new Issue Area No. 8 for states that only allow AVR to occur at DMV facilities. Some

states open this up and institute the AVR process at other state agencies. In all, we developed a four-item ordered scale (see table 2.2) that scores states with Back-End AVR "0" and states without AVR "3."

Issue Area No. 9: The Number of Early Voting Days
There has been a considerable expansion in the number of states that allow early voting in the period studied. In 1996 there were only nine states, and by 2020 there were twenty-seven. The expansion and popularity of early voting have caused us to rethink this consideration and led us to adopt a new stand-alone Issue Area No. 9. Specifically, we begin counting each state's early voting days.[49] In 2020 Virginia was most generous, giving voters forty-two days before the November election to cast an early ballot. We treat vote-by-mail states uniquely, assuming that vote-by-mail precludes the need to vote early.[50]

Figure 2.4 reports the number of early voting days for each state in 2020. Note that we do not include the five vote-by-mail states and that Virginia, followed by Illinois, is the least restrictive. In 2020 Maryland, Louisiana, Kansas, and Florida allowed only one week, or seven days, of early voting. Note that the mode is still "0," indicating that no early voting is still quite common. Again, we imagine that Issue Area No. 9 remains dynamic, making it necessary to track changes in state laws carefully. The popular media explains the dramatic increase in voter turnout in the 2020 election cycle as a function of early voting. The Current Population Survey, conducted by the Census Bureau in November 2020, reveals that 69 percent of voters cast their ballots early (by mail or via early voting). Only 40 percent of voters took advantage of these alternative ballot methods in the 2016 election cycle.[51]

UNDERSTANDING THE COST OF VOTING INDEX

One way to understand the COVI is to visualize a three-mile race. Figure 2.5 displays the hypothetical race. We use the value "0" to represent the beginning of the voting process, and this is where everyone would start if all states had the same election policies. The finish line is just past the −3 in the figure, indicating the completion of the three-mile race. Moreover, a closer position, shown by a negative number on the line, suggests less effort is required to vote or complete the race. In the other direction, the positive values indicate that the runner needs to run further or that more effort is required to vote.

In the hypothetical race, all eligible voters are the racers. However, there

State	Days
VA	42
IL	40
NE	30
CA	29
AZ	22
GA	19
NC	16
AK	15
ND	15
TN	15
AR	14
NM	14
NV	13
TX	13
WV	10
DE	8
MA	8
NY	8
FL	7
KS	7
LA	7
MD	7
AL	0
CT	0
IA	0
ID	0
IN	0
KY	0
ME	0
MI	0
MN	0
MO	0
MS	0
MT	0
NH	0
NJ	0
OH	0
OK	0
PA	0
RI	0
SC	0
SD	0
VT	0
WI	0
WY	0

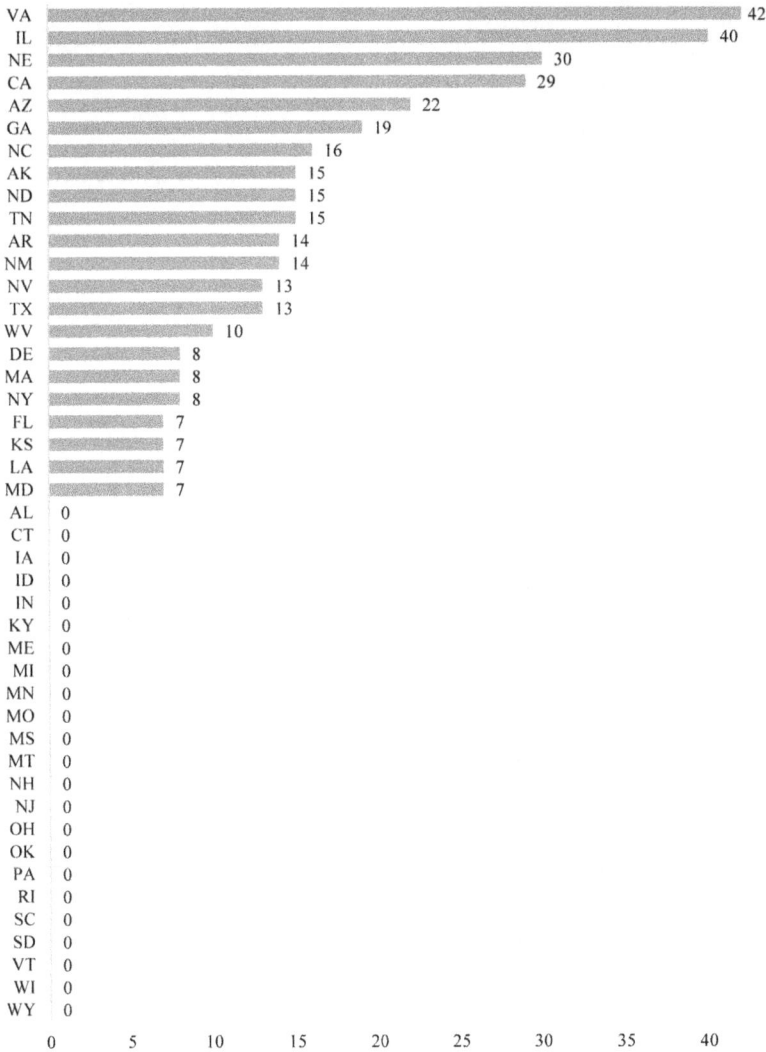

Figure 2.4. The number of early voting days by state: 2020

Source: Michael Pomante, Scot Schraufnagel, and Quan Li

are fifty unique starting spots, each representing where state citizens begin the race. Individuals must run the same distance when participating in a traditional race, but not so with voting in the United States. Instead, each state's policies determine the length an individual must run to vote. When states implement policies that make voting easier, participants in these states move

Finish Line |__|_____|_____|_____|_____|_____|_____|

       -3.0   -2.0   -1.0   0*   +1   +2   +3

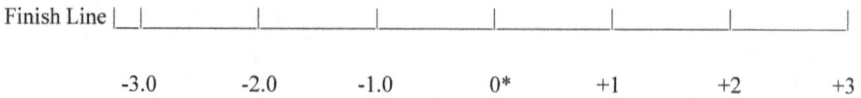

Figure 2.5. Voting as a three-mile race

* = Starting Line: This is where all eligible voters would start if there were no variations in state election law.

Source: Michael Pomante, Scot Schraufnagel, and Quan Li

closer to the finish line. On the other hand, individuals who live in states with more restrictive policies move further away.

To illustrate, Issue Area No. 1 is each state's in-person registration deadline. These deadlines range from "0" for states with EDR to 30 days before the election. If an individual's state has EDR, they get to start some distance closer to the finish line. If a state has a registration deadline of thirty days, its eligible voters are required to run further. Individuals living in states with the median number of days (fifteen days in 2020) begin at "0," or the original starting line. After everyone moves their designated distance, the process repeats for each issue area (see table 2.2). Once the process considers each issue area, individuals in each state have established their unique starting position, and at that point, the race to vote starts.

A More Technical Explanation

We assemble the COVI using PCA. In 2020 state scores in each of the nine issue areas are the variables, or columns of numbers, used. We construct issue area scores so that a larger number indicates a greater cost. Each row in the database represents a state's unique election laws or issue area score during a specific election cycle. We use PCA to produce each state's overall index value.

Specifically, PCA extracts underlying dimensions to the data called principal components. The first component explains the most interitem variation between the columns of numbers. In our case, the variables appearing in the columns represent a summation of each state's laws in a specific issue area, such as "poll hours" or "early voting days." The second component explains the second most amount of variation after removing the first component, and so forth. We weigh the first three or four components, depending on the year, by the amount of variation explained by the principal component, and then add the three or four values. This mathematical process produces a single estimate for each state in each election cycle, which taps the overall difficulty of voting. We call the total state scores the Cost of Voting Index.

Notably, the COVI values we obtain comport with conventional wisdom regarding states that maintain a more or less inclusive electoral arrangement. For instance, most observers recognize Texas as a state where voting is more difficult and Oregon as a state that has gone out of its way to make voting easier. The COVI values we obtain are consistent with these expectations. The intrinsic value of the COVI becomes evident when we move to hypothesis testing in subsequent chapters.

Conclusion

Our scrutiny of state election law, together with academic research, identifies forty-six unique electoral-institutional arrangements in the American states to include in the 2020 COVI. Each consideration represents unique state policies with the potential to influence interstate variation in the time and energy it takes to vote. Because many states created new laws and processes during the period studied, there is considerable unevenness in the number of items included in the building of the COVI each presidential election year. For instance, in 1996, there were only twenty-one considerations used to determine COVI values. Crucially, we consistently use the same PCA for each version of the COVI and the same weighting and aggregation methods.[52] One can find specifics on the construction of the index in appendix B, our sensitivity analysis that explains alternative weighting considerations in appendix C, and a construct validity check of our measurement strategy in appendix D.[53]

This chapter has been long, and we hope not too tedious. We have attempted to make the explanations as concise as possible. The problem we confront is the need to be transparent. Our measurement approach must be reliable and replicable. To this end, we provide all state values on each item and a detailed codebook on a companion website.[54] The large number of laws discussed also contributed to length. Nevertheless, we hope the reader appreciates our attempt at thoroughness.

Chapter 3 is more descriptive. Specifically, we turn to the relative state ranks and changes thereto that occurred over the seven election cycles studied. This examination allows us to test the soundness of our measurement strategies. It is essential to show that a state's rank changes when it changes its election laws. Mainly, we test whether restricting laws or making voting more accessible changes the relative state rank in the manner one would expect. We aim to leave no doubt in the reader's mind that our measurement strategy has merit. Once this is established, in chapter 4, we move forward to explore explanations for across state variation in COVI values in the contemporary era.

3: Falling Behind or Jumping Ahead: Movement in the State Cost of Voting Rank

Since James King (1994) developed a registering to vote index for the fifty American states, academics have been less inclined to create an index representing the totality of the time and effort associated with participating in elections.[1] We have filled this gap with the newly developed Cost of Voting Index. In seeking to provide a theoretical foundation for our work, we note it was Anthony Downs who spurred the contemporary discussion on the cost of voting when he argued that "time is the principal cost of voting: time to register, to discover what parties are running, to deliberate, to go to the polls, and to mark the ballot" (1957, 265).

The COVI by Presidential Election: 1996–2020

The primary focus of this chapter is to examine how the adoption of new policies alters the relative cost of voting for state citizens, as indicated by changes in state rank on the COVI. Our index construction process calculates a single value for each state in each presidential election year since the NVRA passed in 1993. Index values represent the amalgam of state laws that exist when we take a measurement. In other words, each set of index values is a product of a time-specific set of state laws. Consequently, the raw COVI values are not comparable over time. However, we can compare state ranks over time. Each new measure of the COVI allows us to rank the fifty American states anew. This chapter examines state rank changes, asking whether state movement in rank comports with expectations.[2]

In 2020 New Hampshire ranked fiftieth or was the state with the most restrictive electoral-institutional arrangement. However, this was not always the case. In 2020 Oregon was where voters found it the easiest to participate in elections. Nevertheless, Oregon has not always been the most inclusive state. Notably, based on our measurement strategy, there can be a change in rank even when a state does nothing. This change occurs if other states alter their laws. For instance, we have observed the increased reliance by some states on new technologies to make voting more accessible, or the creation of voting centers. Some states have taken advantage of these innovations more than others have; the states that do not fall in rank even when they have not altered their laws in a more restrictive direction.[3] In effect, it becomes more costly to vote in a state when it fails to adopt a modernization policy relative to other states.

The following sections provide state ranks for each presidential election cycle studied. Once we get to the second election cycle, the election of 2000, we begin tracking changes in state rank and explain the specific state law changes that cause movement in state rank. These changes allow us to test our measurement strategy's dependability and provide context for the type of law changes that affect state rankings. In the figures, we note that the state with the lowest cost of voting in each election year (ranked first) is at the top of the diagram. In contrast, one can find the state with the greatest cost of voting (ranked fiftieth) at the bottom of each figure. A larger number, or state rank, indicates more costly voting relative to other states.

1996 COVI VALUES

We begin with the 1996 presidential election, in which the Democratic incumbent president Bill Clinton faced off against Republican senator Bob Dole. Figure 3.1 displays the 1996 raw scores and rankings. This year, index values range from −2.591 for North Dakota to 1.011 for Tennessee. Considering the raw scores, as is the case with state ranks, larger numbers indicate greater cost. North Dakota voters started closest to the finish line in 1996, largely because the state does not require citizens to register to vote before Election Day. Tennessee, which still required citizens to register thirty days before Election Day, ranked last in 1996. The state was also one of only two states with a photo identification requirement to cast a ballot. Hawaii, which ranked twenty-fourth that year, was the other.

2000 COVI VALUES

There was the addition of one more cost of voting consideration in 2000. That year, the state of Oregon adopted vote-by-mail. It began circulating ballots to all registered voters ahead of the election, significantly reducing the cost of voting. This option causes us to score Oregon as though it has "early voting,"

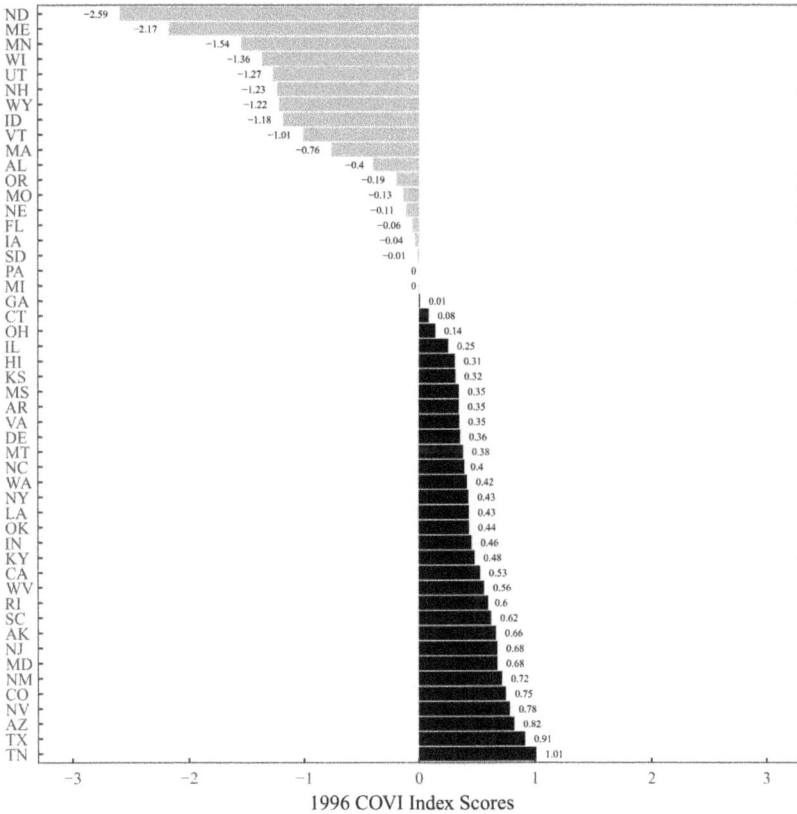

Figure 3.1. State COVI ranks: 1996

Source: Michael Pomante, Scot Schraufnagel, and Quan Li

under the assumption that voting by mail precludes the need to vote early. Finally, it is important to note that other states experienced movement in their ranks between 1996 and 2000 as they adopted policies included in the 1996 COVI. Figure 3.2 shows the raw COVI values and the fifty state ranks in 2000.

It bears repeating that the determination of state ranks reflects a state's specific policies compared to other states' policies. Consequently, states can and do change rank when they do nothing. Table 3.1 displays the change in rank from 1996 to 2000 for the least and most costly states. In addition, we show the change in state rank associated with the adoption of vote-by-mail, a significant new state law that many recognize as reducing the cost of voting. The convenience of having an official ballot mailed to one's home should be obvious.

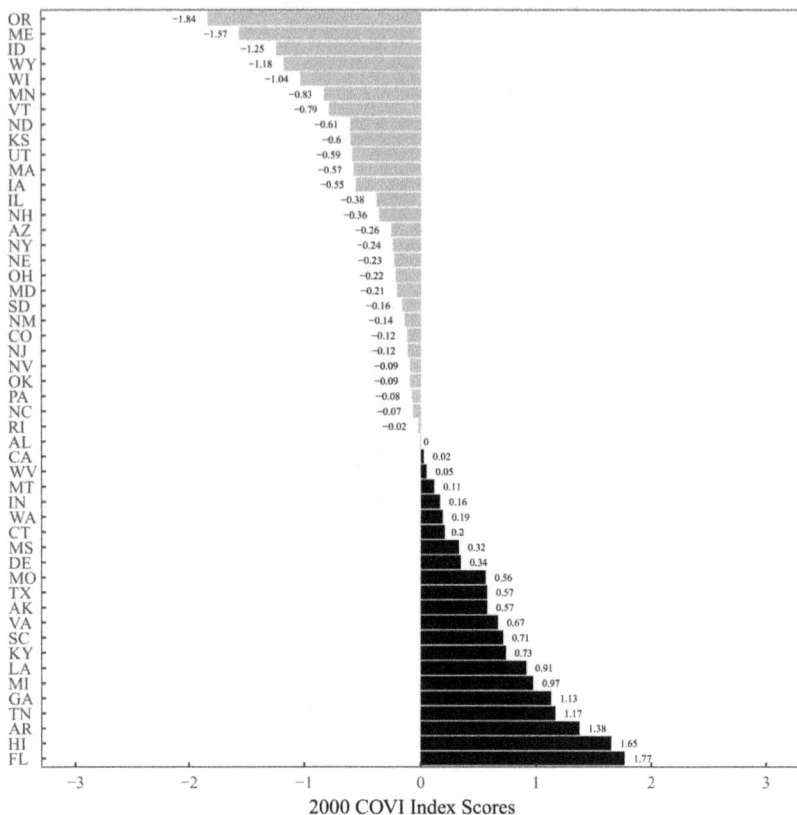

Figure 3.2. State COVI ranks: 2000

Source: Michael Pomante, Scot Schraufnagel, and Quan Li

Therefore, because Oregon adopted all mail voting we see Oregon moving eleven spots toward the most accessible voting state (ranked first), indicating that its electoral environment had become less burdensome.

In 1996 Florida was the fifteenth most accessible state for voting. Yet, by 2000 the state was fiftieth, dropping thirty-five places. This change is due, in part, to other states adopting policies that make voting less burdensome. But more importantly, in 1998 the Republican majority in the Florida State Legislature passed a photo ID law and further stipulated that old voter registration cards were no longer an acceptable form of identification. Moreover, in 2000 Florida still maintained a twenty-nine-day voter registration deadline, which meant no same-day voter registration or polling place registration, an

Table 3.1. Select State Ranks and Rank Changes: 2000

	State	Rank in 1996	Rank in 2000	Rank change
Least costly state	OR	12	1	– 11
Most costly state	FL	15	50	+ 35
New Election Law				
Introduction of all-mail voting	OR	12	1	– 11

Source: Michael Pomante, Scot Schraufnagel, and Quan Li

innovation other states were adopting. Still more, in 2000 the Sunshine State had no early voting, no in-person absentee voting, and no state holiday, as in other states. Finally, regarding Oregon and considering vote-by-mail, it is essential to remember that this change has a ripple effect. Specifically, vote-by-mail causes change in the coding of other considerations. Therefore, the change of eleven places for Oregon is not surprising.

2004 COVI Values

Construction of the 2004 index saw three new policies in Issue Area No. 2, the registration restriction additive subindex, and we added one other consideration to the voting inconvenience scale (Issue Area No. 4). Specifically, this is the first election when online voter registration appears, and we include this innovative law in the registration restriction issue area (No. 2).[4] In addition, the 2004 election cycle is the first where data on mental competency requirements for voter registration are reliably available.[5] Still more, Wyoming became the first state to restrict registration drives during this period. Finally, we add vote centers to the mix in the voting inconvenience issue area. Some states began allowing citizens to cast their ballot somewhere other than their home precinct.[6] The 2004 index finds North Dakota regaining the top spot (–2.039), and Tennessee falls to last place with a COVI value of 1.038. Figure 3.3 displays the location of all fifty states on the 2004 COVI.

Although North Dakota jumps back into the first position, Oregon only drops one spot, becoming the second easiest state to vote in during this election cycle. We can note that it makes sense that the two states are jostling for the top position. The first stage of voting, registering to vote, does not exist in North Dakota, and Oregon's vote-by-mail law makes the second stage of voting, casting a ballot, very convenient. Moreover, we can explain North Dakota's ascension back to the top of the ranking by including one of the new

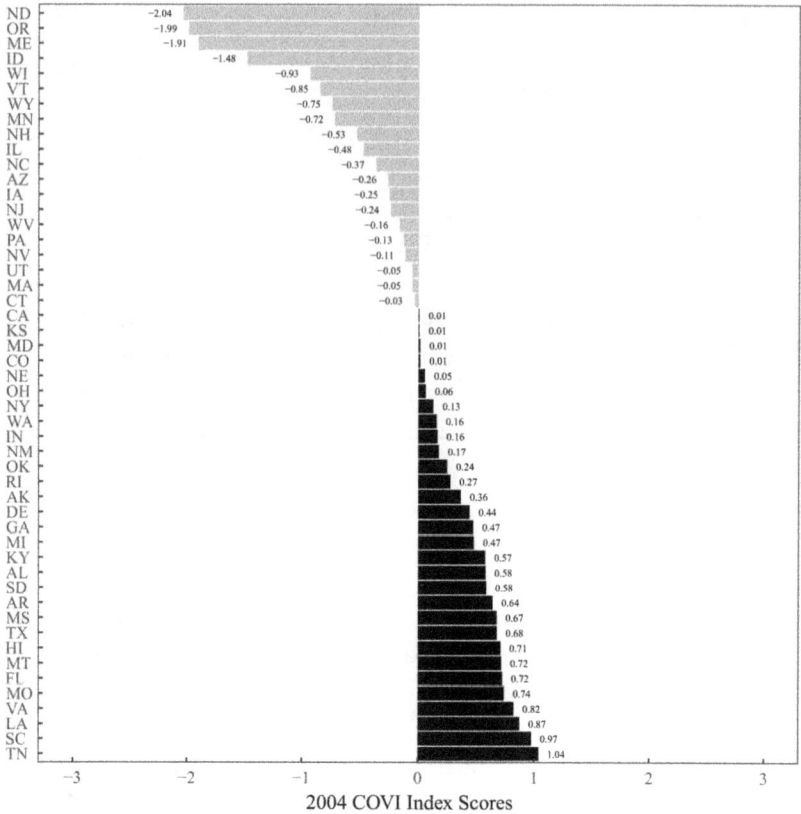

Figure 3.3. State COVI ranks: 2004

Source: Michael Pomante, Scot Schraufnagel, and Quan Li

considerations. When we add online voter registration, North Dakota joins Arizona as the only states that scored "0" because North Dakota does not require voter registration. Moreover, North Dakota adopted early voting before the 2004 general election.

Considering table 3.2, Tennessee's fall is predictable. The Volunteer State maintains a thirty-day voter registration deadline and scores "1" on three of the four new considerations; the state does not adopt online voter registration, maintains a mental competency law, and does not create vote centers. Florida stays near the bottom, tied with Montana as the forty-fourth most challenging state for voting. Florida's move out of last place occurred because the state adopted an early voting law before the 2004 general election.[7]

Table 3.2. Select State Ranks and Rank Changes: 2004

	State	Rank in 2000	Rank in 2004	Rank change
Least costly state	ND	8	1	–7
Most costly state	TN	47	50	3
New voting laws				
Online voter registration	AZ	15	12	–3
No registration drives allowed	WY	4	7	3

Source: Michael Pomante, Scot Schraufnagel, and Quan Li

Again, considering table 3.2 and the new voting laws, Arizona's adoption of online voter registration moves the state from fifteenth to twelfth, indicating that the state made it easier to vote relative to other states. On the other hand, Wyoming's ban on registration drives causes it to move from fourth to seventh. We see that this consideration continues to weigh down Wyoming's ranking, as will the state's failure to adopt early voting and other election law innovations in subsequent years.[8]

We can also note a significant change in state rank for North Carolina between 2000 and 2004 (see figures 3.2 and 3.3). In the previous election cycle, the Tar Heel State was ranked twenty-seventh, but the state climbed to eleventh in 2004, a move forward of sixteen places. Notably, North Carolina did not add to its cost of voting by having a mental competency requirement for voter registration. However, the most significant change between the two election cycles was the adoption of in-person absentee voting and early voting. In 2004 South Dakota fell nineteen spots, coming in at thirty-ninth. The state's adoption of a photo ID law, a mental competency law for voter registration, and the failure to adopt an online voter registration option for citizens explain the move.

2008 COVI VALUES

In 2008 we saw the inclusion of three new considerations to the voting inconvenience subindex (Issue Area No. 4). Although laws allowing workers time off from work to vote, with or without pay, had been around before 2008, this is the first year we could gather reliable data for all fifty states. Recall that 2008 was also the first election cycle that California began allowing voters to obtain permanent absentee voter status, a law that looks something akin to vote-by-mail. Voters who sign up with their election supervisor's office can consistently

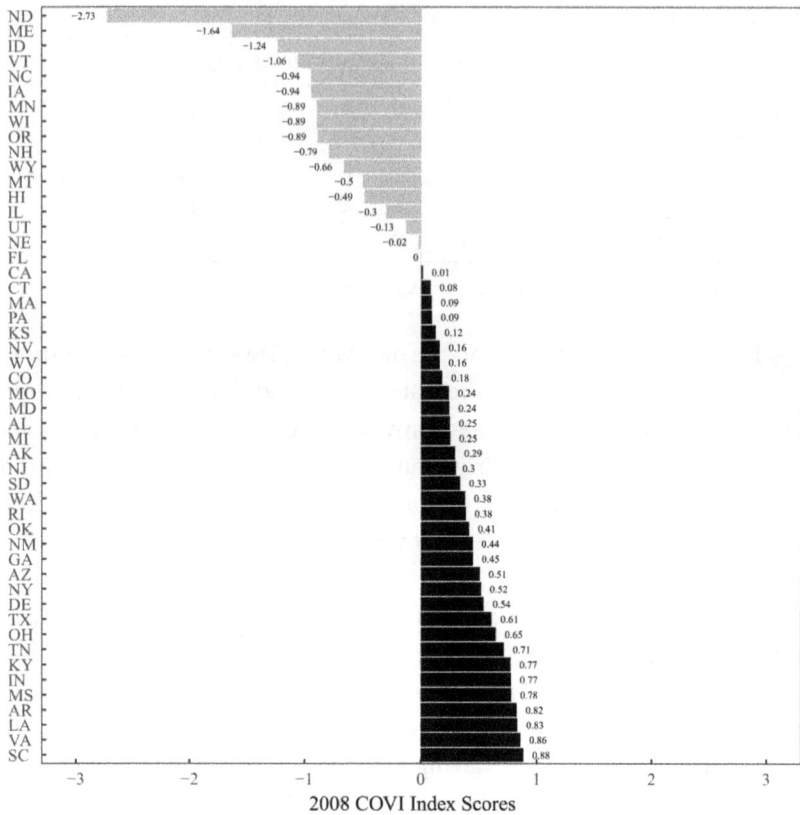

Figure 3.4. State COVI ranks: 2008

Source: Michael Pomante, Scot Schraufnagel, and Quan Li

and predictably have a blank ballot mailed to them before scheduled elections in the same manner as today in vote-by-mail states. Moreover, California already had no-excuse absentee voting. Consequently, the option of permanent absentee voter status was available to anyone. In 2008, the opportunity to vote by mail in California was only for registered individuals.[9]

In 2008 index values ranged from –2.727 in North Dakota to .883 in South Carolina. Figure 3.4 exhibits the raw values and rankings for all fifty states. At this time, the Midwest states of Iowa, Minnesota, and Wisconsin are among the top ten states where it was easiest to vote. Note, however, that Indiana, another Midwest state, is in the bottom ten most difficult states to vote. The Hoosier state and Ohio join mostly southern states in the bottom ten.

Table 3.3. Select State Ranks and Rank Changes: 2008

	State	Rank in 2004	Rank in 2008	Rank change
Least costly state	ND	1	1	0
Most costly state	SC	49	50	1
New voting law				
Permanent absentee status	CA	21	18	–3

Source: Michael Pomante, Scot Schraufnagel, and Quan Li

In table 3.3 we note that North Dakota holds the top spot as the least costly state. South Carolina dropped one spot to become the costliest state to vote in 2008. As noted, between 2004 and 2008, three new policies were included in COVI construction. North Dakota did not fare well with these policies, as the state did not have a state law allowing workers time off to vote or time off with pay. It also did not establish permanent absentee voter status for voters. However, the Peace Garden state did open vote centers for the 2008 election cycle. This development seems to offset private sector employees' lack of time off. Most important, North Dakota still did not require voter registration, which gave it the lowest possible score for the considerations used to tap the first stage of voting in the United States.

We can explain South Carolina's replacement of Tennessee as the most challenging state to vote in by including the two variables associated with giving workers time off to vote. Tennessee requires some private employers to give some hourly workers time off to vote with pay, and South Carolina does not. In 2008 these policies reduced the relative cost of voting in Tennessee and the state moved from fiftieth to forty-third. We also see a significant change in Montana's relative cost of voting between 2004 and 2008. The state moved thirty-two spots from the forty-fourth to the twelfth easiest. In 2004 Montana required citizens to register to vote thirty days before Election Day. However, by 2008 the state adopted same-day voter registration, a variable that receives considerable weight in index construction because it relates so well to other restrictions. Moving in the other direction between 2004 and 2008 is the state of Arizona. The Grand Canyon state moved from the twelfth easiest state to thirty-eighth when it began strictly enforcing its ID law at polling locations.

Considering California's adoption of permanent absentee voting in 2008, it is worth noting that this is an important change because it makes a move to vote-by-mail more straightforward. Before 2008 the state required any individual who wished to obtain an absentee ballot to request the ballot each time they wanted to vote absentee. Now, the ballot would routinely appear in the mail. The new California law especially reduced the burden of voting on individuals with disabilities, who find traveling to polling locations more challenging than other voters. Unsurprisingly, California's new law moved the state from twenty-first in 2004 to eighteenth easiest in 2008.

2012 COVI VALUES

Following the election of President Barack Obama, some states passed legislation to make voting more costly. For instance, apparently in reaction to the fact that successful registration drives helped propel Obama's victory, several states adopted voter registration drive restrictions. This spate of new state laws caused us to create a new issue area in 2012—registration drive restrictions (Issue Area No. 7). We folded the ban on registration drives, which first occurred in Wyoming, into a new five-item additive subindex. We also added one new consideration to the registration restriction additive subindex (Issue Area No. 2) in 2012. Rhode Island allows voters to register to vote on Election Day in presidential election years. We added this new consideration, imagining other states would make a parallel move, and indeed Alaska passed such a law in 2021. Still, Rhode Island was the only state to have this law in 2012. In Obama's reelection year, Oregon retook the number one spot from North Dakota with an index value of −1.674, while Tennessee resumed its place as the most challenging state to vote in, with a value of 1.088. Figure 3.5 shows all states' raw values and rankings on the 2012 COVI.

Since the adoption of vote-by-mail in 2000, Oregon has consistently ranked near the top, suggesting it is one of the states where it is easiest to vote. Washington State joined Oregon near the top in 2012, coming in second. The Evergreen State's dramatic move in 2012 up the rankings occurred because it was the second state to adopt an inclusive vote-by-mail law. Recall that this law causes other coding changes. We now score Washington "0" on absentee and early voting considerations. Again, the operating assumption is that vote-by-mail precludes the need to vote early or absentee. Moreover, Washington reduced the state's voter registration deadline from thirty days to eight days between 2008 and 2012, which also helps explain the state's dramatic move up the rankings. In table 3.4 we see Tennessee falls seven spots, back to fiftieth, a

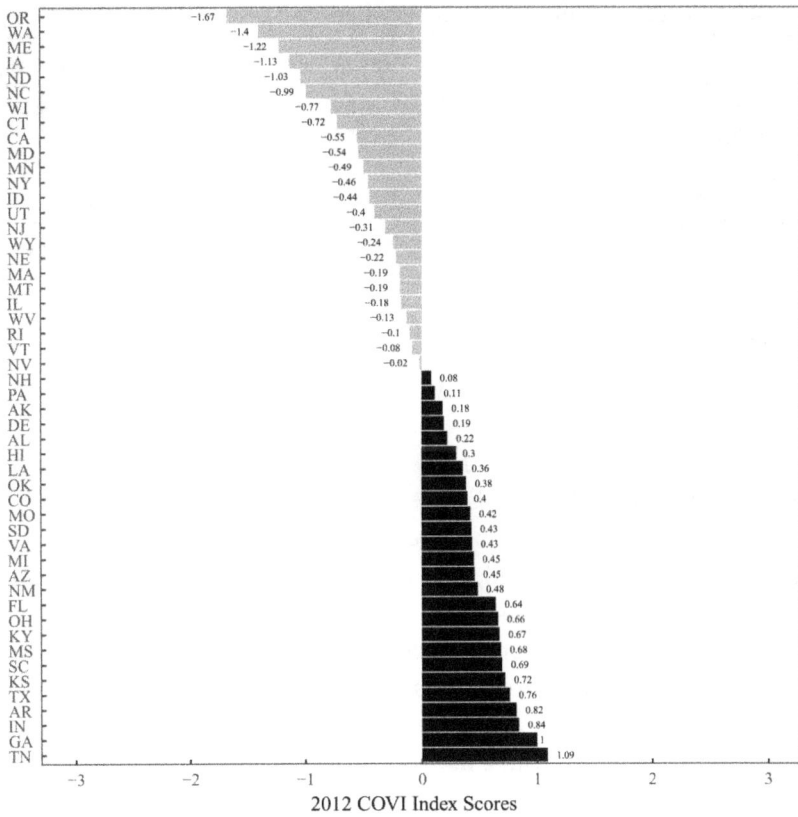

Figure 3.5. State COVI ranks: 2012

Source: Michael Pomante, Scot Schraufnagel, and Quan Li

fall due primarily to the state's strict enforcement of its photo ID requirement (before the 2012 election cycle, enforcement was not strict).

Between 2008 and 2012, Kansas was also busy making changes to state election law, but with the opposite intentions of Washington. First, Kansas increased the registration deadline from fifteen days to twenty-one days before an election. The Sunflower State also adopted a strict photo ID law for the 2012 election cycle. Because of the two new restrictive policies, Kansas moved from the twenty-second to the forty-fifth-ranked state between 2008 and 2012.

Turning back to table 3.4, we learn that new laws limiting voter registration drives and Rhode Island's new EDR law changed state ranks as expected. For

Table 3.4. Select State Ranks and Rank Changes: 2012

	State	Rank in 2008	Rank in 2012	Rank change
Least costly state	OR	9	1	−8
Most costly state	TN	43	50	7
New voting laws				
Registration drive restrictions	CO	25	33	8
	NH	10	25	15
	TX	41	46	5
	WY	11	16	5
EDR—presidential race only	RI	34	22	−12

Source: Michael Pomante, Scot Schraufnagel, and Quan Li

example, four states scored "3" or higher on the new five-item additive registration drive restriction subindex (Issue Area No. 7): Colorado, New Hampshire, Texas, and Wyoming. As a result, these four states' average drop in rank is seven spots. On the other hand, Rhode Island rose twelve spots and became the twenty-second easiest state to vote in by 2012 once it adopted a limited form of EDR. Notably, between 2008 and 2012, Rhode Island also started to allow citizens as young as sixteen to preregister to vote, which also helps explain the state's move up the ranking. In chapter 2 we made the case that preregistration allowances are consistent with a more inclusive electoral-institutional climate and the data in the 2012 COVI seems to back up this assertion.[10]

2016 COVI Values

We added one new consideration in 2016, automatic voter registration, as part of the registration restriction subindex (Issue Area No. 2). Although no state laws are the same in this regard, we can note that Connecticut, Georgia, and Oregon have passed new policies that made registering to vote at state driver licensing facilities much more straightforward. Figure 3.6 exhibits the values and rankings for the 2016 COVI. Oregon maintained the number one spot with a COVI value of −2.016. New Hampshire supplanted Tennessee as the state where voting is most burdensome. The New Hampshire COVI value in 2016 was 1.218, and the state dropped twenty-five spots down the rankings. Note that adopting AVR in Oregon stretched its relative lead. As a result, we see a widening gap over the second-place finisher in 2016, California. Oregon continued to be the least costly state to vote in, primarily because the state

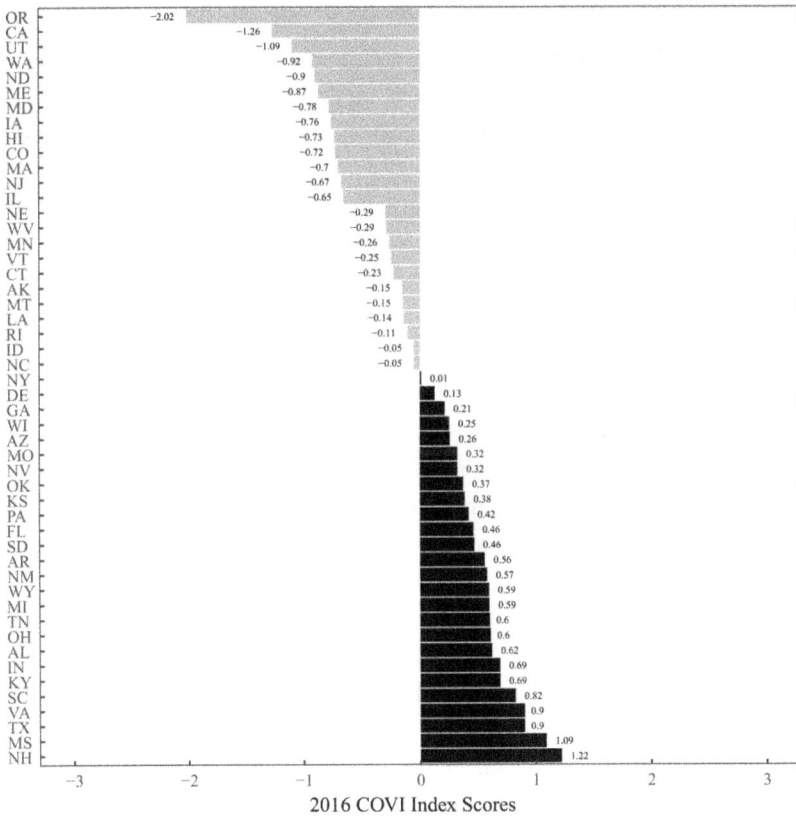

Figure 3.6. State COVI ranks: 2016

Source: Michael Pomante, Scot Schraufnagel, and Quan Li

consistently adopted policies that reduce the burden of voting. In addition to the AVR provision, the state had removed felon and mental competence restrictions by 2016.

Notably, New Hampshire moved from the twenty-fifth easiest state to vote to fiftieth place. Between 2012 and 2016, New Hampshire passed only one new law associated with elections. Specifically, the state passed a voter ID law. Previously, the state had only required a voter's signature that matched the signature on the registration roll. Since 2016 voters need to show their registration card or another form of ID to vote. This change alone might not seem sufficient for such a drastic change in rank. However, the ID consideration is one of the weightier considerations in index construction, and New Hampshire generally failed to move in a more inclusive direction, as many other states were doing at this time. For example, in New Hampshire, in 2016, citizens still needed to travel to a central government facility other than the polling place if they wished to register to vote on Election Day. From 1996 to 2004, it was the only state with this requirement.[11]

Moreover, New Hampshire continued to restrict who can register to vote, with limits on felons, those who do not meet mental competency consider- ations, and those under eighteen years of age. Still more, in 2016 citizens in the Granite State still could not register to vote online, were subjected to a ban on registration drives, and were not allowed to vote early. Still more, the state did not require employers to give workers time off from work for voting, there was no state holiday or in-person absentee voting, and if one wanted to vote ab- sentee in New Hampshire, they needed to provide a state-sanctioned excuse. In short, New Hampshire's failure to adopt any policy that makes voting easier reinforced the new ID requirement and caused the state to take up last place in the rankings.

Table 3.5 displays New Hampshire's precipitous drop down the rankings. While the state was reluctant to adopt inclusionary voting policies, other states like Colorado worked diligently to make voting easier. As a result, the Centennial State jumped twenty-three spots from the thirty-third to the tenth most accessible state to vote in. In 2012 Colorado required voter registration twenty-nine days before an election. However, by 2016 it had adopted EDR and allowed EDR at the actual polling location and not some government of- fice in a different part of town. Perhaps most significantly, Colorado adopted vote-by-mail for the 2016 presidential election, which we know has ripple ef- fects. Still more, Colorado passed a law in 2013 allowing sixteen-year-olds to preregister to vote when they get their driver's license.[12]

Table 3.5 shows an apparent anomaly associated with Connecticut's new AVR law. The state made registering to vote less burdensome but fell in ranking from eighth to eighteenth. This fall occurred because the state did not make the second voting stage easier between 2012 and 2016, while other states were moving in that direction. Specifically, the Constitution State in 2016 still had no preregistration law, state holiday for voting, or in-person absentee voting, required a state-sanctioned excuse to vote absentee, and had yet to adopt early voting. Making registering to vote easier in Connecticut failed to offset the extra costs associated with neglecting to change policies in the second voting

Table 3.5. Select State Ranks and Rank Changes: 2016

	State	Rank in 2012	Rank in 2016	Rank change
Least costly state	OR	1	1	0
Most costly state	NH	25	50	25
Largest reduction in cost	CO	33	10	−23
Largest increase in cost	NH	25	50	25
New voting law				
Automatic voter registration	CT	8	18	10
	GA	49	27	−22
	OR	1	1	0

Source: Michael Pomante, Scot Schraufnagel, and Quan Li

stage. Meanwhile, Georgia experienced a significant climb up the ranking when it passed AVR. The Peach State moves from forty-ninth to the twenty-seventh most accessible state to vote in. Overall, Oregon, which had already been number one, held its position, likely because it also adopted a more automated voter registration process.

2020 COVI VALUES

Unlike in 2016, when we added only a small number of considerations to index construction, the 2020 version tracks several new state policies. However, there are no new stand-alone laws to consider. Instead, as explained in chapter 2, we created two new issue areas. Specifically, we included an automatic voter registration additive subindex (Issue Area No. 8) and began to consider the specific number of early voting days (Issue Area No. 9). Moreover, we started paying closer attention to the elimination of polling locations, especially noting states that were aggressive in this regard. Despite the changes to the construction of the index, Oregon retained its spot as the least costly state (−2.917), and New Hampshire holds on to last place as the costliest state (1.437) to vote in. Figure 3.7 exhibits the raw values and rankings in 2020.

Figure 3.7 exhibits a significant gap between Oregon and Washington and third-place finisher Illinois. In recent election cycles, the two states in the Pacific Northwest have been at the forefront of adopting inclusionary voting practices, usually with Oregon taking the lead and Washington following quickly behind. Both states passed new laws allowing sixteen-year-old citizens to preregister to vote just before the 2020 election. Interestingly, Oregon still

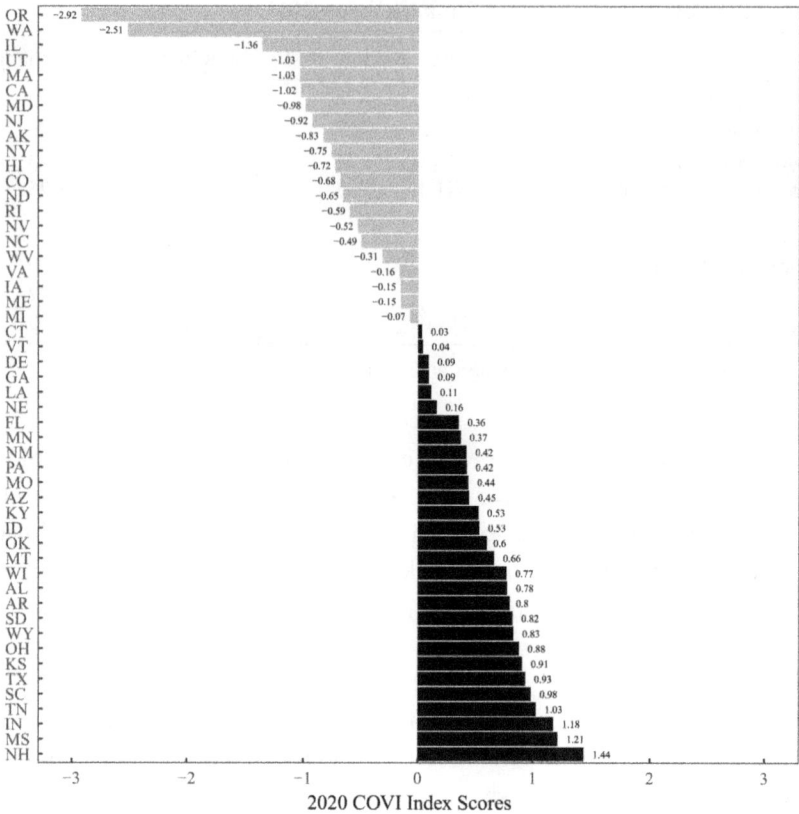

Figure 3.7. State COVI ranks: 2020

Source: Michael Pomante, Scot Schraufnagel, and Quan Li

maintained a registration deadline (twenty-one days) in 2020, while between 2016 and 2020, Washington dropped their registration deadline and adopted EDR or same-day voter registration.[13] However, Washington still maintained a voter identification requirement in the second voting stage. This law, arguably, allowed Oregon to edge out the Evergreen State as the state where it was easiest to vote in 2020. At the bottom of the ranking, in 2020, we find Tennessee, Indiana, Mississippi, and New Hampshire.[14]

Table 3.6 details the rank and rank changes for the easiest and most difficult states. Notably, there was no change in first or fiftieth place. Moreover, there is nothing to track because we do not adopt any wholly new law in the 2020 index construction. However, we can display the change in state rank for three states

Table 3.6. Select State Ranks and Rank Changes: 2020

	State	Rank in 2016	Rank in 2020	Rank change
Least costly state	OR	1	1	0
Most costly state	NH	50	50	0
Significant changes in rank 2016 to 2020				
Largest reduction in cost	VA	47	18	−29
2nd largest reduction in cost	MI	40	21	−19
Largest increase in cost	MT	20	37	17

Source: Michael Pomante, Scot Schraufnagel, and Quan Li

that did experience considerable movement from 2016 to 2020. Specifically, we note that Virginia and Michigan made voting much more accessible between 2016 and 2020, while Montana made voting more restrictive; our scoring reflects these changes.

Virginia's changes occur as part of a standard legislative process. Specifically, the state legislature in Virginia passed a law that dropped the voter registration deadline, which meant voters could now register to vote at polling locations on Election Day. The state also instituted early voting and adopted Election Day as a state holiday. Next, Virginia relaxed absentee voting procedures, allowing voters to vote absentee in-person and to request an absentee ballot without a state-sanctioned excuse. These rather dramatic changes, occurring all at once, cause the Old Dominion state to rise from forty-seventh to eighteenth. Virginia would have increased even further in the rankings if the state had passed a preregistration policy to address youth mobilization.

Michigan also made voting much more accessible between 2016 and 2020. However, the Great Lakes state changed its policies through a voter-backed constitutional initiative, or referendum. During the 2018 midterm election, 67 percent of Michigan voters supported adopting same-day registration. Moreover, the newly approved state constitutional amendment relaxed absentee voting procedures and implemented an AVR law. Adopting same-day registration was a significant change to Michigan's previous law, which had a deadline of four weeks. Although the state's changes failed to provide voter registration at polling locations, voter registration now occurs when movers, or new state residents, visit a Michigan DMV facility. As a result, Michigan moves from the fortieth to the twenty-first easiest state to vote in between 2016 and 2020.

In contrast, in 2020 Montana saw the most significant voting cost increase from the previous presidential election cycle, dropping seventeen spots to thirty-seventh. The fall down the ranking occurred partly because Montana reduced the number of polling locations available to citizens. Moreover, the state failed to adopt additional policies that other states were adopting, such as EDR, AVR, and early voting. Therefore, inaction largely explains Montana's fall in the rankings.

State Movement from 1996 to 2020

So far, we have focused on the shifts in the cost of voting between each presidential election cycle. However, this last section selects a few states and examines their journey over the seven election cycles studied. Specifically, we look at the states that were ranked first and last in 1996 (North Dakota and Tennessee) and the states that ranked first and last in 2020 (Oregon and New Hampshire). We also scrutinize Maryland's movement because it experienced the largest relative reduction in voting costs over the past twenty-five years. Figure 3.8 provides a graphic display of the movement in rankings for the five states.

Perhaps most notably, there is considerable constancy when considering three of the five states. Oregon joins North Dakota as a state that consistently retains a more inclusive electoral-institutional arrangement. The Beaver State started as the twelfth easiest state for voting in 1996, and as time progresses, it occupies the easiest slot in four of the seven election cycles studied, including the most recent iteration in 2020. North Dakota's lack of a voter registration requirement causes that state to maintain a less restrictive electoral climate. However, one must note that during the 2020 election cycle, the state briefly contemplated aggressive restrictions on Native Americans' voting eligibility.[15] Overall, the state was the easiest to vote in for the other three of the seven election cycles and only recently, in 2020, fell out of the top ten, landing at thirteenth in 2020. The recent drop in North Dakota has to do with the failure of the state to adopt mail-in voting and more inclusive absentee voting processes. In all, it is safe to claim that the two northern states (Oregon and North Dakota) have maintained a less restrictive or more inclusive electoral climate relative to other states in the twenty-first century.

On the other hand, Tennessee started as the most restrictive state to vote

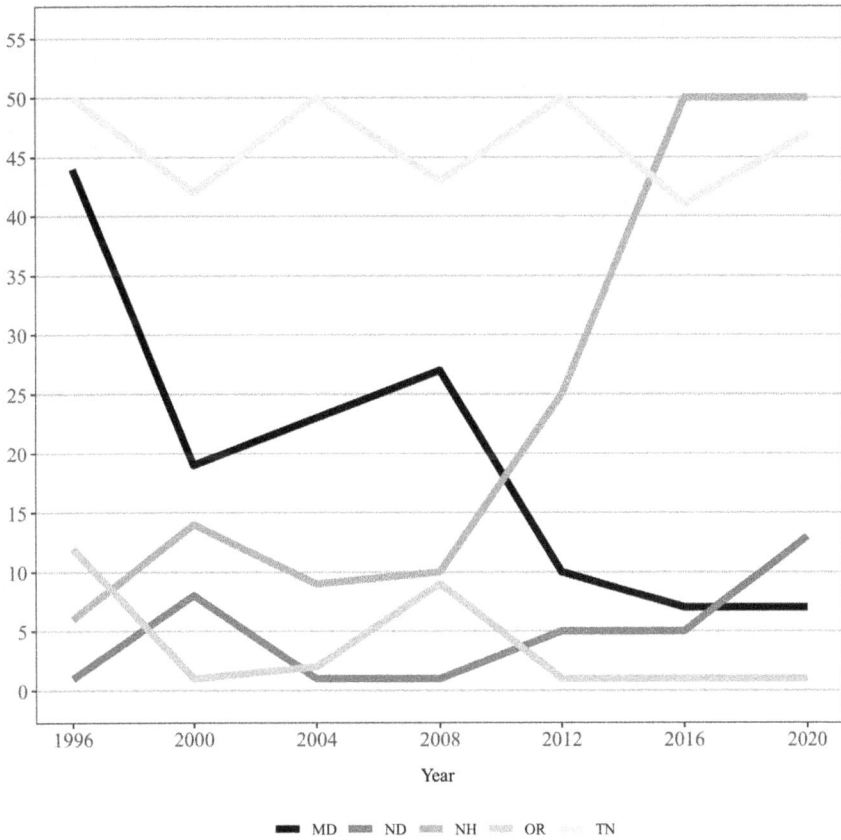

Figure 3.8. Change in rank of select states: 1996–2020

Source: Michael Pomante, Scot Schraufnagel, and Quan Li

in 1996 and only advanced three spots by 2020. Tennessee's inability to move out of the bottom ten is due primarily to its unwillingness to adopt policies to make voting easier. The Volunteer State, in 2020, was still requiring citizens to register thirty days before an election, the maximum number of days allowed by national law. While the thirty-day requirement was more common in 1996, technological advancements have allowed states to adopt same-day voter registration and other policies to make voter registration easier. Moreover, the Volunteer State still has not adopted an online voter registration system, let alone any automated voter registration process. In terms of ballot casting, Tennessee continued, through 2020, to require a state-sanctioned excuse to vote absentee (even during the COVID-19 pandemic election of 2020). Moreover, the state maintained strict enforcement of a photo ID, even though voter impersonations are extremely rare. However, the state did adopt early voting in time for the 2004 election, and the additional fifteen days of early voting arguably kept Tennessee out of last place in 2020.

Considering the other two states in figure 3.8, we see Maryland and New Hampshire move dramatically in the opposite direction during the period studied. Note that Maryland was ranked forty-fourth in 1996 and, with changes over time, became the seventh least restrictive state by 2020. This move up the rankings was the most significant among all fifty states. The focus of all voting law changes made by the Free State during the twenty-five years was in the direction of more accessible voting. Perhaps the greatest impact came when the state adopted early voting between 2008 and 2012. Note the precipitous drop in the figure (or climb up the rankings) from twenty-seventh place in 2008 to tenth place by 2012. Moreover, by 2020 the state had done away with its twenty-nine-day voter registration deadline, adopting EDR, with an option to register to vote at polling locations. Maryland also made significant progress in other areas associated with voter registration. Between 2008 and 2012, the state adopted OVR and began to allow citizens as young as sixteen to preregister. Moreover, in 2020 Maryland continued as one of the sixteen states that allow a voter's signature to suffice as identification at poll locations.

In stark contrast to Maryland, New Hampshire was in 1996 the sixth easiest state to vote in but fell to fiftieth by 2016 and stayed there in 2020. Over the years, the Granite State has largely failed to act on any significant legislation that would have reduced the state's cost of voting. Ironically, New Hampshire was one of only seven states with an EDR option in 1996. However, since 1996 the state requires an ID to vote, reduced the number of polling locations available to voters, and restricted voter registration drives. Yet, inaction is also responsible for the state's fall. The state has failed to adopt new technologies that allow for early voting, online voter registration, or AVR.

Figure 3.9 displays the American states by quintiles. In other words, we show the ten states where it is easiest to vote, followed by the ten states that are second easiest, and so forth. The ten states where it is easiest to vote are colored black in the figure, and the ten states where it is most difficult to vote are the lightest shade of gray. We do not assume that our measurement strategy is flawless or that it is impossible to challenge a given state's rank in a particular

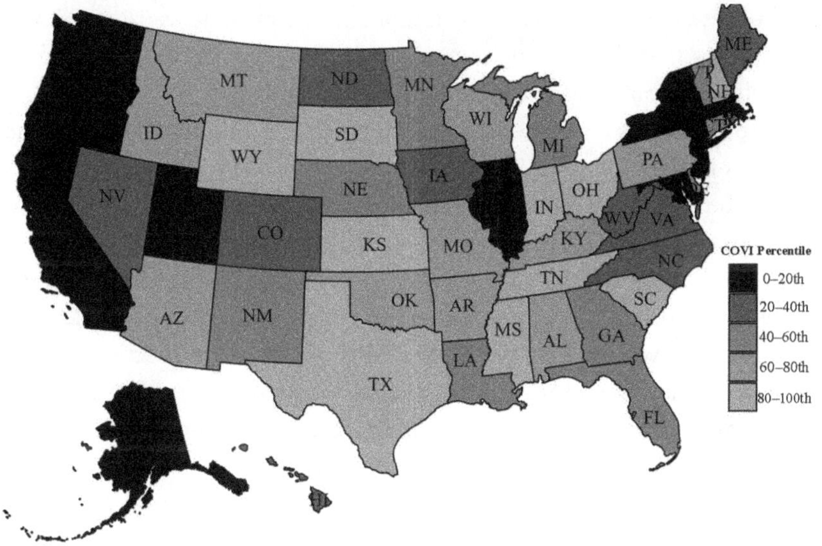

Figure 3.9. The cost of voting in 2020: ranked by quintile from lowest to highest cost

Source: Michael Pomante, Scot Schraufnagel, and Quan Li

year. However, we are confident that the cost of voting is much greater in the lightest shade of gray states than in the black states. No one should suggest it is easier to vote in Ohio than in Utah. Moreover, we are confident that the time and energy associated with voting in the states in the 40–60 percentile is greater than in the black states and less costly than in the lightest shade of gray states. Ironically, early in 2021 the governor of Georgia claimed, based on a select few voting laws, that it is easier to vote in Georgia than in New York.[16] Our analysis suggests that it is an inaccurate assessment.

Conclusion

As noted at the beginning of this chapter, we also calculated a COVI in 2020 that considered changes in the state election process in response to the COVID-19 global pandemic. These results are available on our website.[17] Again, we can report that changes to raw values and state rank meet expectations. For instance, the four states that adopted vote-by-mail for the 2020 election (California,

Nevada, New Jersey, and Vermont) jumped in the ranking as expected. Conversely, states that did nothing to accommodate voters during the pandemic either fell in the rankings or maintained a high rank.

Throughout this chapter, we have explored the ranking of all fifty American states in the last seven presidential election cycles. In each election, we uncover the specifics explaining a state's rank change. Unsurprisingly, when states adopt laws that ease the burden of the two-stage voting process in the United States, their relative cost of voting decreases. These findings lead us to inquire, what contributes to a state's adoption or nonadoption of policies that alter the cost of voting? Given that Jim Crow–era voting restrictions resulted from a perceived racial threat, in chapter 4, we explore the effect the size of state minority populations has on the relative cost of voting. We also look to uncover what role political parties play in making voting more or less costly. Historically, the Democratic Party was responsible for adopting restrictive voting policies to disenfranchise formerly enslaved people. Have the parties fully reversed roles in this regard? Is the Grand Old Republican Party now more likely to associate with a restrictive electoral-institutional climate? We turn to answer these questions in chapter 4.

4: Minority Populations, Republicans, and the COVI

In a republic like the United States, voting is one of the most fundamental and common forms of political participation. A republican form of government, or a "representative democracy," suggests sovereignty resides with the citizenry but elected representatives make the political decisions that affect everyday life. This type of political system empowers citizens to vote for those who they wish to represent them. Unfortunately, effective representation suffers if the system systematically excludes specific subpopulations from the selection process. Hence, scholars, and other members of the attentive public, place considerable attention on elections, paying particular attention to developing and maintaining free, fair, and inclusive voting practices. An important motivation for this book was to learn if systematic discrimination in state voting laws in the United States hampers quality representation and competent government.

Historically, the United States has been a world leader in democratic institution building. For instance, the country was the first to drop property requirements as a condition for voting (Engerman and Sokoloff 2005). Furthermore, efforts to expand voting rights to women found strong, early advocates in the United States (Cooney 2005). Although some countries, like Brazil, grant the franchise to sixteen-year-olds, the United States was among the leaders in extending voting rights to eighteen-year-olds. Yet, what are we to make of alleged attempts by some state governments to restrict voting in the twenty-first century? This question is especially salient as countries like Australia, Canada, and Estonia are moving forward more quickly with the technology that allows for convenient and secure voting via cellular phones.

Scholars studying US exceptionalism find there is much we could learn from other countries (Stephanopoulos 2013) in terms of electoral law. Indeed, moves by other democracies suggest the United States is no longer the beacon of democratic inclusion that so many imagine. In fact, in 2016 a democracy index developed by the *Economist* downgraded the United States from a full democracy to a flawed democracy.[1]

Scholars have long understood that elected representatives in a republic are more responsive to the people and groups who vote (Berelson 1952; Almond and Verba 1963; Griffin and Newman 2005). Consequently, a comprehensive investigation into voting practices is crucial, especially if specific subpopulations are discouraged from voting in predictable ways. The concern is for the quality of the electoral process and, by extension, the legitimacy of government institutions. Laws intended to disenfranchise specific segments of a country's population are commonplace in authoritarian regimes where leaders manipulate elections to illegitimately boost their support while discouraging their opposition (Levitsky and Way 2010; Schedler 2002; 2006). These practices should not be obvious or exist in the United States, a country once seen as a leader in democratic institution building.

Unfortunately, in the United States, we can note instances when state policymakers have made their motivation to pass restrictive voting laws reasonably clear. For example, in November 2012 Jim Greer, the former chair of the Republican Party in Florida, told the press that the goal of the passage of restrictions on early/absentee voting and voter registration was to make voting more difficult and inconvenient. He expounded that more convenient voting "is bad for Republican Party candidates."[2] Similarly, in July 2013 Pennsylvania House Majority Leader Mike Turzai boasted that the state's new voter identification law intended to "allow Governor Romney to win the state of Pennsylvania."[3] Likewise, in April 2016 Wisconsin State Representative Glenn Grothman bragged that 2016 would be different from previous elections because "now we have photo I.D., and I think photo I.D. is gonna make a little bit of a difference."[4] Finally, Justin Clark, a senior political adviser and senior counsel to President Donald Trump's 2020 reelection campaign, noted, "traditionally it's always been Republicans suppressing votes in places," but now it is possible to begin "protecting our voters. We know where they are . . . Let's start playing offense a little bit."[5]

These claims indicate that Republican Party operatives, in recent years, have been anxious to make voting more difficult for Democrats, at least in some states. Yet, the quotes point to partisan motives and do not suggest a systematic attempt to disenfranchise protected groups covered by civil rights legislation. This distinction is important because civil rights abuse prompts serious legal wrangling in the United States. As of 2021 the demographic considerations protected by national civil rights laws are race, gender, color, ethnicity, religion, age, and disability. One might imagine that Republican Party operatives are making policies, when and where they can, to gain an electoral advantage without malice toward a particular group with civil rights protections. However, suppose their efforts produce election practices that disproportionately affect the representation of Black or Hispanic subpopulations. If this were the case, one would move quickly into a sticky legal situation with potential implications for due process and equal protection under the law, which form the basis for civil rights protections.

In a republic, if specific subpopulations are systematically discouraged from voting and elections produce significant underrepresentation of certain groups, it follows that there may be less effective representation of that group's interest (Avery and Peffley 2005; Fraga 2018, Hajnal and Trounstine 2005; Hill and Leighley 1992).

Previous research has uncovered that specific state policies, such as voter identification laws, have a larger demobilizing effect on Hispanic populations and other minorities (Government Accountability Office 2014; Hajnal, Lajevardi, & Nielson 2017). Other researchers find that photo ID laws disproportionately disenfranchise the elderly, the less educated, and those with lower incomes because these groups are less likely to have a driver's license (Barreto, Nuño, and Sanchez, 2009).[6] Notably, we included these policies in the Cost of Voting Index (COVI: Issue Area No. 5). In chapter 5, we use the COVI to make clearer why some people are more likely to vote than others. However, it is important to test whether partisan inclinations, combined with state racial and ethnic demographics, can predict COVI values or a more restrictive electoral-institutional climate. These tests are the focus of this chapter.

In much of what follows, we use each state's raw COVI value as the dependent variable or the phenomenon we wish to explain. We wonder whether demographic and partisan conditions in each state can explain index values. The COVI provides an advantage because we are not limited to analyzing a single election law or a single election. Instead, we look for explanations for the broad electoral-institutional climate of each state, testing the totality of state variation in electoral restrictiveness over a quarter century. For example, we test whether states with larger Black or Hispanic populations have more restrictive election laws. In addition, we explore whether the Democratic or Republican Party's dominance of the state legislative process can explain restrictions.

Notably, others have found connections between the size of state minority populations and antiminority legislation. Specifically, the frequency of restrictive immigration laws in the American states occurs more commonly in states with faster-growing Hispanic populations (Márquez and Schraufnagel 2013). Others find stricter death penalty policies in states with a higher percentage of Black citizens (Jacobs and Carmichael 2002). Relatedly, scholars find that growth in the Hispanic population influences the policy attitudes of whites (Rocha and Espino 2009). Still more, scholars find that Republican state governments generally speaking are more likely to pass legislation requiring citizens to have a photo ID to vote (Rocha and Matsubayashi 2014; Hicks et al. 2015), and others find that Republicans are more likely to favor restricted voting policies, generally (Bentele and Obrien 2013). Unlike much of this previous work, which is limited to an analysis of a single election law, or a single election cycle, our investigation examines the broad swath of state laws captured by COVI values.

Bivariate Testing: Black and Hispanic Populations, and Republicans

We begin by testing whether the sheer size of minority populations in each state correlates with state COVI values. Table 4.1 displays the relationship between Black and Hispanic subpopulations and COVI values in the past seven presidential election years. Notably, because COVI values measure unique state election laws in each election cycle, it is advisable to examine each presidential election year independently. Nevertheless, we can note that the percentage of each state's Black population is statistically associated with higher COVI values in six of the seven election cycles studied. Put differently, there is a positive correlation between state COVI values and the percentage of state residents identifying as "African-American or Black" on US census forms. In 2020, however, the relationship was no longer statistically significant using a conventional determination of statistical significance ($P > .05$).

In table 4.1, we note that the size of the Hispanic population positively correlates with a higher cost of voting in the first five presidential election cycles studied (1996–2012). Still, there is no solid statistical relationship using a robust two-tailed test for statistical significance, except in 1996. Nonetheless, it is the case in the earlier period that states with a larger percentage of

Table 4.1. Percent Black and Hispanic Populations and the Variable Costs of Voting in the American States: Presidential Election Years

Pearson-R Correlation Coefficients: P-values are a two-tailed test

	% Black population	% Hispanic population
1996	.382 (*P* < .00)	.324 (*P* < .03)
2000	.484 (*P* < .00)	.025 (*P* < .87)
2004	.501 (*P* < .00)	.050 (*P* < .74)
2008	.511 (*P* < .00)	.185 (*P* < .20)
2012	.370 (*P* < .00)	.058 (*P* < .69)
2016	.342 (*P* < .02)	−.081 (*P* < .58)
2020	.157 (*P* < .28)	−.191 (*P* < .19)
In each test n = 50		

Note: We gathered minority population estimates from the United States Census Bureau. Specifically, we used 1990 census numbers for the 1996 election and 2000 values for the 2000 and 2004 elections. Still more, we used 2005 values (population estimates) for the 2008 election, 2010 values for the 2012 election, 2014 values (population estimates) for the 2016 election, and we use 2019 population estimates for 2020 (United States Census Bureau, "Quick Facts," accessed July 21, 2022, https://www .census.gov/quickfacts/fact/table/AK,US/PST045221,). Cost of Voting Index values are available at Cost of Voting Index, last accessed July 21, 2022, https://www.costofvotingindex.com.

Source: Michael Pomante, Scot Schraufnagel, and Quan Li

people who identify as "Hispanic or Latino" on census forms garnered higher COVI values. Interestingly, the bivariate relationship turned negative in 2016 and 2020. A negative correlation suggests that states with a greater percentage of Hispanic residents have lower COVI values, on average. Although this is not a statistically significant relationship, one might imagine that the growing Hispanic population in the period studied and the increased voting strength of this group might have changed things. For instance, California has a substantial Hispanic population (39.4 percent in 2019) and relatively low COVI values, particularly in 2016 and 2020. In 1996 (1990 US census), California had only an above-average state Hispanic population size and a much lower COVI rank. The Hispanic consideration begs further scrutiny because others have found that the growth of state Hispanic populations leads to different policy outcomes (Márquez and Schraufnagel 2013) and policy attitudes among whites (Rocha and Espino 2009).

Table 4.2 provides three related tests of the relationship between the growth in each state's Hispanic population from 1990 to 2019, using Census Bureau data and different COVI considerations. In the first instance, we correlate the percentage of growth in Hispanic populations with raw COVI values in 2020.

Table 4.2. Percent Growth in the Hispanic Populations (1990–2019) and Three Measures of the Cost of Voting
Pearson-R Correlation Coefficients: P-values are a two-tailed test

Years	Raw COVI values
2020	.308 ($P < .03$); n = 50
	State COVI rank
2020	.355 ($P < .02$); n = 50
	Change in COVI state rank
2020–1996	.304 ($P < .04$); n = 50

Source: Michael Pomante, Scot Schraufnagel, and Quan Li

Next, we complement this test by correlating Hispanic state population growth with the COVI state ranks in 2020. Finally, the third test measures the relationship between the change in state rank from 1996 to 2020 and the change in Hispanic state population size from 1990 to 2019, as reported by the Census Bureau. In each of the three tests, the growth of state Hispanic populations correlates significantly with COVI values. This test indicates that in the period studied, voting was more restrictive in states where state Hispanic populations grew the fastest.

We attempt to test correlations in three ways to determine the robustness of the relationship between growth in each state's Hispanic population and voting restrictions. If a statistical relationship exists using one measurement strategy but disappears with a different strategy, we would need to conclude that we are uncertain if there is a strong relationship. However, we obtain positive, statistically significant coefficients in each of the three tests. Therefore, it does not matter how we measure things. When state Hispanic populations increase in size as a percentage of a state's total population, there is a corresponding higher cost of voting during the period studied.

We now turn to the question of partisanship or the political party controlling state governments. We cannot simply ignore the quotes from Republican sources, which suggest the modern Republican Party is interested in selective voter demobilization. With this in mind and consistent with other literature, we hypothesized that the Republican Party's control of state legislative processes would associate with more voting restrictions. The hypothesis is somewhat ironic. The Democratic Party was clearly most closely associated with election restrictions in the Jim Crow era, as former enslavers in the South who went out of their way to prevent Black citizens from voting were predominantly Democrats. Nonetheless, in the contemporary era, we expect COVI values to associate positively and significantly with Republican (GOP) sway over the state legislative process.

To test this thesis, we measure the GOP's influence over state election laws in two ways. First, we examine the percentage of state legislators (House and Senate combined) from the Republican Party each year before the presidential election when we calculate the COVI values. For instance, we use Republican Party sway in state government in 1995 as a predictor of restrictiveness in 1996, and 1999 GOP numbers for 2000, and so forth.

Second, we use a simple dummy variable, lagged by one year, which scores a case "1" if the GOP had majority control of each state legislative chamber and the governor's office. Then, again, we use multiple measures of our key explanatory variable, GOP control, to ascertain the strength of our findings.

We report the results of the political party test in table 4.3, and we learn that only in the two most recent presidential election cycles (2016 and 2020) does Republican sway over state legislatures correlate positively and significantly with COVI values. Interestingly, we find a negative link between more GOP control of the state legislative process and COVI values in the first two presidential election cycles studied. Moreover, in the first instance, the association is statistically significant. However, post-2008, it seems the GOP switched positions regarding voting restrictions. Not long ago, the GOP was more likely to associate with inclusion or laws that make voting easier. It is only very recently that the party, on average, associates with restrictive voting policies. However, in the middle years, especially in 2004 and 2008, one must accept the null hypothesis of no relationship between partisan control of the state legislative process and voting restriction. Put differently, in the first decade of the twenty-first century, the political party with sway over state legislative processes was unrelated to the overall cost of voting in the American states. However, by 2012 the GOP was becoming more likely to associate with restriction.

Notably, after the successful election campaign of Barack Obama in 2008, the political parties seemed to switch positions as it relates to voting restrictions. As a result, by 2020, there was a very high correlation between GOP influence over the state legislative process and the COVI. Analyzing the raw data, we note that the growth in the relationship between the GOP and restriction

Table 4.3. GOP Control of State Government and the Variable Costs of Voting: Presidential Election Years 1996–2020

Pearson-R Correlation Coefficients: P-values are a two-tailed test

	% GOP members (both chambers)	GOP maj. control of both chambers + gov.
1996	−.322 (*P* < .03)	−.342 (*P* < .02)
2000	−.361 (*P* < .02)	−.141 (*P* < .34)
2004	−.261 (*P* < .08)	.001 (*P* < 1.00)
2008	−.078 (*P* < .61)	−.089 (*P* < .55)
2012	.169 (*P* < .25)	.289 (*P* < .05)
2016	.455 (*P* < .01)	.443 (*P* < .01)
2020	.530 (*P* < .01)	.431 (*P* < .01)

n = 49

(Nebraska's nonpartisan state legislature omitted)

Source: Republican Party members and majority control obtained from the National Conference of State Legislatures using values from the year preceding the election.

Source: Michael Pomante, Scot Schraufnagel, and Quan Li

occurs when these more conservative states fail to implement innovative practices that reduce voting costs. For instance, many Republican-leaning states have yet to adopt automatic voter registration for citizens who change residence.

However, there is more to the story. When we scrutinize the raw data more carefully, we learn that before 2012, many states, primarily in the rural West, were characterized by Republican control of the state legislative process while still maintaining reasonably low COVI values. For instance, in 1996 Republican Wyoming had the seventh lowest COVI value. Kansas, another Republican Party stronghold in 1996, was in the middle of the pack with the twenty-fifth lowest COVI value.[7]

This additional scrutiny also reveals that Republican Party control and easier voting in the rural Western states (i.e., North Dakota and Utah) coincides with small Black and Hispanic populations. Is it possible that the relative size of a state's Black population interacts with Republican Party control to produce higher COVI values? In other words, are Republican lawmakers more likely to restrict voting only when the state's minority populations are larger or growing? If this is the case, we may have uncovered voter suppression concerns. Importantly, it is not the case that, in 1996, the first year we study, the GOP was the party more sympathetic to the plight of Black Americans, as was the case earlier in the twentieth century (Bullock III 1988). By 1996 the GOP was already more white and more rural (McKee 2008). Yet there was no meaningful positive correlation between the Republican Party and higher COVI values until 2012 and not in a robust, statistically significant manner until 2016.

Moving beyond the Bivariate Tests

Considering a possible interaction between state minority populations and partisan control of state legislatures suggests the need to move beyond bivariate correlational analyses. So far, all we have uncovered are some unfortunate anecdotes. Some of these narratives comport with expectations, specifically, that Black Americans are more likely to face voting restrictions and that the Republican Party has, in very recent years, embraced more restricted voting. However, the preliminary analyses raise new questions. Indeed, our first test of the Hispanic population size across the fifty states provided an incomplete picture. However, with a little more digging, we found that growth in this subpopulation correlates with higher COVI values.

Importantly, we still do not know how these bivariate relationships hold up when we control for other considerations, not the least of which is the "benefits" of voting or the competitiveness of each state's electoral climate (Filer and Kenny 1980; Colomer 1991). For example, one might imagine that in more electorally competitive states, state legislators in control of the legislative process might be especially keen to maintain the status quo and refuse to innovate election law to make the process more inclusive. After all, those in power obtained office using the prevailing state election laws.

Backing up, we reconsider the question of the size of state Black populations and voting restrictions and create an interaction term. An interaction occurs when the effect of one variable depends on the value of another variable. In our case, we have already found that Republicans are not robustly associated with more restrictive voting until 2016. First, however, we want to determine if the relationship between Republicans and voting difficulty depends upon the size of a state's Black population. To do so, we calculate an interaction term by multiplying the percentage of the Black population in each state by the percentage of Republicans in that same state's legislature. We do this for each of the seven presidential election cycles. Then, we use this interaction term, and its component parts, in a base regression model to test for an association with the cost of voting in each state in each presidential election year. This test tells us if both factors, larger Black populations and GOP sway over the legislative process, need to occur in tandem to obtain higher COVI values or more voting restrictions. In other words, is it the case that Republican Party control of state legislatures, in the contemporary period, is associated with higher COVI values only when there is a larger Black population in the state? We display the results in table 4.4.

Looking at the interaction variable (% Black Population * % GOP Members), we find that the cost of voting is higher in five of the seven election cycles when there are more GOP state legislators and a larger percentage of Black residents in the state. The exceptions are the 2008 and 2016 election cycles. However, in both cases, the coefficient for the interaction term is positive and larger than the standard error, suggesting it is moving toward statistical significance. We know from table 4.3 that the percentage of the GOP in state legislatures was neither necessary nor sufficient to move the costs of voting higher during the first five presidential election cycles studied (1996, 2000, 2004, 2008, and 2012). However, we now learn that when considering larger state Black populations, the Republican Party does associate with a higher cost of voting as far back as 1996. The evidence suggests that from 1996 to 2004, before Republicans began to associate with more restriction in our bivariate tests, larger Black populations in the state and Republican Party control of state legislative processes interacted and, on average, associated with a more restrictive electoral-institutional climate.

When interpreting the regression results that use an interaction term, it is quite rare to pay much attention to the results associated with the individual parts of the interaction. Nevertheless, these results can be enlightening because the tests tell us something about the effect of the independent variable on the dependent variable when the value of the second part of the interaction term equals "0." For instance, in our case, the coefficient representing the effect of the percent GOP on COVI values tells us what this would be if there were no Black residents in the state. Conversely, the test of the nature of the association between the Black subpopulation and the COVI is the effect under a scenario wherein there were "0" members of the GOP in a state's legislature. Although both scenarios do not represent real-world events, the interpretation of these coefficients can be revealing, especially concerning the relationship

Table 4.4. Explaining Cost of Voting Index Values Using an Interaction between the Percent Black Residents in the State and the Percent GOP State Legislators: Presidential Election Years 1996–2020

Ordinary Least Squares Regression: Dependent variable is each state's COVI value

		Coefficient (standard error)
1996	% Black population	−.039 (.030)
	% GOP members (both chambers)	−.021 (.009)*
	% Black population* % GOP members	.0017 (.0007)*
	F-statistic; adjusted R²; n	5.49*; .22; 49
2000	% Black population	−.039 (.032)
	% GOP members (both chambers)	−.021 (.008)*
	% Black population* % GOP members	.0018 (.0008)*
	F-statistic; adjusted R²; n	8.15*; .31; 49
2004	% Black population	−.025 (.031)
	% GOP members (both chambers)	−.015 (.008)ᵗ
	% Black population* % GOP members	.0014 (.0007)*
	F-statistic; adjusted R²; n	7.34*; .28; 49
2008	% Black population	.003 (.038)
	% GOP members (both chambers)	−.008 (.009)
	% Black population* % GOP members	.0008 (.0008)
	F-statistic; adjusted R²; n	5.82*; .23; 49
2012	% Black population	−.049 (.035)
	% GOP members (both chambers)	−.002 (.007)
	% Black population* % GOP members	.0015 (.0007)*
	F-statistic; adjusted R²; n	5.27*; .21; 49
2016	% Black population	−.027 (.039)
	% GOP members (both chambers)	.012 (.007)ᵗ
	% Black population* % GOP members	.0009 (.0007)
	F-statistic; adjusted R²; n	7.66; .29; 49
2020	% Black population	−.059 (.043)
	% GOP members (both chambers)	.014 (.008)ᵗ
	% Black population* % GOP members	.0013 (.0007)ᵗ
	F-statistic; adjusted R²; n	7.84*; .30; 49

Note: We follow the lead of other researchers who omit Nebraska's nonpartisan state legislature from analyses of variation in inter-state outcomes (Gary and Lowery 1995; Emmert and Traut 2003; Sanbonmatsu 2003). When we assign Nebraska the same partisan value as neighboring Kansas, we obtain no appreciable difference in the results reported in the table.

*$P < .05$; ᵗ $P < .10$ (two-tailed tests)

Source: Michael Pomante, Scot Schraufnagel, and Quan Li

between the GOP and the COVI if there are no Black residents in the state. Notice a statistically significant association in the first three election cycles (1996, 2000, and 2004) between GOP sway over the state legislative process and lower COVI values. This negative value indicates that if there were zero Black residents in the state, the Republican Party associates, on average, with lower costs or less restrictive voting laws. This finding is revealing because some states in this earlier period have minimal Black populations. As a result, more Republicans in a state legislature did not predict higher COVI values in these states.

Developing More Fully Specified Models

Because our data are arrayed over time (1996–2020 with gaps) and across sections (each of the forty-nine states with a partisan legislature), we can run a variation of the Generalized Least Squares regression model to test what other considerations might be affecting state COVI values.[8] In this instance, controlling each state's electoral competition level seems wise. Legislators in states with a more competitive electoral climate might be anxious to make voting easier, lest higher voter turnout affects election outcomes in unpredictable ways. We operationalize this consideration using the closeness of the previous presidential election in each state. For example, in Utah in 2008 the absolute value of the difference in vote percentage between the two major political party candidates (John McCain and Barack Obama) was about 46 percent. John McCain received about 73 percent of the vote to Barack Obama's 26 percent.[9] Because electoral competition in the state is minimal, we imagine that state legislators would not be as concerned with trying to restrict voting. In 2008, the absolute value of the difference between the two major political party candidates was about 5 percent in Florida. We use this quantity to predict Florida's 2012 COVI value. Smaller numbers on this measure indicate more electoral competition, and we anticipate smaller numbers lead to greater restriction. In other words, we expect a negative association with the cost of voting.[10]

Next, we imagine that state legislative professionalism might produce a higher or lower cost of voting value. Some state legislatures are decidedly part-time bodies, and state legislators in these states routinely hold other full-time jobs. One can imagine that states with more "professional" or full-time legislatures are distinct in important ways from states where the legislature meets for only a minimal amount of time each year.[11] We use Peverill Squire's (2007; 2017) measure of state legislative professionalism, which measures "unlimited legislative sessions, superior staff resources, and sufficient pay to allow members to pursue legislative service as their vocation" (Squire 2007, 211). Thus, we include state rank on the Squire Index in our models to control the likelihood that each state legislature is predisposed to restriction. Specifically, we hypothesize that less professional state legislatures are more likely not to modernize or keep pace with election innovations such as online or automatic voter registration. Larger rank values indicate a more part-time or "amateur" state legislature of the type found in states with more "traditional" state cultures (Elazar 1966). Therefore, we hypothesize a positive coefficient or that higher state ranks associate with a higher cost of voting value.

We report the precise results of the model run in appendix E (table E4.1). When considering all seven election cycles in the same model, we learn right away that the interaction between the size of the Republican state legislative delegation and the size of the state's Black population work together to explain between-state variations in the cost of voting. When the two considerations rise in tandem, voting costs are higher. More Republicans and more Black residents predict more significant state restrictions. Many states in these election cycles have consistently small Black populations. For example, using the 1990 census, Idaho, Maine, Vermont, and North Dakota had less than 1 percent Black populations at the time. By 2020 each state's Black population was relatively unchanged. Correspondingly, we can note that each state's COVI rank is relatively low throughout the period studied, indicating it is easier to vote in these states.

Notably, many recognize Idaho and North Dakota as states with significant Republican representation in elected offices. However, the size of the Republican delegation in these states' legislatures does not associate with a more restrictive electoral-institutional climate. Put differently, Republican control of the state legislative process alone does not explain higher COVI values. When the percentage of each state's Black population is larger and the percentage of Republican state legislators is larger, however, we obtain higher COVI values, on average. The two considerations work together. Importantly, this is the case after controlling for other possible explanations for interstate variation in COVI values. The model predictably returns a negative coefficient for electoral competition and a positive coefficient for the Squire Index.

To understand the effect of the GOP delegation size in state legislatures on COVI values more completely, we create figure 4.1. The figure depicts the relationship between GOP sway over the legislative process and the predicted cost of voting (the COVI value) under two different scenarios. The two lines represent the minimum (0.3) and maximum value (37.8) of the state's Black population, as reported by the Census Bureau in the twenty-five years studied. The light gray line represents the maximum observed value, and the dark gray line represents the minimum value. The figure shows that when the size of a state's Black population is minimal (dark gray line), very near zero, the size of the GOP delegation in state legislatures does not increase the cost of voting much. The line is nearly flat. However, when the size of the Black population is larger (light gray line), the cost of voting rises significantly as the percentage of the GOP in the state legislature grows.

Next, we study the growth in state Hispanic populations during the study period. We already know (see table 4.1) that the percentage of state Hispanic populations alone does not always correlate with higher COVI values, especially recently. The lack of a bivariate relationship diminishes the possibility of finding anything consistent with the results reported in table 4.4, which showed that the interaction of state Black populations and the percentage of GOP state legislators produce more costly voting.[12] However, we uncovered that state Hispanic population growth correlates positively with higher COVI values, which deserves more attention.[13] Again, we report the detailed results in appendix E (table E4.2). Sure enough, the interaction term produces a coefficient more than three times the size of the standard error, representing a highly statistically significant relationship. Intrastate positive change in the size of the Hispanic population, in combination with intrastate variation in the size of the GOP state legislative delegation, produces higher COVI values or a more restrictive state electoral-institutional climate on average, all else being equal. Considering the control variables, the electoral competition's effect on COVI values is not evident in the Hispanic population growth model (see table E4.2). However, we find that higher Squire Index ranks, or a more amateur state legislature, predict higher COVI values as expected.

To illustrate our findings related to Hispanic population growth, the GOP,

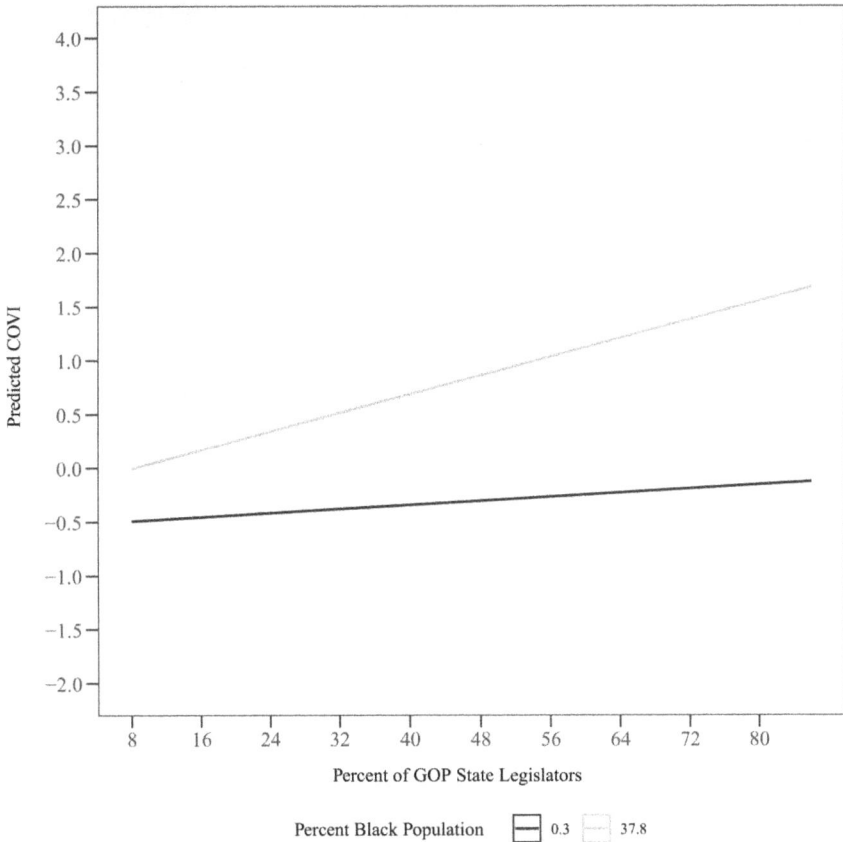

Figure 4.1. GOP sway over state legislative process and the cost of voting when Black Populations are small and large: 1996–2020

Source: Michael Pomante, Scot Schraufnagel, and Quan Li

and the COVI, consider the state of California. During the studied period, California witnessed some growth in its Hispanic population, but not as much as in many other states. In 1990, 25.8 percent of California's population was Hispanic, which grew to 39.4 percent by 2019, representing a 52.7 percent increase. Notably, California was the sixth most inclusive state to vote in during the 2020 presidential election. Evidently, this Hispanic population growth was insufficient to drive the higher voting cost.

In contrast, consider a state like Alabama. According to the 1990 census, only 0.6 percent of state residents identified as Hispanic or Latino. However,

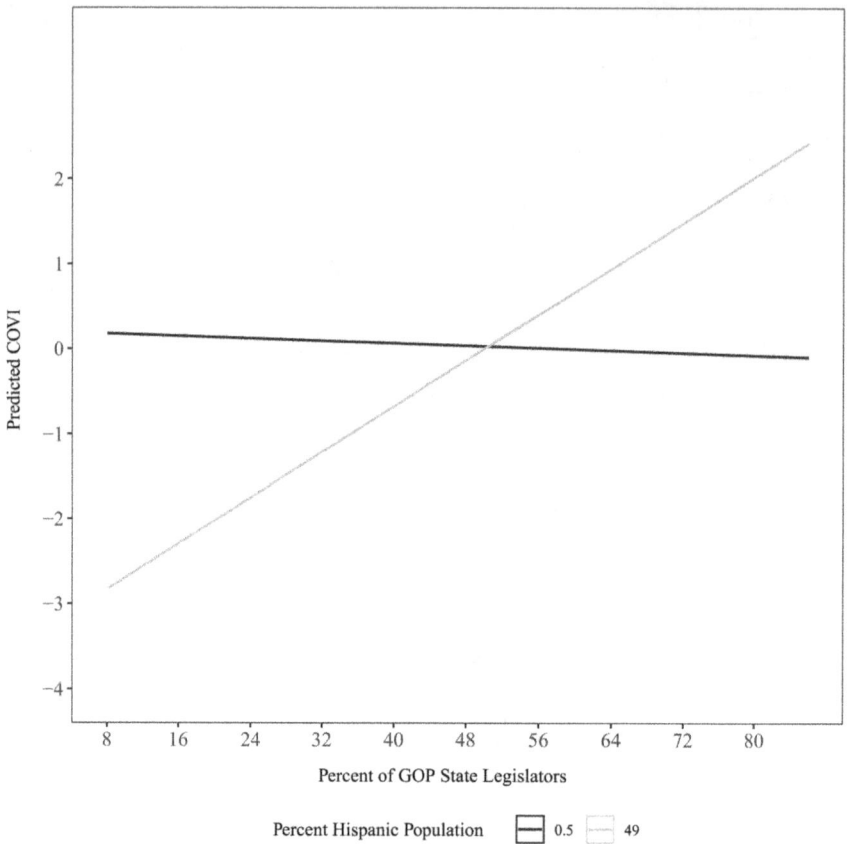

Figure 4.2. GOP sway over state legislative process and the cost of voting when Hispanic populations are small and large: 1996–2020

Source: Michael Pomante, Scot Schraufnagel, and Quan Li

2019 Census Bureau estimates suggest the percentage of the state's Hispanic population had grown to 4.6 percent, representing a 766 percent increase. Many also recognize Alabama as a state that is decidedly more Republican.[14] The substantial growth in the state's Hispanic population, working in tandem with Republican sway over state election law, produces a COVI value ranked thirty-ninth in 2020. In 1996, when Alabama had less than a 1 percent Hispanic population, the state was ranked eleventh. We provide a graphic display of the results in figure 4.2 to substantiate our findings.

The dark gray line represents the relationship between the size of the state

Table 4.5. The Effect of Larger Black Populations, Growing Hispanic Populations, and Republican Control of State Legislatures: The Cost of Voting in 49 States, 1996–2020

Random-Effects Generalized Least Squares Regression

Variable	Coefficient (standard error)
%Black population	.009 (.015)
%Hispanic population growth	−.074 (.017)*
%GOP state legislators	−.009 (.005)[t]
%Black population* %GOP state legislators	.0005 (.00027)[t]
%Hispanic population growth* %GOP state legislators	.0015 (.0003)*
Electoral competition	−.002 (.004)
Squire index (legislative professionalism)	.007 (.005)
Constant	−.002 (.312)
Wald Chi²	49.10*
Overall R-squared	.18
n	343

Note: We follow the lead of other researchers who omit Nebraska's nonpartisan state legislature from analyses of variation in interstate outcomes (Gary and Lowery 1995; Emmert and Traut 2003; Sanbonmatsu 2003). When we assign Nebraska the same partisan value as neighboring Kansas, we obtain no appreciable difference in the results reported in the table.

*$P < .05$; [t] $P < .10$ (two-tailed tests)

Source: Michael Pomante, Scot Schraufnagel, and Quan L

GOP legislative delegation and the COVI when the state Hispanic population is at the minimum value in our database (0.5). The light gray line is the average relationship when the Hispanic population is at the maximum state value (49.0). Considering the dark gray line, we can note that the cost of voting does not change much when the size of the GOP delegation grows when there are almost no Hispanic citizens in the state. In fact, the line has a slight negative tilt, suggesting that the GOP may favor fewer restrictions if there are no Hispanic citizens in the state. However, this changes when considering the maximum Hispanic population size (light gray line). Now, when there are more GOP legislators, the predicted cost of voting increases sharply. In other words, when the Hispanic population is large, GOP sway over the state legislative process is associated with a more restrictive electoral-institutional climate.

We also create a model that considers both Black and Hispanic state populations. We report these results in table 4.5.[15] This modeling provides, arguably, the most robust test of our thesis, specifically, that GOP control of the state legislative process drives up the cost of voting when there is a perceived racial threat, defined by a larger Black population or a growing Hispanic population.

Both interaction terms, presented in the middle of table 4.5, return positive coefficients as expected.[16] Therefore, this tells us that during these presidential election cycles, when states have larger Black populations and/or growing Hispanic populations, GOP-controlled legislatures associate with more costly voting, on average. As a possible illustration of this finding, we can note that before the 2012 presidential election, Florida, which had a considerable Black population and a growing Hispanic population, reduced the number of early voting days from fourteen to eight. In addition, the state eliminated the final Sunday of early voting. This change, arguably, occurred because on the final Sunday before Election Day, many Black churches conduct "souls to the polls" voter drives where congregants travel to early voting locations and cast their ballots as a group.

Considering the components of the interaction, the %GOP State Legislators associates with fewer restrictions, on average, under a scenario where a state has no Black population and no growth in the Hispanic population.[17] Of course, this is not a real-world scenario. However, it is not so far-fetched as not to provide insight. Recall that Black populations are pretty small in some western rural states and New England states. Importantly, we obtain these results after controlling for the competitiveness of a state electoral climate in presidential elections and the professional versus the amateur status of the state legislative process.

Conclusion

Our results uncover evidence in support of the "racial threat" theory. Scholars developed the concept of racial threat as a determinant of public policy outcomes as far back as the 1940s when V. O. Key (1949) observed that as the size of the Black community increased, so did fear within the white population. He found that fear led to an increase in the controlling behaviors of whites. Moreover, we know that Republican-leaning states became more restricting after the country elected Barack Obama, the first Black president. Before the

2008 election, there was a negative link between COVI values and a larger percentage of GOP members in each state's legislature (see table 4.3). Put differently, in the earlier period, the GOP, on average, was associated with a less restrictive electioneering posture. The bivariate and the statistically significant relationship between the GOP and election restrictions does not materialize until after Obama's electoral success.

Moreover, in the aftermath of the Supreme Court ruling in *Shelby County v. Holder*, and in time for the 2016 election cycle, we witness the relationship between GOP control and a more restrictive climate grow even stronger. The 2016 election cycle was the first to allow states with a history of racist policies to change their laws without preclearance or oversight from the federal government.[18] Yet, before the landmark 5–4 Supreme Court decision, we found evidence that the Republican Party associated with more costly voting in states with larger Black populations and growing Hispanic populations. However, it is essential to note a more extensive shift in GOP focus coinciding with the 2008 presidential election cycle. Notably, the 2008 presidential election saw the highest levels of voter turnout in contemporary times until 2020. We surmise that political operatives in US state legislatures interpreted the spike in voter turnout as responsible for President Obama's electoral success. Because Obama was a Democrat, his party brethren began to make voting easier in states they controlled. Conversely, his GOP opponents tried to make voting more difficult in the states where they held sway.

In chapter 8 we test whether making voting easier creates a decidedly partisan advantage. We can note, for now, that missing from the prevailing literature is any systematic evidence that increased voter turnout always benefits the Democrats. In the end, we find that the increase in voter turnout witnessed in the 2020 election benefited President Trump. As far back as the late 1970s, James DeNardo (1980) argued that "the joke's on the Democrats" and that one cannot assume that higher voter turnout always creates an advantage for the Democratic Party.

This chapter has used COVI values as the dependent variable and tried to understand why some states have higher COVI values than others. We learn there is an extraordinarily high positive correlation between state Black populations and the cost of voting. This relationship may be left over from the Jim Crow era (before 1965) when it was evident that state legislators, particularly in the South, were making voting more difficult for Black Americans.

In the contemporary era, the GOP's influence over state legislative processes, by itself, does not relate strongly to a higher cost of voting until the 2016 presidential election cycle. However, there is evidence of a partisan shift in this regard post-2008. Ultimately, when we create new variables that interact with the percent of a state population that is Black, Hispanic population growth, and the size of the GOP delegation in each state legislature, the interactions are positively associated with COVI values going back to 1996.

In earlier work (Li, Pomante, & Schraufnagel 2018), we showed that the relative cost of voting affects state-level voter turnout levels. In appendix D we replicate these tests and bring the analysis current through the 2020 election cycle.[19] Unequivocally, higher COVI values associate with lower statewide voter turnout. In the next chapter, we use individual survey respondents as our unit of analysis to explore the impact of the difficulty of voting on individual-level voter turnout. This test allows us to control for various considerations that scholars argue influence citizens' likelihood to participate in elections. Specifically, we hypothesize that more restricted voting decreases voter turnout, especially for minority Americans, the undereducated, and renters.

5: The COVI and Reported Voter Turnout

In this chapter, we test whether state laws that raise voting costs disproportionately influence the turnout of underrepresented groups. Using the US Census Bureau's Current Population Survey data on reported voter turnout after the 2016 presidential election and our COVI values for 2016, we test whether Black, Hispanic, Asian Americans, and citizens without a high school diploma are less likely to report they voted when a state has a more restricting electoral climate.

Normatively, the underrepresentation of the undereducated is concerning. This group might be in special need of government policies to promote their well-being. Moreover, misinformation campaigns that attempt to sway or rally public opinion in support of a particular unworthy cause might prey on the undereducated, a group that is arguably more easily misled. At the same time, we know Black and Hispanic Americans drop out of high school at higher rates than whites.[1] In this case, lower educational attainment might reinforce other considerations that lead to lower political participation levels for members of the two largest minority communities in the United States.

In the preceding chapters, we learned there is no random assignment of COVI values. For instance, when states change their voting laws, voting becomes easier or more difficult relative to other states. Moreover, it is unquestionably the case that since 1996, there have been higher COVI values in states with larger Black populations and states with growing Hispanic populations. What we do not know yet is whether restricted voting leads to lower participation levels for Black and Hispanic citizens. To be certain, we are not the first to address the question (Spring 2012; Juelich and Coll 2020; Ritter and Tolbert 2021).[2] However, many previous efforts focus on the effect a particular restriction, or set of restrictions, has on minority voter turnout. They have also failed to uncover consistent evidence that minorities are negatively and systematically affected by restrictive voting laws (Hood and Bullock 2012; Rocha and Matsubayashi 2014).

This chapter provides a comprehensive look at minority voter demobilization under different levels of aggregate voting restrictions, or COVI values.

The newly created index allows us to test the minority demobilization thesis further, using a broader set of state laws and practices. Our hunch is that higher costs, defined by higher COVI values, negatively influence the turnout of Hispanic and Asian Americans. Scholars find that socioeconomic considerations (Highton and Burris 2002; Jackson 2003; Xu 2005) explain the lower voter turnout of both groups. Jackson (2003) contends that the difference in socioeconomic status is probably the paramount consideration explaining the lower turnout of Hispanics. Controlling for socioeconomic factors, we hypothesize that greater voting restrictions place an additional burden on both groups. We contend that cultural differences, as exemplified by language differences, make voting restrictions even more draining or inconvenient (see Uhlaner, Cain, and Kiewiet 1989; Barreto 2005).

Concerning Black Americans, after keeping education and income constant, researchers find that Black citizens vote at a higher rate than white citizens (Olsen 1970; Verba and Nie 1972; Guterbock and London 1983; Tate 1994). Nevertheless, on average, Black Americans obtain lower education and income levels (Rosenstone 1982; Leighley and Vedlitz 1999), which scholars know depresses voter turnout (Filer, Kenny, and Morton 1993). Hence, the situation is more complicated. Correspondingly, we do not have strong expectations regarding voter turnout among Black Americans, especially given that we control for socioeconomic considerations.

Importantly, in our efforts to learn more about voting restrictions and voter turnout, we pay particular attention to the role of education. Lower education can make trying to steer through state election laws more difficult. Nothing is straightforward about keeping track of registration deadlines, finding a new polling location, or ensuring one has the proper identification to vote, and these processes might be especially difficult for the undereducated. In our modeling, we test whether a more restrictive state electoral climate places a greater burden on citizens without a high school diploma. We believe that not finishing high school associates with more difficulty navigating voter registration and balloting processes and that consequently this group is less likely to vote than their more educated peers.

Complicating the voter turnout prospects of members of minority groups and the undereducated is that they are less likely to own their own home (Cahill and Franklin 2013). To check our measurement strategies, we also test for differences between survey respondents from the four subpopulations (Black,

Hispanic, and Asian Americans, as well as the undereducated) who own their own homes versus those who do not. If a higher COVI value depresses voter turnout, this should especially be the case for the more mobile—nonhomeowners, who need to reregister to vote each time they change their address. Research has shown that voter registration restrictions disproportionately burden people who move often (Highton and Wolfinger 1998; Hershey 2009). On average, more mobile people might find it particularly difficult to keep track of interstate and even intrastate differences in voting processes. In addition, residential mobility requires voters to relearn election laws and procedures each time they relocate.

To test these hypotheses, we run several new models with interaction terms to learn if a more restrictive state electoral climate places a greater burden on citizens from each group.[3] In all, we expect Hispanic, Asian, and undereducated respondents to report voting less often when the cost of voting is higher.[4] As noted, our outlook regarding individuals representing the Black community is somewhat mixed. We do some extra digging in this case because as mentioned, compared to whites and all else being equal, Black citizens tend to vote at a higher rate (Tate 1994). Specifically, we anticipate a negative coefficient derived from our test of Hispanics, Asians, and those without a high school diploma. We also hypothesize that an interaction term (Test Group * COVI) returns another negative coefficient. In other words, being Hispanic, Asian, or undereducated works in tandem with higher COVI values to reduce the probability of voting even further.

To address the issue of homeownership for each test group, we calculate the probability that individuals report voting if they do not own their own home and compare this to the same group members who own a home. Our concern is somewhat different from those who argue that homeownership gives citizens a more significant stake in government policies and, correspondingly, they are more likely to vote (Squire, Wolfinger, and Glass 1987; Timpone 1998, 149; Highton and Wolfinger 2001). Previously research found that homeownership causes citizens to be more concerned with zoning, property tax, and traffic congestion, among other concerns, as they seek to protect the investment they have in their homes. We concur with this thinking but also wish to use homeownership, or the lack thereof, as a surrogate for individuals who are more mobile or more likely to change addresses. Because of the different theoretical expectations, we keep home ownership in all modeling while looking for changes in the predicted probability of voting for the four test groups under the two scenarios: homeowners and renters.

As noted, we use the Census Bureau's Current Population Survey (CPS) for all the tests reported in this chapter. Most specifically, we use the 2016 November Voting and Registration Supplement Survey, which asks respondents whether they voted in the 2016 presidential election, along with various other questions representing demographic considerations. We use 2016 state COVI values as a primary predictor variable in the models. Notably, in 2016, COVI values ranged from −2.02 in Oregon to 1.22 in New Hampshire. We repeat the state-level values for all respondents who reside in each state. We wish to learn if state COVI values interact with Black, Hispanic, and Asian respondents, along with those who do not hold a high school diploma, in a manner that associates with lower self-reported voting.

Measuring Reported Voting

Unfortunately, the CPS survey does not verify that individual respondents voted in the relevant presidential election. Roughly 72 percent of respondents in the 2016 CPS survey reported voting. Overall, voter turnout that year was closer to 55 percent. Scholars routinely argue that how one measures voter turnout matters (Holbrook and Heidbreder 2010; McDonald 2002). This measurement is especially true if one is concerned with reporting aggregate turnout for comparison purposes over time. In our case, we are using individuals as our unit of analysis and a single cross-section of time. We do not employ a comparison over time.

We do not mean to gloss over the potential problem of survey respondents overreporting that they voted.[5] Yet, in this instance, the bias works against our hypotheses or suspicions regarding the cost of voting. In other words, overreporting makes it more difficult to find that the COVI reduces voter turnout. If our testing finds lower voter turnout associated with higher COVI values, this is the case under less-than-ideal circumstances created by the overreporting of turnout. Therefore, if the cost of voting affects turnout, we may be underestimating the actual effect the COVI has on turnout if individuals in these groups are prone to overreport voting.[6] Importantly, for the sake of our argument, one notable scholar argues that when using individuals as a unit of analysis, overreporting is unlikely to adversely affect the "substantive conclusions about the factors that influence voting or nonvoting" (Sigelman 1982, 47).

Minority Populations, the COVI, and Reported Voter Turnout

We are fully aware that the cost of voting is not the only explanation for individual-level voter turnout decisions. However, we imagine that it matters and matters predictably. Besides restrictive voting laws, we believe education and being a homeowner determines whether an individual participates in elections (Squire, Wolfinger, and Glass 1987). Moreover, scholars find that being married (Wolfinger and Wolfinger 2008), female (Lopez, Kirby, & Sagoff 2003), and older and wealthier each increase the likelihood that a citizen turns out to vote. On the other hand, being unemployed (Rosenstone 1982) has been found to decrease the likelihood of voting. Therefore, we control for each of these considerations.

Regarding income and age, scholars note the possibility of a nonlinear relationship or that the effect of income and age on voting is a little more complicated. For instance, at the lowest income levels, how much someone makes does not seem to produce greater voter turnout (Filer, Kenny, and Morton 1993; Tolbert and McNeal 2003). An unemployed individual may have no income but more time to vote, whereas someone with a low-wage job may have more income but less time to vote. Consequently, we include both income and income squared in our models. We expect a negative relationship with reported voting for the income test and a positive relationship with the faster-accelerating income squared. We also include age squared, but now we expect reported voter turnout to decrease at the highest age levels (Alvarez, Bailey, and Katz 2011, 28; but also, Tolbert and McNeal 2003). Alternatively, we anticipate a positive coefficient derived from the test of age and a negative coefficient for age squared.

Beyond the state-level COVI values and the demographic considerations just discussed, we add one additional state-level predictor of voter turnout to each model. Specifically, we add a marker of each state's level of electoral competition in the 2016 presidential election cycle. Again, we repeat the value for all respondents from a particular state. In this instance, we use the closest race at the top of the ticket (president, governor, or senator) as a surrogate for electoral competition or the "benefits" of voting. We hypothesize that smaller election margins at the top of the ballot indicate a more competitive electoral climate. We believe more competitive races mobilize voters because they imagine their vote is more consequential. In other words, the perception is that the benefits of voting are greater, increasing the likelihood that an individual votes.

We begin by looking at simple bivariate relationships between individual reported voting and COVI values using respondents from all fifty states, weighted by voting eligible population.[7] Next, we report the results in table 5.1 with data related to our deeper dive into Black voter turnout. When considering the entire sample, the bivariate relationship between reported voting and a state's COVI value is negative (–.025) and statistically robust at $P < .001$ (see row 1 of table 5.1). In other words, we can be 99.9 percent confident that, in 2016, fewer respondents reported voting when a state had a higher COVI value. An individual-level analysis and a large sample size (n = 79,348) means that the bivariate coefficient is not particularly large. This small coefficient is due to the many factors that explain individual-level voter turnout. However, statistically speaking, the relationship is very strong.

We noted, in chapter 4, that when the Black population in a state is relatively small, any "racial threat" appears minimal. We found voting was easier in states with small Black populations. Table 5.1 displays the relationship between the COVI and reported voting in states where the Black population is less than 1.5 percent and where the Black population exceeds 1.5 percent. Specifically, we use state Black population estimates from the 2015 Census Bureau to test turnout in 2016. In the 2015 Census Bureau estimates, there were seven states where the Black population was less than 1.5 percent of the state population. The states in alphabetical order are Idaho, Maine, Montana, New Hampshire, Utah, Vermont, and Wyoming. We learn there is no negative relationship between 2016 state COVI values and reported turnout in these states. In fact, the coefficient is positive and statistically significant, suggesting that a higher cost of voting in these seven states does not matter or that reported voter turnout is higher when the cost of voting is greater. However, looking at the other forty-three states where the Black population exceeds 1.5 percent, the now-familiar negative and statistically significant relationship between voting and the COVI returns. We suggest this is additional evidence that state lawmakers

Table 5.1. The COVI and Reported Voting: 2016

State population	Bivariate correlation (*P*-value)	No. of respondents
All states	−.025 (*P* < .001)	79,348
Less than 1.5% Black	.022 (*P* < .04)	8,825
Greater than 1.5% Black	−.030 (*P* < .001)	70,523

States with very small Black populations (n = 7) compared to other states (n = 43).

Source: Michael Pomante, Scot Schraufnagel, and Quan Li

are especially inclined to restrict voting under conditions of larger state Black populations.

We can do something similar when considering the Hispanic population in each state. However, the 2015 census estimates do not identify any state with less than a 1.5 percent Hispanic population. Therefore, we use a different demarcation. Due to a natural break in the data at 5 percent, we use this as our threshold and check for the relationship between COVI values and reported voter turnout in two groups of states.[8] It turns out that fourteen states in 2015 had a Hispanic population below 5 percent. Alphabetically they are Alabama, Kentucky, Louisiana, Maine, Michigan, Missouri, Mississippi, Montana, New Hampshire, North Dakota, Ohio, South Dakota, Vermont, and West Virginia. On the other hand, there were thirty-six states with more than a 5 percent Hispanic population. Table 5.2 displays the strength and direction of the relationship between state COVI values and individual level reported voting in the two groups of states.

Again, we note that when the minority population in the states is relatively small, less than 5 percent, any "racial threat" is presumably reduced. Under

Table 5.2. The COVI and Reported Voting: 2016

State population	Bivariate correlation (*P*-value)	No. of respondents
Less than 5% Hispanic	.010 (*P* < .15)	22,582
Greater than 5% Hispanic	−.035 (*P* < .001)	56,766
All states	−.025 (*P* < .001)	79,348

States with small Hispanic populations (n = 14) compared to other states (n = 36).

Source: Michael Pomante, Scot Schraufnagel, and Quan Li

these circumstances, higher COVI values do not relate to lower reported voter turnout. However, when we examine the thirty-six states where the Hispanic population is more sizable, we obtain the predicted negative and statistically significant association between the COVI values and turnout. Because of the relatively low percentage of Asian Americans in most states, it is more challenging to conduct a similar test. Moreover, we know that states with larger Asian populations, such as California and Washington, make voting relatively easier. This fact alone suggests that the racial threat consideration relating to the Asian minority does not present itself. Additionally, there may be a different perception of Asian minorities as compared to Black and Hispanic subpopulations (Wong, Lai, and Nagasawa 1998). However, we still hypothesize that higher cost of voting values can demobilize Asian Americans. In this instance, the demobilization, we suggest, occurs because of considerations other than "racial threat," such as language and cultural barriers.

We theorized that the undereducated, identified as individuals without a high school diploma, would be less likely to vote in states with more constrained voting laws. In this case, it is doubtful that state legislators have purposefully singled out the undereducated.[9] Nevertheless, there is a confounding problem. Ricketts and Sawhill (1988) find that minorities, on average, are overrepresented among the underclass of Americans who attain lower education levels. Moreover, the 2016 CPS reports that 10.27 percent of all respondents reported not having a high school diploma. This number grows to 24.08 percent of Hispanic respondents, 15.01 percent of Black respondents, and 11.52 percent of Asian respondents.[10] If election restrictions disproportionately affect the undereducated and voting becomes more difficult for these groups, the unfairness disproportionately affects minority group members in the United States.

We now turn to the results of the fully specified model, which tests individual level reported turnout for survey respondents belonging to the four subpopulations we have discussed. Ultimately, we test whether those respondents who report belonging to any of the subpopulations are less likely to vote when they reside in a state with a larger COVI value. To do this, we create interaction terms, which multiply the zeros and ones representing respondents from each group with their state's COVI value.

Before we present our findings related to the interactions, we first check if the COVI and other considerations are performing as hypothesized and investigate more completely the overreporting of Black survey respondents.

Table 5.3. The Effect of the COVI on Individual Reported Voting in the 2016 Election

Model: Logistical regression

Independent variables	Model 1 Coef. (s.e.)
COVI values (cost of voting)	−.158 (.015)*
Electoral competition (benefit of voting)	.014 (.001)*
Black	.491 (.035) ^
Hispanic	−.279 (.032)*
Asian	−.970 (.050)*
No high school diploma	−.370 (.037)*
Education	.385 (.009)*
Income	−.003 (.012)
Income squared	.003 (.001)*
Married	.286 (.023)*
Homeowner	.449 (.024)*
Female	.195 (.020)*
Age	.022 (.003)*
Age squared	.000 (.000)
Unemployed	−.145 (.057)*
Constant	−2.57 (.093)*
F-Statistic	556.91
No. of observations	150,673

$* P < .05$ (two-tailed tests); ^ statistically significant in the hypothesized wrong direction

Source: Michael Pomante, Scot Schraufnagel, and Quan Li

Model 1 displays the results of this base analysis in table 5.3. Weighting the data grows our sample size from 79,348 to 150,673. This increase occurs because the process adds cases, in specific states, based on considerations such as race, gender, and the age of respondents. The procedure causes the sample to represent the target population better.[11]

Looking especially at the reported voter turnout of the three minority groups and the undereducated, we uncover the negative relationship we imagined in three of the four instances. The exception is Black Americans, who were more likely to report they voted in 2016 after controlling for all the other considerations. The Hispanic and Asian respondents reported voting at a lower rate, as is the case for respondents without a high school diploma.

Importantly, in the modeling, all the other variables perform as hypothesized. Unfortunately, the coefficients derived from a LOGIT regression are not easy to interpret. For now, we look at the direction of the relationships (whether positive or negative) and the strength of the associations based on standard conventions of statistical significance. When we test the interaction of state COVI values with the subpopulation markers, we can report our results in terms of the average proportional change in reported voting, given different scenarios, which are easier to explain and understand.

The statistically significant negative coefficient obtained for the test of the COVI indicates that reported voting decreases when respondents reside in states with a more restrictive electoral-institutional climate. Correspondingly, we obtain a statistically significant and positive coefficient for the benefits of voting. A more competitive election at the top of the ballot in a respondent's state is associated with an increased likelihood of voting. Our nonlinear hypotheses regarding income and age also perform as expected. There is no relationship between income and voting at the lowest income levels. However, as income increases (income squared), we get a positive and significant association with voter turnout, as anticipated. Regarding the respondent's age, at lower levels, age is strongly associated with an increase in reported turnout. However, the positive relationship falls off at the highest age levels (age squared).

Black Americans, Reported Turnout, and the COVI in 2016

There is considerable evidence that survey respondents, generally, are prone to overreport voting. Scholars argue that this occurs because of a "social desirability response bias" (Holbrook and Krosnick 2010, 37). Survey participants misreport because they wish to portray themselves positively to the interviewer (Lyons and Scheb 1999; Blais et al. 2004). Moreover, there is evidence that Black Americans are particularly susceptible to overreport voting on surveys (Deufel and Kedar 2010). This behavior presents a particularly challenging situation for our testing.[12] Still, as already indicated, researchers found that once one controls for income and education, Black Americans vote at the same or even higher rates than whites, and this has been the case since the 1960s (Verba and Nie 1972, 149–173). Of course, there is still an underrepresentation of Black voters, but this is not a function of race. Instead, the explanation is that Black Americans, on average, have lower education and income levels than others.

Table 5.4. Reported Voter Turnout: The Effect of the COVI on Black Voting in the 2016 Election

Model: Logistical regression

Independent variables	Model 2 Coef. (s.e.)	Model 3 Coef. (s.e.)	Model 4 Coef. (s.e.)
COVI values (cost of voting)	−.136 (.013)*	−.075 (.014)*	−.134 (.015)*
Electoral competition (benefit of voting)	.014 (.00)*	.016 (.001)*	.016 (.001)*
Black	.005 (.03)	.311 (.033)*	.542 (.035)*
COVI* Black			.149 (.052)*
Education		.408 (.007)*	.420 (.008)*
Income		.072 (.003)*	.006 (.011)
Income squared			.003 (.001)*
Married			.260 (.022)*
Homeowner			.465 (.024)*
Female			.186 (.020)*
Age			.024 (.003)*
Age squared			.000 (.000)
Unemployed			−.149 (.056)*
Constant	.60 (.02)*	−1.50 (.03)*	−2.85 (.09)*
F-Statistic	99.48*	1145.44*	595.44*
No. of observations	150,673	150,673	150,673

* $P < .05$ (two-tailed tests); ^ statistically significant in the hypothesized wrong direction

Source: Michael Pomante, Scot Schraufnagel, and Quan Li

In table 5.4, we report three progressively more complete models that examine more closely Black reported voter turnout in the 2016 survey. In model 2, we test whether Black Americans reported voting more often than others in 2016 after controlling for the COVI and state electoral competition. Holding these two state-level considerations constant, we find the coefficient representing the test of "Black" is positive, but it is not even close to being statistically significant. In this instance, we must accept the null hypothesis of "no difference" between the reported voting of Black citizens and others.

Moving to model 3, we now control for education and income and find that Black respondents report voting at a higher rate. This finding is what researchers have argued would be the case. In model 4, this relationship holds when we interact being Black with the respondents' state COVI value. In other

words, we do not find support for our thesis that restrictive voting laws disproportionately demobilize Black Americans. Of course, we are concerned that
overreported voting is biasing the result. For now, however, we cannot report
any evidence that higher state COVI values are more likely to demobilize Black
Americans, at least not in 2016. However, we can turn back to insights garnered
from racial threat theory (Enos 2016; Goldman 2017) to modify our expectations. It is possible that in states where the Black population has been growing
the fastest, higher COVI values cause less Black voting.

To perform this auxiliary test, we look only at those states with the fastest-
growing Black populations. In these states, one can imagine the perceived racial threat is greater for some white legislators. We measure growth in state
Black populations using Census Bureau figures from 1990 and census population estimates from 2019. During this roughly thirty-year period, seventeen
states saw an increase in Black populations greater than 25 percent.[13] The seventeen states in alphabetical order are Arizona, Delaware, Idaho, Iowa, Maine,
Massachusetts, Minnesota, Montana, Nebraska, New Hampshire, North Dakota, Rhode Island, South Dakota, Utah, Vermont, Wisconsin, and Wyoming.
While the Black population was stable in most states, thirty-three states had
less than a 25 percent increase in Black residents from the end of the twentieth
century to the beginning of the twenty-first.

In the modeling, we use the exact specifications as in model 4 in table 5.4
but run the test using only the seventeen states with the fastest-growing Black
populations. If something akin to a racial threat is present, we should expect
higher values on the interaction term (Black * State COVI Value) to associate
with a lower likelihood of reported voting. This testing is particularly relevant
because it assesses the demobilizing influence of the COVI in states where
Black political power should be or could be growing. Growing population size
should lead to more political influence.

One can find the results table in appendix G (table G5.1). To display our
findings, we created figure 5.1, which reports the predicted probability of reported voting associated with being Black in the seventeen states under different COVI scenarios. On the horizontal axis, we display the different COVI
values. The figure does not report the full range of the COVI because we only
use COVI values from the seventeen states with the fastest growing Black populations. The line in the figure is not particularly steep; however, the relationship is negative and statistically significant. In addition, we learn that reported

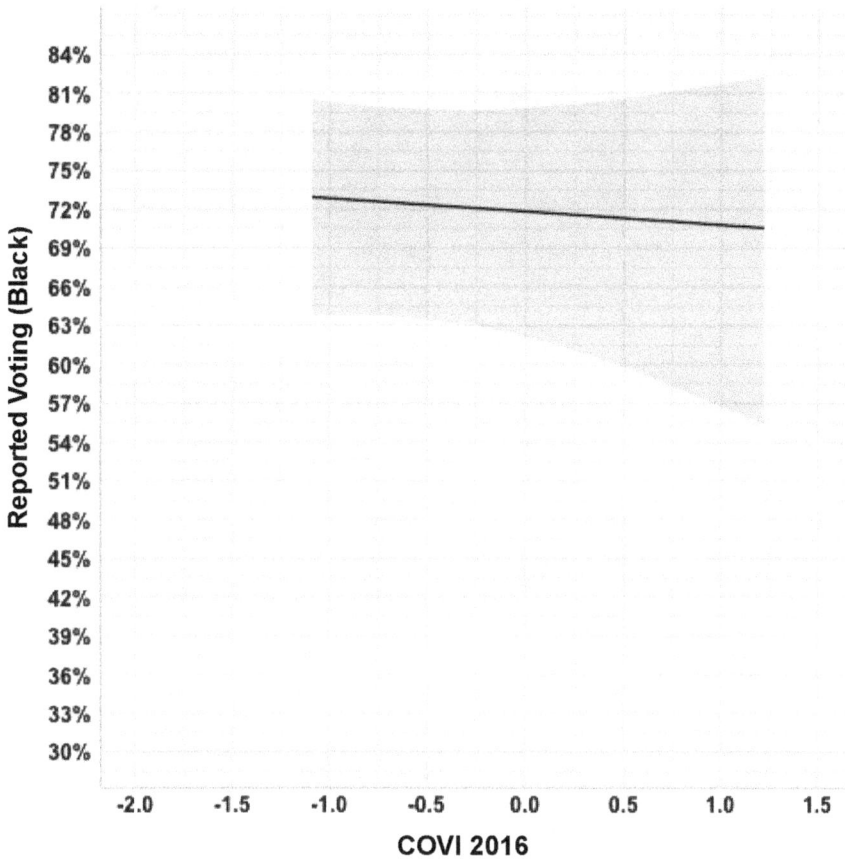

Figure 5.1. Change in the predicted probability of Black reported voting and the COVI in the seventeen states where the Black population has been growing the fastest

Source: Michael Pomante, Scot Schraufnagel, and Quan Li

Black voting goes down in these seventeen states as we move from the least restrictive state (Utah) to the most restrictive state (New Hampshire). Moreover, this is the case with the potential overreporting of voter turnout by Black Americans in these states. This finding suggests we may be underreporting the true effect of the cost of voting on Black voter demobilization.

Figure 5.2 reports the predicted probability of reported voting for Black homeowners versus the more mobile nonhomeowners in the seventeen states where the Black population has been growing the most rapidly over the past

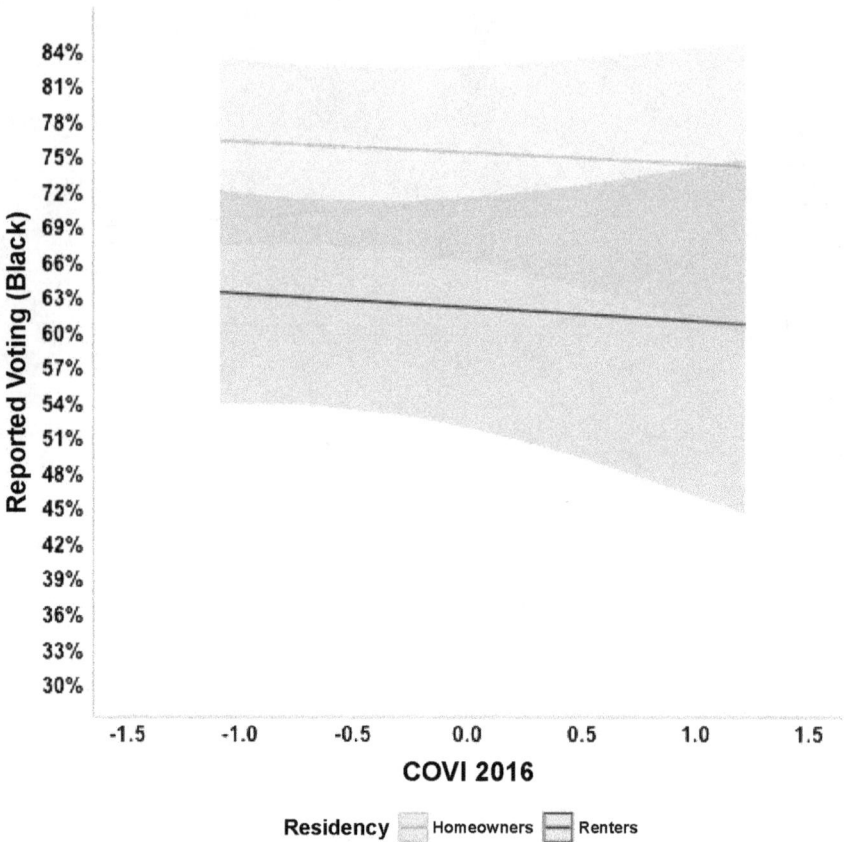

Figure 5.2. Change in the predicted probability of Black reported voting and the COVI in the seventeen states where the Black population has been growing the fastest: homeowners versus renters

Source: Michael Pomante, Scot Schraufnagel, and Quan Li

thirty years. If extended, the dark gray line representing nonhomeowners (principally renters) would intersect the y-axis at a much lower level. Moreover, the slope is slightly greater. The change in the predicted probability of reported voting for nonhomeowners is greater than 2 percent versus a change of less than 2 percent for homeowners. When we examine the descriptive data, we learn that in these seventeen states, 56 percent of all Black homeowners (2990/5340 * 100) who responded to the survey claimed they voted. In contrast, only 34 percent of Black renters (107/314 * 100) reported voting. This

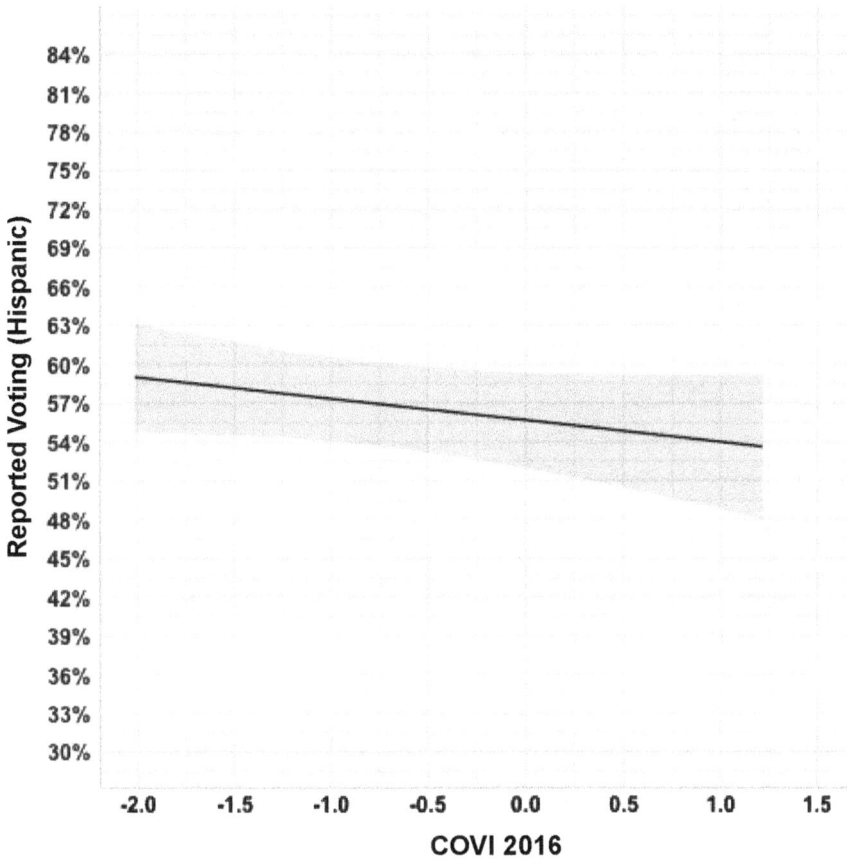

Figure 5.3. Change in the predicted probability of Hispanic reported voting and the COVI

Source: Michael Pomante, Scot Schraufnagel, and Quan Li

difference is what we imagined. Restrictive voting is especially burdensome for renters (and the homeless).

HISPANIC AMERICANS, REPORTED TURNOUT, AND THE COVI IN 2016

Figure 5.3 displays the change in the predicted probability of reported voting associated with being Hispanic under the different cost of voting scenarios, or COVI values. The full results of the model run are available in appendix G (table G5.2). Again, we test the interaction between being Hispanic and the respondent's state COVI value. In this instance, we examine all fifty states and

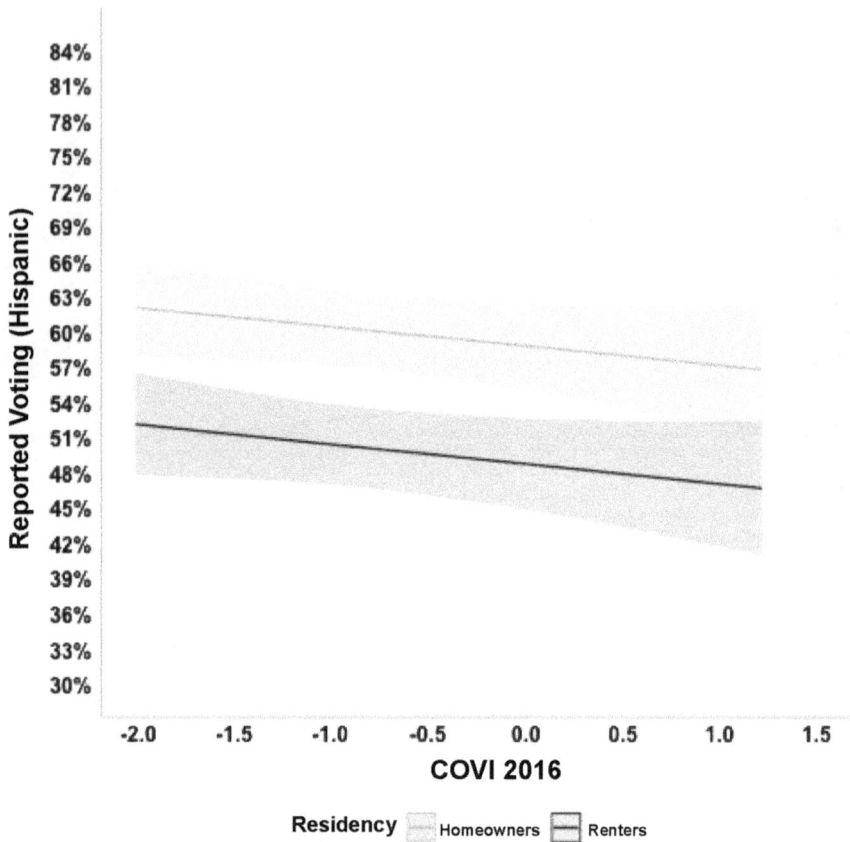

Figure 5.4. Change in the predicted probability of Hispanic reported voting and the COVI: homeowners versus renters

Source: Michael Pomante, Scot Schraufnagel, and Quan Li

find that being Hispanic is associated with less reported voting when the cost of voting is higher. The full range of COVI values is associated with about a 5 percent decrease in the likelihood that a Hispanic respondent reports they voted in 2016, and the decline is easily statistically significant.

Figure 5.4 shows the difference between Hispanic homeowners versus nonhomeowners or renters. Again, the slope for renters, the dark gray line, is slightly steeper than for homeowners. This reduction in reported voting is occurring, on average, after controlling for a whole host of other considerations that influence reported voting. Moreover, considering Hispanic homeowners, raw descriptive statistics suggest that more than 65 percent of Hispanic respondents who own a home reported they voted versus less than 35 percent of Hispanic nonhomeowners.

ASIAN AMERICANS, REPORTED TURNOUT, AND THE COVI IN 2016

Figure 5.5 displays the change in predicted probability associated with being Asian American. Appendix G provides the full results of the model run in table G5.3. Note the much lower predicted probability that an Asian American respondent reports voting in 2016 when the cost of voting is higher. For example, in the most accessible state to vote, Oregon (COVI –2.02.), about 45 percent of Asian American respondents reported voting. The rate drops to less

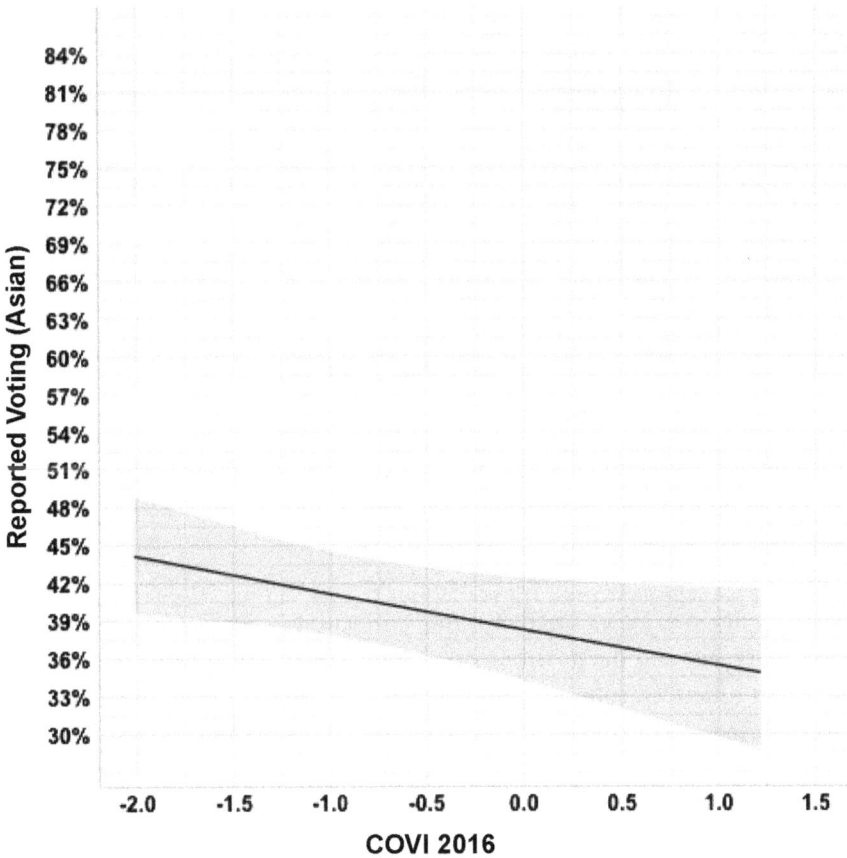

Figure 5.5. Change in the predicted probability of Asian American reported voting and the COVI

Source: Michael Pomante, Scot Schraufnagel, and Quan Li

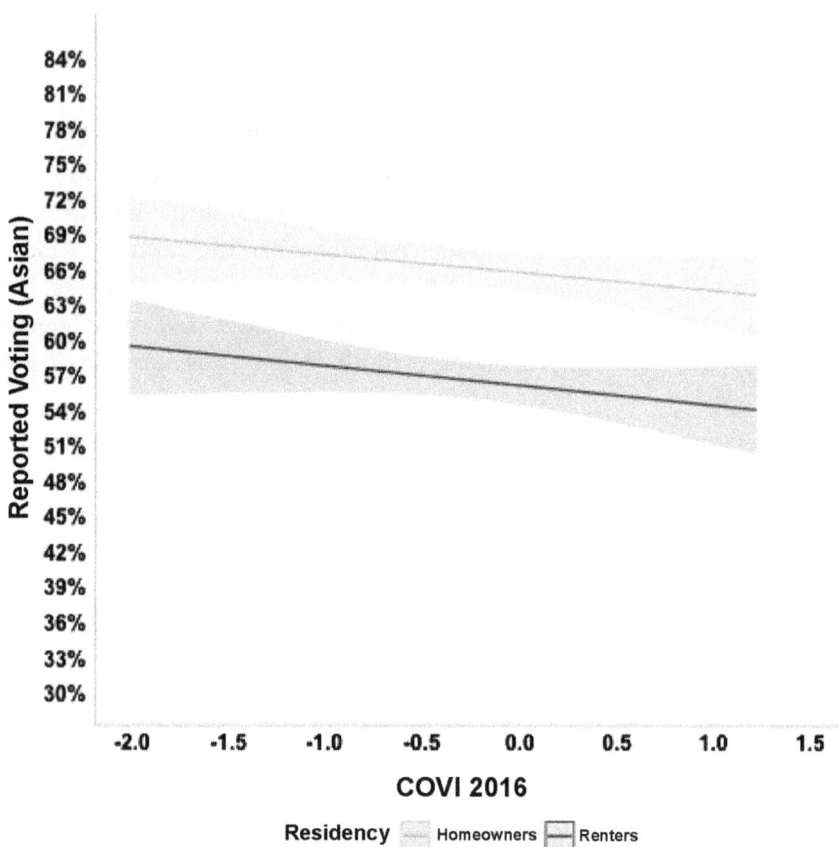

Figure 5.6. Change in the predicted probability of Asian American reported voting and the COVI: homeowners versus renters

Source: Michael Pomante, Scot Schraufnagel, and Quan Li

than 36 percent in states where it is more difficult to vote. Supposing a social-desirability bias and the possibility that some respondents overreport voting, the Asian American subpopulation appears less susceptible to this tendency. The reported voter turnout, in this instance, is much more in line with the actual turnout as defined by exit polls and other post hoc investigations of voter turnout in the 2016 election (Masuoka et al. 2018; Masuoka, Ramanathan, and Junn 2019).

Considering the difference between Asian American homeowners and nonhomeowners, in figure 5.6, we find a particularly significant disadvantage for more mobile Asian Americans under the different cost of voting scenarios. Considering the results, as we move from Oregon to New Hampshire, the percentage of Asian Americans who report they voted drops from about 47 percent to 38 percent for homeowners. Under the same scenario, the decline for nonhomeowners is from about 37 percent to 29 percent, all else equal. One must imagine that cultural and language considerations are a particular burden for the more mobile Asian American subpopulation. Movers must familiarize themselves with voting processes each time they relocate. Eligible voters changing addresses within a state must reregister before voting in the next election cycle. If there is no automatic voter registration, no online voter registration, or a restrictive voter registration deadline, each of these considerations can demobilize those who might otherwise exercise their right to vote.

UNDEREDUCATED AMERICANS, REPORTED TURNOUT, AND THE COVI IN 2016

Leaving the precepts of racial threat theory behind, for a time, along with cultural and language barriers, we wonder if a more restrictive state electoral-institutional climate suppresses the turnout of the undereducated or, more specifically, respondents without a high school diploma. Importantly, the raw data suggests that the three minority groups are each overrepresented among respondents who have not reached this level of educational attainment. Figure 5.7 displays the change in predicted probability associated with lower education under the different cost of voting scenarios. Again, appendix G reports the full results (table G5.4).

Note that there is a statistically significant negative slope indicating that the undereducated are less likely to report voting when voting costs grow. Only about 57 percent of those without a high school diploma report voting in 2016 in the most inclusive electoral climate (Oregon). This rate drops to approximately 51 percent in the most restrictive state (New Hampshire). Recall that over 72 percent of all respondents reported voting in 2016. We predicted that reported voting would be lower for the undereducated group, and this is the case.

Moreover, it is essential to remember that the model run also controls for years of education, which is a statistically significant consideration (see table G5.4). Putting both education variables in the same model provides an exceptionally robust test of the relationship between education and voting under the

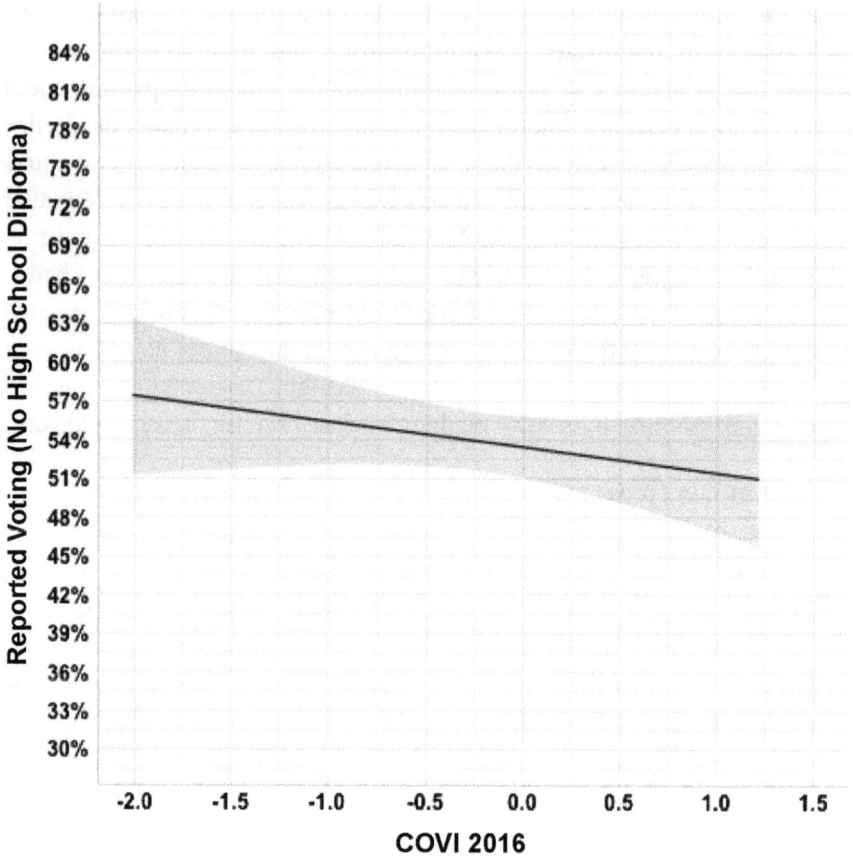

Figure 5.7. Change in the predicted probability of reported voting among those without a high school diploma and the COVI

Source: Michael Pomante, Scot Schraufnagel, and Quan Li

different cost of voting scenarios. We learn that reported voting goes up for those with more years of education, but there is also a corresponding decrease in reported voting when the respondent does not have a high school diploma and the cost of voting is higher. The results of this vigorous test strongly suggest that a higher cost of voting disproportionately demobilizes undereducated citizens.

Considering the undereducated further, we again find that nonhomeowners are notably less likely to report voting. Moreover, the different costs of voting scenarios produce a steeper dark gray line in figure 5.8. The change

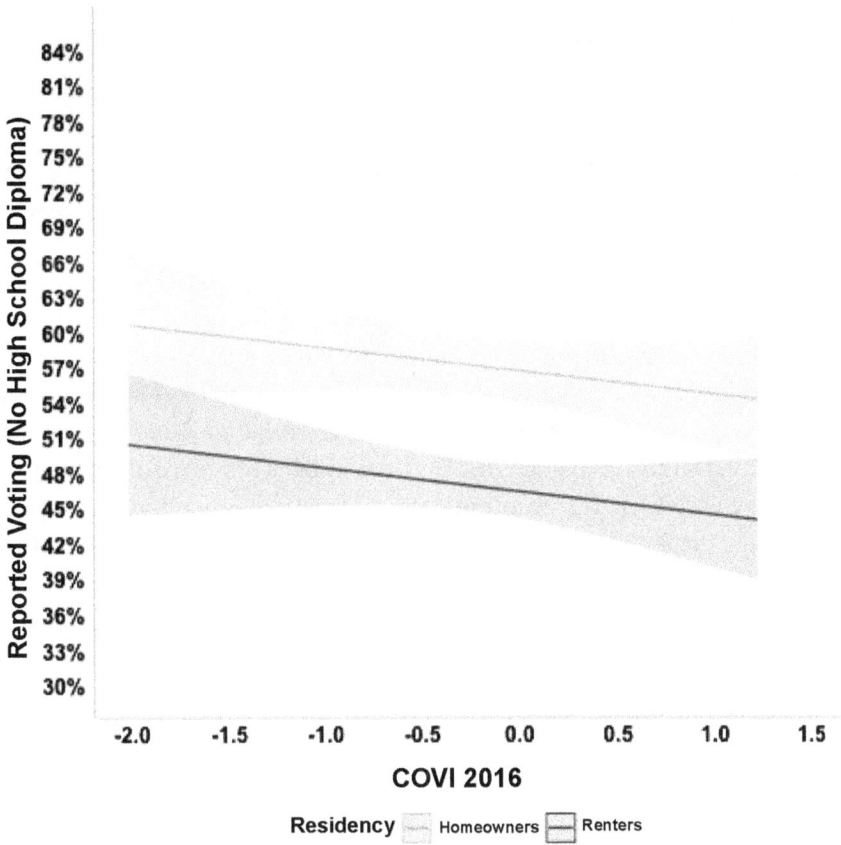

Figure 5.8. Change in the predicted probability of reported voting among those without a high school diploma and the COVI: homeowners versus renters

Source: Michael Pomante, Scot Schraufnagel, and Quan Li

in the predicted probability of reported voting, associated with the range of COVI values, creates a drop of around 6 percent for homeowners. The drop grows to over 7 percent for nonhomeowners. As noted at the beginning of the chapter, we meant our test of the role of homeownership to be a validity check of our modeling assumptions. If our thesis regarding the relative cost of voting is correct, we should find that renters who need to reregister to vote more often are particularly disadvantaged. Indeed, we see this when we consider all four subpopulations. Homeowners in each group are likelier to report that they voted than renters.

Conclusion

Importantly, our investigation corroborates research published in 2021 by Michael Ritter and Caroline Tolbert. These authors also use the COVI to predict changes in the probability of voting across racial subgroups. Both sets of researchers, operating entirely independent of one another, find that Hispanic citizens are especially disadvantaged when the cost of voting is higher. Moreover, we both find demobilization for all voters under the scenario of more costly voting. Still more consistent with our analysis, Ritter and Tolbert (2021) did not find evidence for an across-the-board demobilization of Black Americans associated with the COVI. However, when we look more deeply, using the insights of racial threat theory, which suggests that growing populations are particularly threatening, we find the demobilizing influence of more costly voting. Specifically, in the seventeen states where Black American populations are growing the fastest, the COVI interacts with being Black in a manner that associates with lower reported voter turnout. This finding is particularly troubling because growing populations should equate to growing political influence, but if the cost of voting demobilizes group members, this would be less likely to occur.[14]

It is worth noting that throughout US history, whites have held a majority of seats in state legislatures in every state. Indeed, there has been a descriptive underrepresentation of minority populations in state legislatures and other elected statewide offices since the foundation of the republic (more on this in chapter 6). It is easy to imagine that many white legislators in positions of power and influence appreciate status quo arrangements and would like to maintain them. However, a radical change in the mobilization of minority voters, the undereducated, and renters might upset the proverbial apple cart and cause turnover in the individuals holding public office. Such a change would threaten existing political arrangements and existing public policies.

It makes sense that many current legislators would be interested in maintaining restrictive election laws, perhaps some legislators more than others. After all, existing officeholders obtained their positions using the prevailing rules, and new voters could change things. Notably, the motivation to maintain status quo arrangements should be greater if restrictions work to demobilize certain populations. This chapter attempted to answer this question, and the answer is a resounding yes! Restrictions do work. In many predictable ways, individuals representing specific subgroups of eligible voters report voting less often when the costs associated with voting are higher. Specifically, we learned that high COVI values disproportionately suppress the reported turnout of Hispanic, Asian, and undereducated Americans.

Although we do not have a direct test of whether the overrepresented white state legislators are sufficiently interested in maintaining their dominant political position to adopt restrictive electioneering policies, we believe something like this must be going on. In chapter 4, we learned voting was more restricted when states had larger Black or growing Hispanic populations. In this chapter, we find that restrictive voting laws disproportionately demobilize certain subpopulations in predictable ways. In all of this, it is difficult to imagine that the motivation for election law changes is always benign and innocent efforts to improve the voting process.

Individuals from three of the four groups are particularly disadvantaged when they must navigate a more restrictive state electoral process: the first two groups perhaps because of language and cultural considerations, and the latter group because the trouble of voting grows when one has a limited education. Moreover, these disadvantages grow when citizens from these subpopulations are renters or homeless. Homeownership arguably increases the benefits of voting (McCabe 2013), but we hold that residential instability is also part of the explanation. The decentralized administration of election processes in the United States means citizens must relearn how to vote each time they move. Suppose a voter moves to a state with a higher COVI value, the bar for learning how to vote becomes higher. However, even intrastate moves require considerable effort to reregister and find a new polling location.

The situation for the United States' second-largest minority group, Black Americans, is somewhat more complicated. Previous researchers have uncovered that people under the most pressure to vote report voting at higher rates (Bernstein, Chadha, and Montjoy 2001; Silver, Anderson, and Abramson 1986). The psychology of why this is the case is beyond the scope of our research. What we do learn, however, is that the adverse effects of higher COVI values are occurring in the seventeen states with the fastest-growing Black populations. When we imagine Black political influence might be growing, state legislative manipulation of election law can limit any increase in political power. From Utah to New Hampshire, when Black populations are growing the fastest, we find that increased COVI values, signaling more restrictions, predict less reported voting by Black Americans. Residential mobility, or lack of homeownership, provides additional concern. Black renters in these seventeen states are even more likely not to vote when the costs of voting are higher.

In chapter 6, we test if higher COVI values prevent some minorities from running for public office and gaining electoral support when they do run. Correspondingly, we test if minorities are less likely to win when they run and whether the descriptive representation of minorities in state legislatures is lower in states with higher COVI values. In an auxiliary analysis, we also check whether the underrepresentation of women is greater when states have higher COVI values. We suspect that the underrepresentation of females in public office is also associated with a more restrictive state electoral climate. In this instance, we again suppose that white male state legislators are potentially trying to hold on to their privileged political position by maintaining election laws that preserve the status quo.

6: Minority Candidate Electoral Success and the Underrepresentation of Minorities and Women

In the 117th Congress (2021–2023), more Black, Hispanic, and Asian Americans served in the US Congress than ever before. However, the underrepresentation of each group persists. The Pew Research Center reports:

> Non-Hispanic white Americans account for 77% of voting members in the new Congress [the 117th], considerably larger than their 60% share of the U.S. population overall. This gap hasn't narrowed with time: In 1981, 94% of members of Congress were White, compared with 80% of the U.S. population.[1]

Particularly troubling is that although the percentage of minorities in Congress has grown, the numbers have not kept pace with the diversification of society. Pew's research finds that the underrepresentation of minorities in Congress has grown more extensive in the past forty years. Specifically, minorities had a 14 percent gap in representation in 1981, which grew to a 17 percent gap by 2021.

Moving beyond voter turnout, in this chapter, we test the electoral success of minority candidates under the different voting cost scenarios. Specifically, does minority candidate success decline when voting costs are higher? We are limited in answering this question by statewide COVI values. Thankfully, there are several statewide offices, such as those of governor and senator, where the electoral constituency is the entire state. Moreover, there are instances when the whole state is a single US House district. When candidates run for the lower chamber in these at-large elections, we can again use COVI values to test minority electoral achievement effectively.[2] All statewide elected offices become our testing ground.

Moreover, women, like minorities, are a subpopulation that has been notoriously underrepresented in elected office in the United States (Smith, Reingold, and Owens 2012; Thomsen 2015; Lowande, Ritchie, and Lauterbach 2019). Therefore, we can test how each state legislature stacks up when considering the descriptive representation of women and Black and Hispanic

Americans. We wish to learn if states with a more inclusive electoral-institutional posture associate with a greater descriptive representation of these underrepresented groups. We hypothesize that more restrictions, or higher COVI values, are less likely to produce state legislator populations that mirror state resident populations. In the testing, we acknowledge that some state legislatures are more amateur or part-time. These legislatures tend to be more elite bodies with lower descriptive representation (Squire 2007, 2017). All of these factors must be considered when we conduct some of our tests.

Minorities, the COVI, and Electoral Success

We begin with several tests of the relationship between each state's electoral-institutional climate and minority electoral success.[3] Specifically, we collect data on all minorities who run for governor, senator, lieutenant governor (when running alone), at-large House seats, and other positions within the plural executive of state governments such as attorney general, comptroller, secretary of state, and treasurer. We examine all statewide races from 1996 to 2020. We include only minorities who run as candidates for one of the two major political parties. Third-party candidates are already disadvantaged (Schraufnagel 2011), which might bias our results, as their inclusion in the analysis would confound our tests of minority electoral accomplishment.

Upfront, we examine Black and Hispanic candidate electoral success in three different ways. In other words, we have three unique dependent variables. We conduct the three tests to determine whether one modeling assumption is driving our results. If we get the same answer for all three tests, we can be more confident that we have uncovered the genuine relationship between the two considerations (minority status and electoral success). We use state COVI ranks as the key explanatory variable in each test and state ranks to standardize our consideration of the cost of voting over the period studied (1996–2020).[4]

To elaborate further on the three dependent variables, or measurement strategies, consider the experience of Kamala Harris (D-CA) when she ran for attorney general in California in 2010 against Steve Cooley (R). Specifically, the future vice president is a minority woman who faced four third-party attorney general candidates besides Cooley. Ms. Harris won the race, obtaining

46.05 percent of the vote to 45.21 percent for Mr. Cooley. Considering our first dependent variable, we scored the Harris case "1" because she won. In cases when the minority candidate loses, we score "0."[5] In the second model, the Harris case receives a score of "46.05," representing her actual vote percentage. Finally, in a third instance, the case receives a score of "0.84" (46.05%–45.21%), equal to the winning vote margin. In a two-candidate race, the Harris vote percentage of 46.05 would otherwise indicate a 7.9 percent loss (53.95%–46.05%).

All three dependent variables are related, and the latter two might seem perfectly correlated. Yet, they are not. Not all statewide races have only two candidates, so the third test examines the difference in vote percentage between the two major party candidates. To illustrate this third measure further, assume a Hispanic candidate receives 40 percent of the vote and loses. In a two-candidate race, the winning candidate would have received 60 percent of the vote and the Hispanic candidate's election margin would equal –20% (40–60). In a different scenario, with a third-party candidate running, the Hispanic candidate may have fared, relatively speaking, much better. In this instance, the Hispanic candidate receives 40 percent of the vote, but now, the winner receives only 45 percent of the vote and the third-party candidate receives the other 15 percent. Under this scenario, the Hispanic candidate's election margin equals a negative 5 percent (40–45). The assumption is that the minority candidate performs better in the second scenario than in the first.

With each of the three dependent variables, or measures of minority electoral support, we expect a negative association with state COVI values. If results show that the COVI negatively influences minority electoral success, we can be confident that more restrictive voting hampers minority electoral success regardless of how we measure it. It is important to remember that each model run represents different measurement assumptions. Recall that when we controlled for education and income, in chapter 5, we learned that Black reported voter turnout is greater than white reported turnout.[6] The initial bivariate relationship was not statistically significant or the whole story. It is necessary to test things in multiple ways to get closer to the truth.

As has been the case throughout this monograph, we begin by examining bivariate relationships. Doing so allows us to check whether we are on the right path in unraveling the genuine relationship between variables. The bivariate tests allow us to compare the strength and direction of the relationship, in this case, between the three indicators of minority electoral success and state COVI ranks. Specifically, we use the state rank in the presidential election cycle before, or contemporaneous with, the statewide race examined. For example, in the 2006 Arizona race for secretary of state, Democrat Israel Torres (D) was the minority candidate. We use Arizona's 2004 COVI rank to predict his success. In the Alabama Senate race, in 2008, between Jeff Sessions (R) and minority candidate Vivian Davis Figures (D), we use the state's 2008 rank. In the time studied, we identified 182 minority candidates running alone for a statewide office representing one of the two major political parties. We do not include the twenty-three Black and Hispanic candidates who ran for lieutenant governor on the same ticket as a gubernatorial candidate, who was most often white.

Table 6.1 displays the correlations between state COVI ranks and the three measures of electoral achievement. The first column in the table displays statistically significant and negative associations between state COVI rank and each of the minority candidate electoral performance indicators. The findings suggest that, on average, minorities perform poorer in states with higher COVI ranks. Recall from chapter 3 that a higher rank, relative to other states, indicates that the cost of voting is greater. Our findings suggest that as the state rank goes up and moves toward fifty, the electoral achievement of minority candidates goes down. Moreover, the bivariate relationships between the three dependent variables (columns 2 and 3) suggest that these alternative measures are dissimilar. As a result, we truly obtain three unique tests of the role of the COVI in depressing minority electoral success.

Of course, bivariate relationships are not the whole story, and we must control for other considerations. For instance, we expect minority candidates

Table 6.1. The Electoral Success of Minority Candidates Running for Statewide Offices and COVI Rank: 1996–2020

	COVI rank	Won office	Own percent	Election margin
COVI rank	1			
Won office	−.27 ($P < .001$) $n = 182$	1		
Own percent	−.23 ($P < .001$) $n = 182$	.71 ($P < .001$) $n = 182$	1	
Election margin	−.25 ($P < .001$) $n = 182$	.77 ($P < .001$) $n = 182$	.94 ($P < .001$) $n = 182$	1

Source: Michael Pomante, Scot Schraufnagel, and Quan Li

to perform better in states with larger minority populations. We also know that minority citizens, especially Black voters (Mangum 2013), are more likely to align with the Democratic Party. Suppose a disproportionate number of the minority candidates in our tests represent the Republican Party. In that case, this could complicate matters and help explain lower electoral accomplishment for Black candidates, unrelated to the cost of voting. Next, we make clear how each control variable is measured.

Control Variables

The candidate's party is the first alternative explanation or control variable.[7] We exclude minority candidates running as independents or representing a minor party from the analysis. We anticipate a positive association between being a candidate of the Democratic Party and electoral success. Therefore, we expect minority Democrats to receive more electoral support, on average, than minority Republicans. It is essential to appreciate that a minority Republican candidate might be less threatening to majority white voters, which could cause these candidates to obtain greater support. For instance, in Vermont, where Black residents make up a tiny portion of the total population, voters elected Randy Brock (R), a Black American, as comptroller in a statewide election in 2004. Once we hold the cost of voting constant, we must be open to the possibility that minority candidates representing the Republican Party will perform better.

Next, we control for the level of electoral competition in the state. In this instance, we are not using a competitive electoral environment to indicate the "benefits" of voting. Instead, our concern is that when electoral contests are tighter, voters don't want to risk voting for a minority candidate out of fear that they may be wasting their vote. We know from previous research that voters do not like to vote for candidates who do not have a realistic chance of winning (Lijphart 1997, 7; Hummel 2014). Suppose an average voter assumes minority candidates are systematically disadvantaged and wants to vote for the eventual winner. In that case, they may opt for the white candidate. We measure electoral competition as the difference between the vote percentages of the two major-party candidates at the top of the ticket (governor, senator, or president) in either the contemporaneous or previous election cycle.[8] We anticipate that a larger margin, indicating less electoral competition, is associated with more minority candidate support. In other words, more competition equals fewer minority candidate votes, and we expect to obtain a negative coefficient in the model runs.

Next, we test whether the gender of the minority candidate makes a difference.[9] Although research has shown that female candidates generally perform on par with men when they have similar experience and campaign resources (Dolan 2014, 3), we also know that minority women have been especially disadvantaged in terms of socioeconomic mobility and social status (Michener and Brower 2020). This disadvantage, in turn, might lead to an underfunded campaign and less electoral support, on average. If women are disadvantaged in society, we might expect minority female candidates to find it particularly difficult to win statewide elected office. Correspondingly, we anticipate negative coefficients in the regression analyses.

Our fourth and fifth control variables are the percent Black population and the percent Hispanic population in each state. In each instance, we use US Census Bureau data. Specifically, we use 1990 values for elections from 1996 to 1999; 2000 figures for the 2000–2004 elections; 2005 population estimates for the 2005–2009 elections; 2010 values for the 2010–2013 elections; 2014 population estimates for the 2014–2018 elections; and 2019 population estimates for the 2019–2020 elections. Table 6.2 displays descriptive statistics for each dependent variable, our key explanatory variable (COVI rank), and each control variable.

Note that the mean value of 0.24 for the "won office" consideration in table 6.2 descriptive statistics table indicates that when minority candidates ran for a statewide office in the period studied, they won about 24 percent of the time. Forty-four of the 182 minority candidates we studied won and 138 lost. Dropping to the third dependent variable or the election margin consideration, we can note that Ed Lopez, a Latino Republican, who lost the secretary of state race in Rhode Island in 1998, represents the minimum value. The maximum value belongs to Jesse White, a Black Democrat, who won the 2010 race for secretary of state in Illinois.

The minimum COVI rank of "2" tells us that no minorities ran for statewide office in a state ranked the easiest to vote (either North Dakota or Oregon) in the period studied. If the most accessible state to vote in were included in one of the 182 races, the minimum value of the COVI rank would have to be

Table 6.2. Descriptive Statistics of Variables Used to Test Minority Candidate Electoral Success in Statewide Races: 1996–2020

	Min. value	Max. value	Mean value	Std. dev.
Dependent variables				
Won office	0	1	.24	.43
Own percent	4.1	71.5	44.04	10.23
Election margin	−63.88	43.53	−11.06	19.02
Key explanatory variable				
COVI rank	2	50	28.66	13.06
Control variables				
Democrat	0	1	.77	.42
Electoral competition	.06	51.41	14.55	9.45
Female	0	1	.32	.47
Percent Black population	.5	37.8	15.33	10.73
Percent Hispanic population	.9	49.3	13.75	13.26
n	182			

Source: Michael Pomante, Scot Schraufnagel, and Quan Li

"1." The mean of 0.32 for the variable representing females indicates that about 32 percent (58/182) of the minority candidates running for statewide office in our study were women.

Using the variables presented in table 6.2, we run the three regression models for each of the three dependent variables discussed and report the results in table 6.3. Our primary concern has been the relative restrictiveness of each state's electoral climate or COVI rank. We learn that a higher COVI rank is associated with less electoral success for minority candidates in all three models. The bivariate relationships were not an anomaly. In the more fully specified models, which include the control variables, we now know that minority candidates have less electoral success throughout the contemporary era when a state's electoral-institutional climate is more restrictive.

Considering the "won office" model, in the first column of results, we find that the test of whether the minority candidate was a Democrat and the test of state electoral competition return signs in the hypothesized correct direction. However, the test of these considerations in the first model does not indicate statistically significant relationships, on average, after controlling for other considerations. In the following two models, both variables are statistically

Table 6.3. Minority Electoral Success When Running for Statewide Office and the COVI

Models: LOGIT Regression/Ordinary Least Squares (OLS) Regression/OLS Regression

Key explanatory variable	Won office Coefficient (s.e.)	Own percent Coefficient (s.e.)	Election margin Coefficient (s.e.)
COVI rank	−.053 (.019)*	−.227 (.080)*	−.454 (.158)*
Control variables			
Democrat	.939 (.592)	5.233 (2.633)*	9.502 (4.649)*
Electoral competition	−.004 (.020)	−.222 (.077)*	−.397 (.145)*
Female	−.215 (.620)	.373 (1.986)	−2.126 (3.835)
Percent Black population	−.013 (.025)	−.014 (.097)	.002 (.161)
Percent Hispanic population	.016 (.017)	.113 (.060) ᵗ	.220 (.113) ᵗ
Constant	−.43 (.66)	47.53 (3.09)*	−1.98 (5.90)
Wald Chi²/F-Statistic /F-Statistic	10.39*	2.99*	3.13*
Pseudo R²/R²/R²	.10	.16	.16
n	182	182	182

* $P < .05$ (two-tailed test); ᵗ $P < .05$ (one-tailed test)

Source: Michael Pomante, Scot Schraufnagel, and Quan Li

linked to minority electoral achievement, as predicted. Considering the results of all three tests, we feel comfortable suggesting that minority Democrats running for statewide offices gain more support, on average, than minority Republican candidates do and that state voters are less likely to support minority candidates for these same offices when there is more statewide electoral competition, defined as a closer race at the top of the ballot.

The number representing COVI rank in the first model is a LOGIT coefficient. We can convert this value back to an odds ratio and learn the predicted probability that a minority candidate wins statewide office. Figure 6.1 provides a substantive understanding of how much COVI rank matters. Here we are amazed at the functionally solid relationship between COVI state rank and minority candidate electoral success. Interpretation of our test suggests that in a second-ranked state, the probability that a minority candidate wins is greater than 58 percent. This probability drops to just a little more than 4 percent if the state is ranked fiftieth. A one standard deviation change in COVI rank is about thirteen places; consequently, a one standard deviation change, down

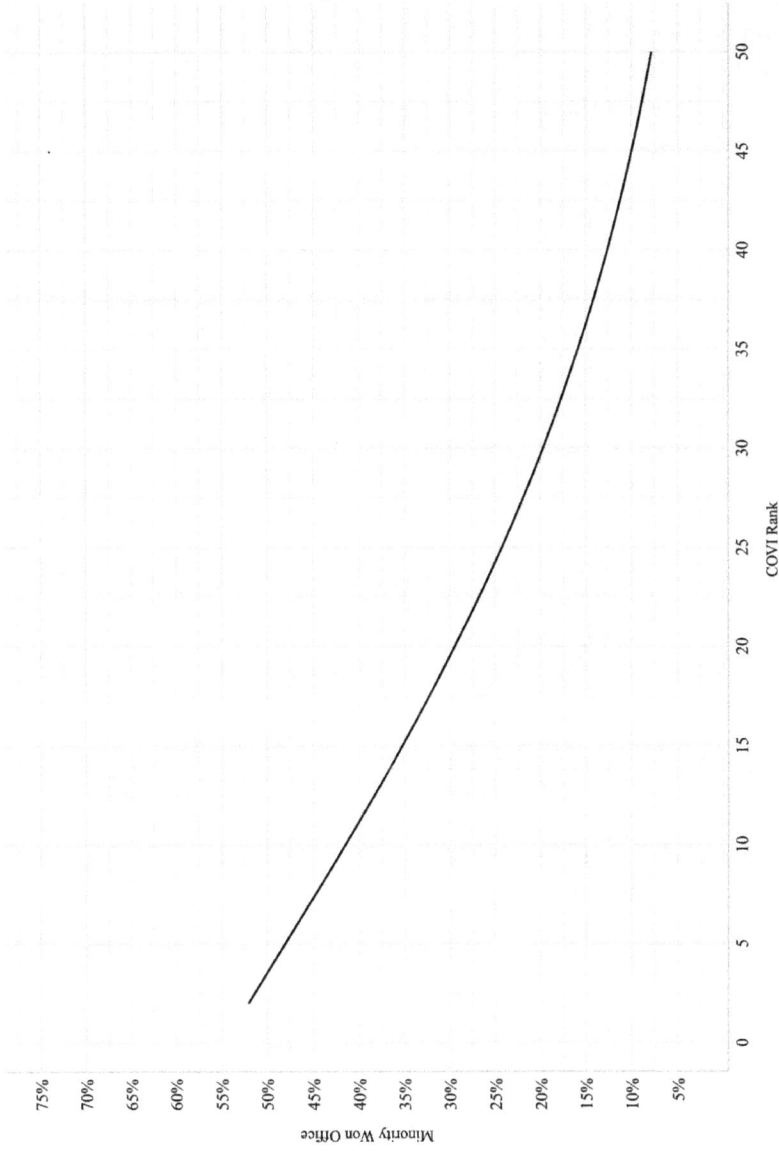

Figure 6.1. The predicted probability that a minority candidate wins under different COVI rank scenarios
Source: Michael Pomante, Scot Schraufnagel, and Quan Li

the rankings, for instance, from twelfth to twenty-fifth place, is associated with a decline in the likelihood that a minority candidate wins from about 46 percent to 30 percent, on average, all else being equal. We hold this to be a meaningful and important explanation of the lack of minority electoral success in races for statewide offices across the country. Moreover, it helps explain the lack of descriptive representation of Black and Hispanic Americans in these statewide offices.

Considering the other two models, we now see evidence that being a Democrat helps minority candidates. Perhaps more interesting, we learn that when electoral competition in a state is greater, minority candidates underperform. One interpretation of this finding is that voters generally are less likely to support a minority candidate if they think their vote may be "wasted." In other words, paradoxically, white voters may be more willing to vote for a minority candidate in a race when the minority candidate is less likely to win. To illustrate this contention, consider Stephen Benjamin, a Black Democrat who ran for attorney general in South Carolina in 2002. Benjamin received a larger vote share than the Democratic Party presidential candidate, Al Gore, in the 2000 South Carolina general election. Benjamin's vote percentage tops Gore's by 2.63 percent. The Palmetto State is a Republican Party stronghold. A vote for a minority Democrat might seem less worrisome for majority white voters because they can safely assume the minority candidate loses. Indeed, Benjamin does lose.

In another instance of the same consideration, we note that former football player Damon Dunn, a Black Republican, ran for secretary of state in California in 2010. Dunn beat John McCain's performance in the 2008 California general election but was not a threat to win the statewide office in a notable Democratic Party stronghold, and he outperformed his political party's presidential candidate in the state. If these occurrences are systematic, and the results from the model suggest they are, we can better understand why minorities perform better, on average, when the electoral environment is less competitive.

Considering the test of COVI rank and a minority candidate's own percentage of votes, we obtain a coefficient of 0.227. Recall that a one standard deviation decline in COVI rank equals about thirteen units. Multiplying the coefficient obtained from the test by thirteen, we can expect approximately a 3 percent drop (0.227 * 13) in electoral support, with a one standard deviation change in state rank. The full range of COVI rank can explain approximately an 11 percent decrease in support for minority candidates (0.227 * 49). This decrease is significant enough to make a difference between winning and losing.

The coefficient representing the electoral margin in the third model equals -.454. Now, a one standard deviation decrease in COVI rank causes the election margin to grow more negative by almost 6 percent (–.454 * 13). For instance, consider Marquita Bradshaw's run for a US Senate seat from Tennessee in 2020. The Democratic Party nominee lost by 27.3 percent to Republican Bill Haggerty. In 2020, Tennessee ranked forty-sixth on the COVI, identifying it as a state with one of the most restrictive electoral climates. North Carolina, on the other hand, in 2020, was ranked thirty-third, a one standard deviation improvement over Tennessee. Another Black Democrat, Yvonne Lewis Holley, ran for lieutenant governor and lost by only 3.26 percent of the vote. Our analysis suggests that the different COVI ranks between Tennessee and North Carolina can explain about 6 percent of the difference in the electoral performance of the two Black females running for statewide office in the same year.

The Underrepresentation of Minorities and Women in State Legislatures

We began this chapter with a question, namely, whether a more restrictive state electoral climate would cause minority candidates who run for statewide office to underperform. The answer is an unequivocal yes. We focused on statewide races because COVI values represent the electoral climate of states, not parts of states. We now wish to learn whether states with more restrictive voting practices witness less minority representation in state legislatures. Moreover, we wish to learn more about female representation in state legislatures and a possible relationship with voting restrictions. Our COVI values allow us to test whether Black and Hispanic citizens, as well as women, have descriptive representation in state legislatures under different levels of voting restriction. But first, we simply measure the volume of minority candidates for statewide offices.

THE VOLUME OF MINORITY CANDIDATES

Before trying better to understand the representation gap of minorities and women, it is possible to test whether minorities, in general, are less likely to run for public office. We suspect that many otherwise qualified individuals from minority groups don't run for public office, given the long history of white male dominance in electoral politics in the United States (Schneider et al. 2016). Understanding that the country's electoral climate is not conducive to minority electoral success, especially in certain states, many rational individuals won't run (Shah 2014). This disbandment is particularly troubling because it suggests a level of political anomie or alienation that undoubtedly results in fewer minorities holding elected office.

To test for minority candidate demobilization, we add the number of possible times a Black or Hispanic could have run in a governor's race, a US Senate race, or an at-large House district from 1996 through 2020. In all, there were 870 opportunities. We learn that fifty-nine minority candidates ran for one of these offices during this time. In other words, 6.78 percent (59/870) of all candidates for statewide office represented one, or the other, of the two largest minority groups in the United States. This rate, of course, is lower than the percentage of these two groups in the broader population. Indeed, during this period, US Census Bureau estimates suggest that over 28 percent of the country's population was either Black or Hispanic. Hence, we get a difference of about 21 percent (28–6.78). This finding alone helps us understand something about the volume of minority underrepresentation that exists at present in the United States.[10]

REPRESENTATION GAPS

Considering demographic representation gaps, we suspect that the underrepresentation of minorities and women occurs more routinely where the cost of voting is higher. Specifically, we test what role higher COVI values play in the demographic underrepresentation of minorities and women that has always existed in state legislatures. Our tests start by counting the number of Black Americans, Hispanics, and women serving in state legislatures and calculating the percentage from each group in 2021. We then use 2020 state COVI values as our primary predictor variable.[11] Although we have not consistently considered gender, we can note the systematic underrepresentation of females in elected office across the United States (Smith, Reingold, and Owens 2012). Therefore, we suspect there is greater underrepresentation of women in state legislatures when the cost of voting is higher. We use the same theory that suggests those in power work to restrict the opportunity of others to unseat them by maintaining status quo voting arrangements.

Again, we look to test things in more than one way to ensure that our findings are not simply the product of a particular measurement strategy. First, we use the demographic representation gap as our dependent variable in bivariate tests. Second, we use the percentage of minorities or women serving in a state legislature and a more fully specified model that controls for the size of minority and female populations in the states. In the first instance, we can note that the Black American representation gap in Mississippi is 6.77 percent. We use the 2019 Census Bureau population estimates and learn that 37.8 percent of the state's citizens identified as Black. In 2021 Black individuals held only 31.03 percent of the seats in the state legislature (40/122 in the House and 14/52 in the Senate). Hence, the Black representation gap in Mississippi is greater than 6 percent. In our second test and the more fully specified models, we use the value 31.03, representing the percentage of Black individuals serving in the state legislature, as our dependent variable. Can the COVI help us systematically understand the representation gap and the raw percentage of minorities and women in state legislatures?

Figures 6.2 and 6.3 display values on the first dependent variable, the representation gap, and their relationship to the cost of voting. We place state markers in the scatterplots to determine where the biggest representation gaps exist. Next, we create a figure for the Black, Hispanic, and female subpopulations we consider. Figure 6.2 displays the strong positive association between the underrepresentation of Black populations in state legislatures and COVI values in 2021. This bivariate relationship is easily statistically significant. Clearly, the underrepresentation of Black Americans in state legislatures is greater when state COVI values are larger.

We also learn from figure 6.2 that Black legislators overrepresent Black constituents in eight state legislatures. The eight states appear below the zero (0.0) horizontal line in the figure: Colorado, Illinois, Missouri, Nevada, New Jersey, Ohio, Oregon, and Washington. Notably, six of the eight states have negative COVI values or are states that make voting easier. Conversely, we find that Black populations are underrepresented in the other forty-two state legislatures. The states with more than a 5 percent gap (see the vertical y-axis) are Arkansas, Louisiana, Massachusetts, and Mississippi. Of those four, only Massachusetts has a negative COVI value. The other three states are ones where voting is more costly.[12]

Now considering the gap in representation of the Hispanic population, we

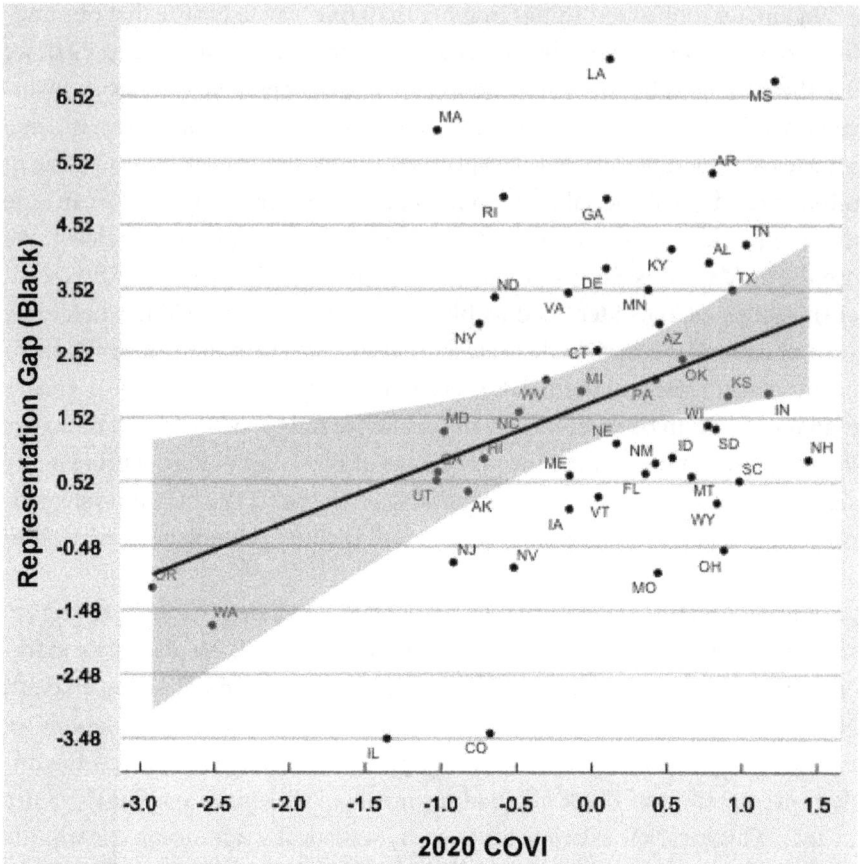

Figure 6.2. The 2020 COVI and the gap between the percent Black state legislators and state Black populations in 2021

Source: Michael Pomante, Scot Schraufnagel, and Quan Li

can note, in figure 6.3, that all states are above the horizontal line marked by zero (0.0). In other words, the Hispanic population is underrepresented in each of the fifty state legislatures. West Virginia is the closest to having proportional representation. Only 1.7 percent of the state residents identify as Latin American or Hispanic, and 1.49 percent of state legislators (2 out of 134) are Hispanic in 2021. Notably, West Virginia is a conservative state and has voted for the Republican Party presidential candidate in the past six presidential election cycles (2000–2020). Yet, West Virginia has a negative COVI value in

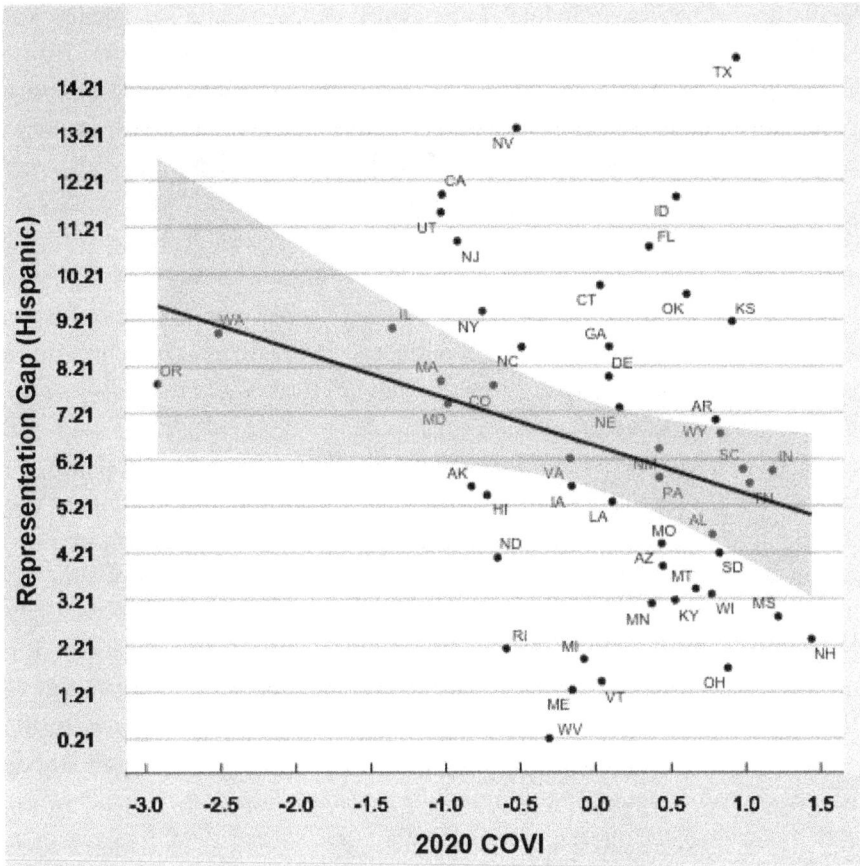

Figure 6.3. The 2020 COVI and the gap between percent Hispanic in state legislature and state Hispanic population in 2021

Source: Michael Pomante, Scot Schraufnagel, and Quan Li

2020, indicating it is a state with a more inclusive state electoral-institutional climate, on average.

Overall, there is no statistically significant relationship between the Hispanic representation gap and COVI values. The variability in the size of state Hispanic populations is, undoubtedly, part of the explanation. In 2019 the state Hispanic population size varied from 1.7 percent in West Virginia to 49.3 percent in New Mexico. In California, one of the states where it is easiest to vote, 39.4 percent of the population identifies as Hispanic. California has a small legislature, with 120 seats in total. In 2021 thirty-three of California's state legislators, or 27.5 percent of the two legislative chambers (22/80 in the state House and 11/40 in the state Senate), were Hispanic. Specifically, there is almost a 12 percent gap (39.4–27.5) in representation in the state ranked sixth easiest to vote during the 2020 election cycle. This finding suggests that states with larger Hispanic populations might find it more challenging to close the Hispanic representation gap, irrespective of the cost of voting. In the following analysis, we exclude states with relatively large Hispanic populations to understand better how higher costs of voting can compromise Hispanic representation. Note, in figure 6.3, that the state of Texas, at the top of the figure, does conform to expectations. It has the most significant gap in representation and one of the highest 2020 COVI values.

Next, we focus on the proportional representation of women in state legislatures and display the results in figure 6.4. We reveal the same pattern, as was the case for Black Americans. Again, we uncover a statistically significant positive association. In other words, as COVI values turn positive or as voting gets more restrictive, the gap in the representation of women grows. Interestingly, Nevada is the only state in the Union where women are overrepresented in the state legislature. In the Silver State, in 2021, 58.73 percent of the sixty-three state legislators (27/42 House and 10/21 Senate) were female. Moreover, the representation gap is less than 10 percent in Colorado, Maine, Oregon, Rhode Island, and Washington. Importantly, like Nevada, all these states make voting easier, on average. Conversely, states that make it harder to vote, such as Alabama, Mississippi, Tennessee, South Carolina, and Wyoming, are among the states with the most prominent female representation gap.

The scatterplots tell an important story. First, however, we want to test if the cost of voting helps determine the percentage of representatives from these groups in state legislatures after controlling for the size of minority and female populations in each state. Specifically, we use the percentage of the Black, Hispanic, and female delegation in each legislature in 2021 as the dependent variable. We combine the representatives from the two chambers, add the two-chamber sizes, and do the division to obtain the proportion of each group and then multiply by one hundred to get %Black Legislators, %Hispanic Legislators, and %Female Legislators. Our key explanatory variable is each state's 2020 COVI value. We use the Census Bureau's 2019 population estimates of each group, including women, as an essential control variable. As the size

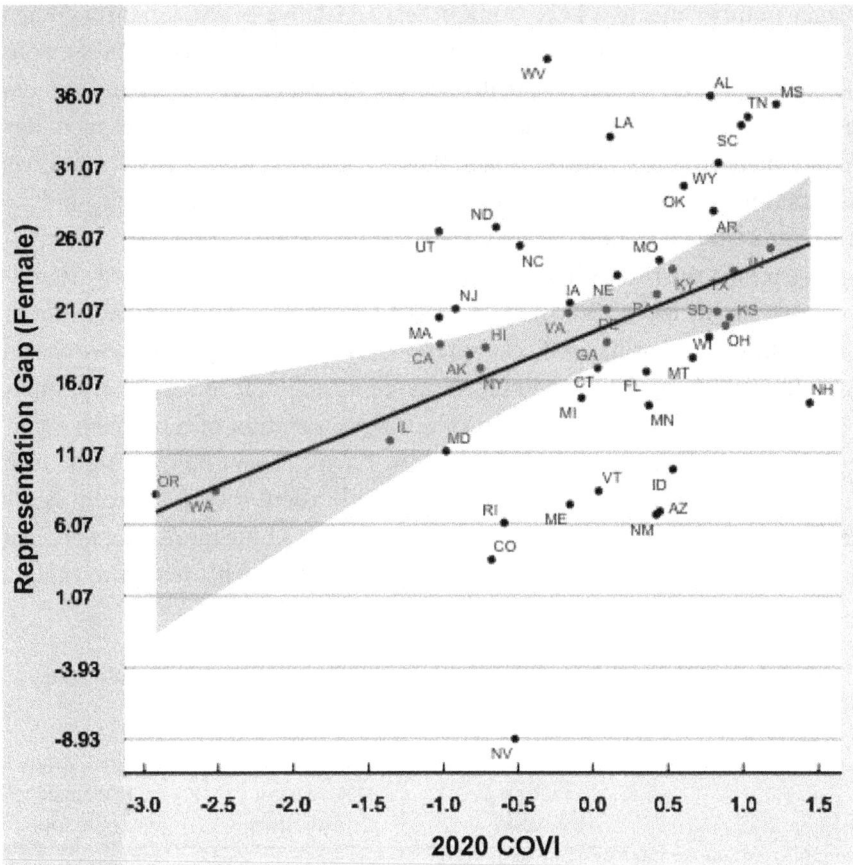

Figure 6.4. The 2020 COVI and gap between percent females in state legislature and state female population in 2021

Source: Michael Pomante, Scot Schraufnagel, and Quan Li

of each group grows as a percentage of all state residents, we expect that the size of the same group will increase in the state legislature. Although there is some variation in the female population by state, we do not anticipate enough variability to pick up a statistically significant relationship in this instance.[13]

In these models, we also control for the Squire Index or the state legislative professionalism indicator. In contrast to what we did in chapter 5, we use the raw Squire Index values. This approach is possible because we are no longer comparing states over time. Squire (2007, 2017) ranked states in a way that a bigger number meant a lower rank or less legislative professionalism. When using Squire Index values, higher values equal greater legislative professionalism. As a result, we expect greater representation of minorities and women in these more full-time legislative bodies, which tend to have fewer members of the socioeconomic elite serving in them. Therefore, we anticipate a positive association between the percentage of representatives from each group and the 2015 Squire Index values.[14]

We report the results in table 6.4. Notably, the COVI is statistically significant in both the Black and female models. In the first model, which tests the effect of the cost of voting on Black representation in state legislatures, we obtain a coefficient of -.736. The 2020 COVI ranges from −2.92 to 1.44 or 4.36 units. Considering this, we see a drop in Black representation of more than 3 percent for the full range of the COVI (−.736 * 4.36). This finding is significant given that the average state legislature has only about 9 (9.43) percent Black legislators. The drop for females (column 3) equals a little more than 1 percent (−.251 * 4.36). However, when we look at the model, which attempts to explain

Table 6.4. The 2020 COVI and the Percentage of Minorities and Female State Legislators in 2021

Model: Ordinary Least Squares Regression

	%Black legislators	%Hispanic legislators	%Female legislators
	Coefficient (s.e.)	Coefficient (s.e.)	Coefficient (s.e.)
2020 COVI	−.736 (.342)**	.637 (.458)	−.251 (.099)**
Black population	.895 (.230***		
Hispanic population		.806 (.039)***	
Female population			−.849 (1.657)
Squire Index	.251 (2.927)	.690 (4.085)	2.344 (13.799)
Constant	−.641 (.754)	−4.280 (.996)***	79.854 (82.664)
F-Statistic	305.53***	158.11***	3.13*
Adjusted R^2	.95	.91	.12
n	50	50	50

*** $P < .001$** $P < .01$* $P < .05$ (two-tailed test)

Source: Michael Pomante, Scot Schraufnagel, and Quan Li

the Hispanic representation in state legislatures, the COVI does not have a statistically significant effect on the percentage of Hispanic state legislators.

Considering the other control variables, as displayed in table 6.4, we learn that the size of each state's Black and Hispanic population explains a great deal of variation in the percentage of legislators from each group. In states like Maine, Vermont, or Wyoming, where minority populations are very low, these states do not elect minority legislators. Conversely, in other states, where minority populations are more prominent, we witness a greater percentage of minorities in the state legislature, as expected. The lack of variability in the state female population arguably compromises an opportunity to find a statistical relationship in the % Female Legislators model.

Considering minority populations in each state, we can note that California and New Mexico have relatively large Hispanic populations but a below-average Black population size. Other states like Louisiana and Mississippi have larger-than-average Black populations but minimal Hispanic populations. These population control variables are highly significant in the models. In other words, there is a very tight fit or relationship between the size of the minority population in each state and the percentage of state legislators from each group. As expected, the Squire Index of legislative professionalism always returns a positive association. Still, it is not statistically significant in the full models.[15]

Next, we examine Hispanic representation in state legislatures more carefully. Specifically, we eliminate the states with relatively large Hispanic populations to explore more thoroughly the relationship between the 2020 COVI and group members serving in state legislatures in 2021. In the past few decades, the Hispanic community in the United States has grown considerably (Abascal 2015, 789). Some states, presumably because they have been more welcoming or perhaps because of greater employment opportunities, have received many new residents from Latin America. In states like Colorado and Nevada, the Hispanic population is well above average, with most of the growth occurring recently (Johnson and Lichter 2008, 334). Presumably, Hispanic representation in these state legislatures has not caught up yet. Indeed, there is likely a lag associated with gaining citizenship, becoming familiar with political processes, and running for elected office.

Colorado and Nevada have lower-than-average COVI values, indicating a more inclusive electoral climate, yet relatively speaking, a lower percentage of

Hispanic state legislators. These states with large Hispanic populations (Colorado's percentage is more than twice the national average, and Nevada's is more than three times the national average) may prevent the hypothesized negative relationship from materializing when considering all fifty American states. We rerun the model to test this proposition, excluding the states with the largest Hispanic populations. When looking at the interstate distribution of the Hispanic population, we noted a break at around 5 percent in chapter 5. There is another natural break, around 15 percent. Specifically, thirty-eight states have less than 15 percent Hispanic residents. Consequently, we test the role the COVI might play on Hispanic representation in state legislatures in the thirty-eight states where Hispanics are a true minority group and report the results in table 6.5.

Using a one-tailed test for statistical significance, we find a negative link between the percentage of state legislative seats occupied by Hispanics and the 2020 COVI values. Again, the full range of the 2020 COVI is from –1.44 (Oregon) to 2.91 (New Hampshire), or about 4.35 points. Oregon and New Hampshire are among the thirty-eight states with less than a 15 percent Hispanic population. The test of the 2020 COVI returns a coefficient equal to -.395. This

Table 6.5. The Percentage of Hispanic State Legislators and the COVI in 2021: State Population Less than 15 Percent of the Total

Model: Ordinary Least Squares Regression

	% Hispanic legislators
	Coefficient (s.e.)
2020 COVI	–.395 (.228) [t]
Hispanic population	.215 (.058)*
Squire Index	4.448 (2.152)*
Constant	–.646 (.636)
F-Statistic	14.03
Adjusted R^2	.51
n	50

* $P < .05$ (two-tailed test); [t] $P < .05$ (one-tailed test)

Source: Michael Pomante, Scot Schraufnagel, and Quan Li

coefficient suggests that, on average, New Hampshire should expect roughly 2 percent fewer Hispanic representatives in their state legislature than Oregon (–.395 * 4.35), all else being equal. This 2 percent drop is significant because, in these thirty-eight states, the range on the dependent variable is only about 5 percent, with a mean value of 1.9 percent and a standard deviation of 1.6 percent. Additionally, table 6.4 shows a positive statistical link between the Squire Index and Hispanic representation in state legislatures, as expected. Of course, in these thirty-eight states, there is a larger percentage of Hispanics serving in the state legislature when the state Hispanic population is larger.

Conclusion

In this chapter, we extended our analysis by examining the effect the COVI has on minority candidate electoral success and the representation gap in state legislators. We measure minority electoral achievement in three ways and always find that a more restrictive state electoral climate is associated with lower minority electoral success. Moreover, the drop in the probability of winning is statistically significant and substantively relevant. For example, we noted that a Black candidate's odds of winning an election in the easiest state for voting was roughly 58 percent. On the other hand, the probability of a Black candidate winning in the costliest state was roughly 4 percent, all else equal (see figure 6.1). We also learn that the Black and female representation gap in state legislatures is larger in states with more restrictive voting laws. Finally, in cases where a state population is less than 15 percent Hispanic, there is also a lower percentage of Hispanics serving in state legislatures when COVI values are higher. Given that our findings so far strongly suggest that racial threat theory is a valid explanation for why states might tighten rules around voting, we now turn to examining the alternative possibility that more election fraud occurs when states make voting easier, the excuse most often given when states tighten restrictions on voting access.

7: The First Big Lie: Accessible Voting Leads to Widespread Voter Fraud

Especially since 2008, Republican Party state legislators, have argued that more convenient voting leads to voter fraud.[1] There is a notable irony in the GOP making these claims. Historically, it was the Democratic Party most concerned with election "integrity," relying on this argument to pass the infamous Jim Crow laws. (Keyssar 2000, 107–108). Alternatively, some southern Democrats claimed "the need to protect peaceable whites from bloodthirsty blacks" (Lichtman 2018, 93). Indeed, the Democratic Party led the states it dominated to restrict voting for the better part of a century, from the late 1860s to the late 1960s. However, since the election of Barack Obama, it has been Republican-controlled state legislators who have been pushing through laws restricting voting under the pretext of maintaining electoral justice or preventing fraud.

Historically, concerns for election integrity are not without merit. For example, research conducted in the 1970s (Benson 1978, 169–85) and 1980s (Summers 1987, 51–67) suggest that during the Gilded Age (1870–1900), election irregularities took place in nearly every state, often with consequences for who won the election. In response to these occurrences, the states adopted voter registration and identification laws to combat fraud. Yet, some researchers note that even then, the motive for some of the laws was the disenfranchisement of immigrant and lower-class voters (Burnham 1986; Gienapp 1982).

Merriam-Webster defines fraud, in part, as the intentional perversion of truth.[2] The reference to "intention" is relevant here because when states catch ineligible individuals voting, court proceedings typically reveal the individual was unaware they were unqualified to vote. Arguably, stricter voter registration laws could have prevented these individuals from registering to vote before they cast a fraudulent ballot. Indeed, this is precisely what many in the GOP have claimed motivates state efforts to restrict voting, especially in the aftermath of the 2020 presidential election cycle.[3] However, lost on many who favor more restrictive voting is that election experts have routinely discredited the notion that widespread fraud occurs or determines election outcomes in the United States (Levitt 2007; Minnite 2010; Ahlquist, Mayer, and Jackman 2014;

Holman and Lay 2018; Udani and Kimball 2018). Moreover, some researchers find that in those rare instances when voter fraud occurs, it is "not threatening the integrity of American elections" (Goel et al. 2020, 468). Hence, reformers intent on voting restrictions seek a solution to a nonexistent problem.

Different Types of Fraud

We suggest that it is important to recognize that there are many different types of fraud. Specifically, it is essential to distinguish "fraud" perpetrated by individual voters from fraud orchestrated by foreign actors, election officials, campaign workers, and candidates for public office. In the first instance, the word "fraud" is in quotes because the individual voter is often unaware they are ineligible to vote. This first category, "voter fraud," contains three subtypes, which we list in table 7.1. The second category is always intentional, and we term this "election fraud." There is some gray area, or overlap, with some of the subtypes of election fraud, but we believe it is possible to identify three discrete categories. Table 7.1 attempts to spell out the different types of electoral hazards.[4] The most vital distinction is that the first broad category involves individual voters, while the second general category involves people more intimately involved in elections as foreign infiltrators, administrators, campaigners, or candidates.

If reformers are sincere about addressing fraud, it is crucial to understand the totality of the problem and the many distinct threats. In other words, if we are to avoid dishonest election outcomes, one must distinguish the unique hazards. The first subtype of voter fraud in table 7.1 includes ineligible voters such as noncitizens and felons. Next, one must add to this category the "mentally incompetent," as many states have laws forbidding voter registration for people with mental disabilities, institutionalized individuals, or citizens living under guardianship arrangements. In the second category, we find voter impersonators. In these instances, the fraudster is likely using a family member's voter registration record or address to vote, perhaps because they forgot to register themselves before the state deadline. The category also includes the notorious voting for a dead person, using a deceased family member's identification or voter registration record. Lastly, there is double voting. These efforts include voting early, or absentee, and again on Election Day or voting in multiple electoral jurisdictions on Election Day, sometimes in two different states.

Table 7.1. Different Types of Potential Voter and Election Fraud

Voter fraud
1. Ineligible voting (noncitizen; felon; mentally incompetent)
2. Voter impersonation (voting for someone else; voting for a dead person)
3. Double voting (voting early and again on Election Day; voting in multiple jurisdictions)

Election fraud
1. Misinformation campaigns (domestic or international operatives spreading deception)
2. Corrupt election official (misreporting vote totals; rigging the vote-counting machinery)
3. Corrupt campaign worker or candidate (buying votes, strong-arming absentee ballots; manipulating people in line to vote for a preferred candidate; falsifying signatures on a ballot petition; lying about eligibility or residence)

Source: Michael Pomante, Scot Schraufnagel, and Quan Li

Turning now to the three categories of election fraud, the first involves foreign interference, and the next two involve corrupt domestic actors. We find misinformation campaigns, hacking of election administration equipment, and even political assassinations in the first subtype of election fraud. In each instance, the perpetrator is a foreign national. In the second subtype, the concern is corrupt election administrators. Scholars routinely find this fraud occurring in developing democracies (Malesky, Schuler, and Tran 2012; van Ham and Lindberg 2015). Moreover, this type of fraud was common in the United States during the Gilded Age (Benson 1978; Summers 1987). These election officials may "rig" the vote-counting equipment or report fallacious vote totals. The last category includes overzealous campaign workers doing what they can to boost the vote total of their favored candidates. It also recognizes candidates for public office who falsify election eligibility paperwork or go out of their way to stack the deck by buying votes.[5]

We hold it is crucial to distinguish the different types of fraud if reformers are sincere about addressing the issue. Importantly, we hold that "voter fraud" is much less of a concern than election fraud. Recall the seminal work by Anthony Downs (1957), introduced in chapter 3, on the irrationality of voting. Because the likelihood that one's vote determines the election outcome is so infinitesimal, it makes sense for people to act rationally and stay home. Riker and Ordershook (1968) developed an equation to explain the logic of Downs's argument: $R = (BP)-C$. Specifically, the authors suggest voting is only rational when the value of R is positive. In the equation, R equals the reward an individual receives from voting, and C is the cost an individual must pay to vote. B is the differential benefit a voter receives if their preferred candidate wins. Finally, P is the probability that a citizen's actions (or vote) bring about that benefit. The point is that "R" usually is negative for anyone who performs the calculation.

If there is a considerable cost to voting, and the probability that one's vote makes a difference is negligible, it makes sense that people abstain from the franchise. This truism explains why the United States, and other democratic countries, never get everyone to vote. Importantly, as we consider voter fraud, if voting itself is illogical, fraudulent voting is even more absurd. When committing voter fraud, one must add to the "cost of voting" the possibility of being caught and punished. Likewise, undocumented individuals who vote illegally must add the potential cost of deportation to their cost calculation. Consequently, voter fraud ought to be rare, and practitioners and scholars routinely find it is.

Particularly relevant, Goel et al. (2020) estimate that "to reduce [one instance of] double voting," it "could impede approximately 300 legitimate voters" from exercising their right to vote (456). That is, by making registration, and by extension voting, more difficult, legislators may prevent some fraud, but the corresponding increase in the cost of voting grows the probability that other citizens won't navigate the extra hassle. Moreover, the new restriction would cause otherwise eligible voters to find the act of voting irrational.[6]

Election fraud is also infrequent. However, the potential payoff or the probability that this fraud produces the desired election outcome is greater. Election fraud, orchestrated by election officials, campaign workers, or bad foreign actors increases the odds of a fallacious election outcome because now the fraud likely involves more than a single vote. However, counterbalancing the increased "B" or differential benefit is an increase in "C" or cost. This malfeasance often comes with severe penalties, including incarceration, if caught.[7] The possibility of this punishment is especially true for domestic election officials, candidates, or campaign workers. However, holding foreign infiltrators accountable is likely more challenging because they are most likely engaging in illegal activities outside US jurisdiction. Therefore, the cost of committing election fraud is nonexistent for these foreign actors.

A mass misinformation campaign, such as the type orchestrated by Russian government officials in their efforts to influence the 2016 presidential election (Wilner 2018, 311), is a particularly troubling fraud scenario. Now the "P" might be pretty substantial and the "C" quite low. To be sure, any of the three types of election fraud is a problem. Corrupt election officials or campaign workers trying to steal a local election surely compromises the legitimacy of all elections. However, we must point out that election fraud, of any stripe, is distinct from individual voter fraud. Notably, attempts to restrict or police election fraud generally do not increase the cost of voting for individual voters. For instance, creating a paper trail to verify vote counts or increasing the penalties for election fraud as a deterrent would not influence the time and effort it takes an eligible citizen to vote. If reformers are sincere about protecting election integrity in the United States, the focus should be squarely on preventing election fraud.

The distinction between the two general categories of fraud is particularly poignant because, unfortunately, many "reforms" passed in Republican state legislatures in recent years call for stricter voter identification processes and limits on absentee voting, which are attempts to address the much less consequential voter fraud. Making voting less convenient for individual voters does little to address the potential for election fraud. For instance, letting someone register to vote online, or vote early, reduces individual costs, making citizens more likely to vote. However, this has little to do with amplifying the more severe threat of election fraud. Said differently, making it easier to vote and reducing the value of "C" in the Riker and Ordeshook equation for individual voters does not improve the odds that a foreign power interferes in our elections or make our elected officials or campaign workers more or less likely to be corrupt. Creating a more restrictive electoral-institutional process for voters to navigate does not address the likelihood of corruption perpetrated by bad foreign or domestic actors.

One might counter that making voting easier opens more windows for swindlers to enter and disrupt election processes. For instance, more early voting sites increase the number of places where corruption might take place. However, this contention does not stand up well when one seriously considers what it means to make voting easier. More convenient voting often decentralizes voting administration. Expanding polling locations and drop box accessibility increases costs for election crooks. The increased cost occurs because their efforts require hacking or, in some way, disrupting a larger number of facilities. Liberal reformers often lament the lack of national election administration, and their concerns are not without merit. However, there is a tradeoff, and the decentralized nature of election administration in the United States makes election fraud less of a concern, especially when considering statewide and national elections.

It is important to repeat that new technology geared toward making voting easier for individual voters can make the entire electioneering enterprise more secure. For instance, an online or automatic voter registration system can use new technologies to close windows of opportunity for corruption. Vote centers, early voting, and mail-in voting can also reduce the possibility that corrupt actors can sabotage election outcomes. These voting options increase the supervision and deliberation of the authenticity of the ballot cast. Supposing one was sincere about avoiding voter fraud, a reasonable approach might be to move to all early or all mail-in voting. Now observers from both political parties can be in the room, judge the authenticity of the signatures on the submitted envelopes, count the ballots, and ensure no dishonesty is in play. This openness would also serve as a check on the potential corruption of election officials. In other words, making voting easier for individual voters can reduce the possibility of voter fraud and election fraud.

Describing Known Fraud Cases

To understand whether there is more fraud in states with a less restrictive electoral-institutional process, we turn to data provided by the Heritage Foundation. This group has tracked instances of fraud in the United States since the 1980s. Notably, the group has kept pace, and its database includes voter and election fraud cases that surfaced in court documents in recent years, including the months following the 2020 presidential election. In the following analyses, we use the fraud cases the group has identified (n = 1,011), which occurred in one of the fifty American states and appeared on the organization's website through March of 2022. In the mix, there are a few cases from the 1980s and 1990s, but most are twenty-first-century occurrences. The earliest reported case occurred in 1982, and there are six cases from 2022.

Table 7.2 lists the fraud cases Heritage has identified using the six-category classification scheme we have developed. For now, we observe the frequency

Table 7.2. Frequency of Different Types of Voter Fraud and Election Fraud: 1982–2022

Voter fraud	Frequency of proven instances
Voter Fraud	
1. Ineligible voters	467
2. Voter impersonation	201
3. Double voting	126
	Total = 794
Election fraud	
1. Foreign interference	0
2. Corrupt election official	33
3. Corrupt campaign worker or candidate	184
	Total = 217

Source: Heritage Foundation, counts calculated by the authors ("Election Fraud Cases," accessed March 30, 2022, https://www.heritage.org/voterfraud).

Source: Michael Pomante, Scot Schraufnagel, and Quan Li

of known fraud in each category. As noted, there are 1,011 cases to consider.[8] The most common case is voter fraud perpetrated by ineligible individuals. Many of these cases involved people with felony records and the "fraud" was unintentional. Minnesota is the state with the most cases. During the period studied, the Heritage Foundation found 131 cases in the North Star State, of which 127 were ineligible voters. Many were citizens voting in the wrong election jurisdiction. Minnesota is an outlier, and we look closely at the state in the supplemental testing. It is also noteworthy, in table 7.2, that there are no cases of misinformation campaigns orchestrated by foreign actors, despite the threat to electoral legitimacy allegedly caused by Russian government operatives in both 2016 and 2020.[9]

The Heritage Foundation quickly points out that they have listed only a "sample" of actual fraud cases. Yet, in recent years, it seems the Heritage Foundation has a comprehensive list of known fraud cases when we conduct an independent check of court documents and newspaper reports. However, let us assume it was more challenging for the Heritage Foundation to get an accurate picture of fraud in the earlier years of their analysis and that their reported fraud cases represent only twenty years from the fifty states. One can think of twenty years as roughly ten election cycles (presidential and midterm elections). Each state conducts its election administration, so there are at least 500 elections (50 states * 10 election cycles) to consider over twenty years. If one divides the proven cases of fraud, 1,011 cases, by 500 elections, there appears to be a little more than two known fraud instances per election per state.

Yet, the above example is a gross *over*estimation of the frequency of proven fraud cases. There are more than ten election cycles in twenty years, and the Heritage Foundation data spans thirty-nine years. In addition, many states have odd-year elections. If one adds primary elections, there is the potential for at least forty elections in twenty years. Indeed, many cases that the Heritage Foundation identifies occur in local elections taking place independently of the federal general election, which occurs nationally in the United States every two years.

Of course, we do not know how many ineligible voters state election officials have not caught. However, without evidence of a widespread voter fraud scheme, the story does not change much, and it is still doubtful that voter fraud would have altered the outcomes of statewide or national races. The likelihood of a fraudulent election outcome at the statewide or national level is even more dubious, considering that the perpetrators likely split their partisan sympathies equally. It is certainly not the case that those who commit voter fraud all support the same candidate. For instance, seventeen voter fraud cases have appeared on the Heritage Foundation website since the 2020 election. Of these cases, it is possible to determine the party affiliation of the fraudster in seven instances. In all seven cases, the perpetrator was a Republican.

This finding alone is not strong evidence that Republicans are more likely to commit voter fraud or even more likely to be caught committing voter fraud in recent years. However, the finding does make the point that Republican operatives around the country, who still believe voter fraud cost President Donald Trump the 2020 election, do not have complete information. Evidence from the Heritage Foundation suggests those caught after the 2020 presidential election were more likely to be conservatives voting for President Trump. We hold it is reasonable to assume that fraudulent voters split their party allegiance in a manner consistent with the eligible voters who properly participate in elections.[10]

To better understand the type of cases the Heritage Foundation uncovers, table 7.3 elaborates more completely on the twenty-eight instances of fraud chronicled from January 1, 2021, through March 21, 2022. We note the state where the fraud occurred, the type of fraud, whether the fraudster(s) were

Table 7.3. Known Incidents of Voter Fraud (VF) and Election Fraud (EF), since 2020

State	Year	Type of fraud	Type of election	Election year(s)	Political party
AZ	2022	VF—Double voting	National	2020	Republican
CA	2022	VF—Ineligible voting	Local	2020	Unclear
CA	2022	VF—Ineligible voting	Local	2020	Unclear
CA	2022	VF—Ineligible voting	Local	2020	Unclear
TX	2022	EF—Corrupt campaigner	Local-Primary	2018	Democrat
TX	2022	EF—Corrupt campaigner	Local-Primary	2018	Democrat
TX	2022	EF—Corrupt campaigner	Local-Primary	2018	Democrat
CA	2021	EF—Candidate residency	Local	2018	Republican
CA	2021	EF—Candidate residency	Local	Unclear	Republican
CA	2021	VF—Voter impersonation	National	2012–14	Unclear
CO	2021	VF—Double voting	National	2020	Unclear
FL	2021	EF—Corrupt campaigner	National-Primary	2020	Republican
FL	2021	EF—Corrupt official	Local	2020	Unclear
KY	2021	VF—Double voting	Local	2019	Republican
MI	2021	VF—Voter impersonation	National	2020	Unclear
MS	2021	EF—Corrupt official	Local-Primary	2020	Democratic
NH	2021	VF—Double voting	National	2016	Unclear
NH	2021	VF—Double voting	National	2016	Unclear
NV	2021	VF—Double voting	National	2020	Unclear
OH	2021	VF—Double voting	National	2020	Republican
PA	2021	EF—Corrupt official	National-Primary	2014–2016	Democratic
PA	2021	VF—Double voting	National	2020	Republican
PA	2021	VF—Double voting	National	2020	Republican
PA	2021	VF—Double voting	National	2020	Republican
TX	2021	EF—Corrupt official	Local-Primary	2020	Democrat
VA	2021	VF—Double voting	National	2020	Republican
WV	2021	VF—Voter impersonation	Local	2021	Unclear
WV	2021	EF—Corrupt candidate	Local	2019	Unclear

Source: Heritage Foundation. The group uses a different classification scheme than the one presented here. Some of their categories are redundant. Ultimately, we combine their nine fraud types into the six categories shown in table 7.1. Note that all three California cases in 2022 involved the same local city council race and all three 2022 Texas cases involved a local Democratic Party primary in 2018.

Source: Michael Pomante, Scot Schraufnagel, and Quan Li

trying to influence a local or national election, the election year the fraud took place in, and the political party the swindler was trying to help when that information is available. As noted, seventeen of the twenty-right instances involved voter fraud. Eleven cases were election fraud.

We find that only ten of the twenty-eight cases are related to fraud in the

2020 presidential election. As noted, seven out of ten times, the person caught was a Republican. It is unclear what party the fraudster supported in the other three instances. Concerning election fraud cases, two of the eleven represent candidates trying to use a former address to justify eligibility to run for a particular local office. Nine of the eleven instances of election fraud involved local elections, and the other two dealt with the 2020 Republican presidential primaries in Florida and Pennsylvania, one case in each state.

Interestingly, in New Hampshire, where voter registration is relatively restricted, we still find two cases of people trying to vote twice. On the other hand, in Colorado, Nevada, and Virginia, states where voting is more accessible and the potential for voter fraud is arguably greater, there was only one case in each state. Moreover, when considering the size of the eligible voting population in New Hampshire, it is much smaller than it is in Colorado or Nevada; we view this as more evidence suggesting a more restrictive electoral climate is not preventing fraud.

The primary point we make in table 7.3 is that the Heritage Foundation, the group that by many accounts is most aggressively trying to track incidents of fraud and make them public, turns up nothing of major consequence. For example, post-2020, they have identified a handful of double voters, some candidates who lied about their official residence, and a few crooked individuals who tried to influence a local election in a county, all of this in a context where there are thousands of such opportunities every election year. Moreover, there is no evidence that the Democratic Party is more likely to engage in these forms of mischief than the Republicans.

Additional Tests

Our concern in this research is not with the count or the frequency of fraud cases.[11] Instead, we wish to test whether restricting voting can reduce fraud. Curiosity begs the question: Is less fraud taking place when voting becomes more restricted? Specifically, we test whether voting restrictions are associated negatively with known incidents of fraud. To do this, we first investigate whether instances of known fraud increase when voting is more accessible. Second, we test whether a state's change in COVI rank produces a corresponding increase or decrease in the incidents of fraud.[12]

We first look at the correlation between the average COVI state rank from

1996 to 2020 and incidents of voter fraud, election fraud, and total fraud by state, as reported by the Heritage Foundation. Because the Heritage Foundation cases cover roughly the same period as the COVI, we use the average of each state's COVI rank over the approximately twenty-five-year period. During this time, many states consistently obtain a higher or lower rank than others. For instance, since 1996, when comparing state ranks, it has always been easier (less costly) to vote in North Dakota and Oregon and more difficult to vote in Tennessee and Texas. In some other states, for instance, Colorado, Maryland, New Hampshire, and Wyoming, there is considerable movement in rank over the seven election periods. Unfortunately, the average rank for these states is less helpful. However, these states provide an excellent opportunity to test if changes in state law, which make voting more or less restrictive, influence known fraud incidents. Moreover, by looking at change within a single state, we hold reasonably constant interstate variation in the policing of fraud.

To be clear, interstate variation in fraud enforcement confounds matters. One cannot be sure that states with more restrictive voting laws are not the same states that are also more likely to go looking for fraud.[13] The irony, of course, is that presumably the restrictions prevent the need for increased scrutiny. Variable enforcement notwithstanding, we should at least know if a higher average state COVI rank, indicating more restrictions, correlates with less reported fraud in the contemporary era. If it does, it might justify increased voter restrictions. Correspondingly, one should obtain negative co-efficients from our tests. As the average COVI rank increases, indicating more restrictions, incidents of fraud should go down.

When calculating the volume of known fraud cases, we find that not every state has a case of voter fraud or election fraud. Over the thirty-nine years of Heritage Foundation data, Delaware and Vermont have zero reported cases. Hawaii, Montana, Rhode Island, South Carolina, and Utah have one case each. The mean number of voter fraud cases by state is slightly less than sixteen. We standardize state values by taking the number of fraud incidents and dividing it by the size of the state's voting-eligible population (VEP) in 2010. We then multiply that value by one hundred to obtain the percentage of known fraud as a function of the size of the VEP. We use the 2010 population value because it is a year in the middle of the period studied.

For example, Minnesota had 131 cases of fraud and a VEP of 3,802,677 in 2010. Moreover, all 131 cases from Minnesota involved one and only one state

Table 7.4. Correlations between the Average COVI Rank and the Frequency of Fraud in US States: Contemporary Era

	Voter fraud	Election fraud	Total fraud
Average cost of voting rank: 1996–2020	–.18; $P < .20$ n = 50	.20; $P < .17$ n = 50	–.11; $P < .44$ n = 50
Association sans Minnesota			
Average cost of voting rank: 1996–2020	–.07; $P < .65$ n = 49	.19; $P < .20$ n = 49	.03; $P < .83$ n = 49

Note: *P*-values based on two-tailed tests of statistical significance.

Source: Michael Pomante, Scot Schraufnagel, and Quan Li

resident. Therefore, if all of Minnesota's cases occurred in one year, which is not the case, we would say about 0.0033% of the VEP engaged in fraud. This percentage is infinitesimal in the state with the highest level of reported fraud. Moreover, this number is an overestimation because the fraud occurred over fifteen years, from 2004 to 2018.

Table 7.4 reports the correlations between the average COVI rank and the frequency of fraud within a state. Theoretically, higher COVI ranks should be negatively associated with instances of fraud. That is, more restrictions should result in less fraud. The table reports the correlations for "voter fraud," "election fraud," "all fraud," and a parallel analysis excluding Minnesota, which is an outlier. Minnesota's count of fraud cases is more than eight times the average level of fraud in the period we study; as such, later in this chapter we take a deeper dive into Minnesota's high count to learn what is driving cases in the state.

Note straightaway in table 7.4 that there are no statistically significant relationships. There is no evidence that we can reject the null hypothesis of no relationship. The strongest association occurs with election fraud (.20; $p < .17$). Unfortunately, the more damning type of fraud is positively associated with restriction. A more restrictive electoral-institutional climate in the American states is associated with more election fraud. When we exclude Minnesota, the bivariate relationship with total fraud also turns positive. Of course, the lack of statistical significance suggests we must accept the null hypothesis of no relationship for all these tests.

Moving a step forward, we might imagine that the COVI, a factor score representing an underlying latent dimension, may be masking something. To test for this, we use the same analysis reported in table 7.4 but with two components of the COVI. The COVI intends to capture the totality of the cost of voting in each state, and the score includes both voter registration restrictions and constraints when it comes to casting a ballot. One of the items in the COVI related to voter registration is whether a state allows people to register to vote on the same day as the election, measured as a dummy variable scored "1" if the state forbids it. One of the ballot considerations is state ID, and we use a five-item ordered scale ranging from (1) only matching the signature required to (5) strictly enforcing a photo ID. Again, given how we measure these variables, one expects a statistically significant negative association with fraud. Table 7.5 reports the results with and without Minnesota. In this analysis, we use 2012 COVI values because the year falls roughly in the middle of the timeline of reported fraud cases.[14]

In the first column of table 7.5, and considering all fifty states, the no same-day voter registration consideration produces a glimmer of evidence that this voter restriction could lead to less voter fraud. However, one must expand the definition of statistical significance to $P < 0.10$ or use a 90 percent confidence interval. This finding would otherwise be good news if not for the positive and slightly stronger relationship between this registration restriction and election fraud. Turning to the analysis of total fraud, not one of the associations produces a statistically significant relationship in the hypothesized correct direction. Again, this tells us that a more restricted state electoral climate does not affect known fraud cases.

When we drop Minnesota, a state that had same-day voter registration in 2012, the near statistically significant relationship between not allowing citizens to register to vote on Election Day and voter fraud disappears. More worrisome, dropping Minnesota does not affect the nearly statistically significant positive association with election fraud. Lastly, considering state photo ID laws, nothing is going on. There is no association between known fraud cases and state laws requiring voters to identify themselves at polling locations.

Lastly, in terms of statistical tests, we check for a significant negative relationship between a more restrictive electoral process and fraud after controlling for additional considerations. Presumably, the hypothesized negative relationship emerges once one holds constant other factors. We must note that after pulling all the known fraud instances from the Heritage Foundation website, one gets a distinct impression that these cases are random. The

Table 7.5. Correlations between Two Voting Restrictions and the Frequency of Fraud in the US States: Contemporary Era

	Voter fraud	Election fraud	Total fraud
No same-day voter registration allowed, in 2012	−.24;*P < .10 n = 50	.25; P < .09 n = 50	−.15; P < .30 n = 50
Voter ID Likert Scale, 0 to 4. "4" equals strict photo ID required, in 2012	−.11; P < .45 n = 50	.06; P < .66 n = 50	−.08; P < .57 n = 50
Association sans Minnesota			
No same-day voter registration allowed, in 2012	−.18; P < .20 n = 49	.24; P < .09 n = 49	−.05; P < .76 n = 49
Voter ID Likert Scale, 0 to 4. "4" equals strict photo ID required, in 2012	−.01; P < .95 n = 49	06; P < .71 n = 49	.02; P < .90 n = 49

* *P*-values based on two-tailed tests of statistical significance.

Source: Michael Pomante, Scot Schraufnagel, and Quan Li

Minnesota outlier is a case in point. The state has a better-than-average COVI rank (average rank of 11.86). This ranking suggests that only ten or eleven states experienced easier voting in the contemporary era. However, voting in Minnesota is not so easy that one would expect it to have more than eight times the average number of total fraud cases. Oregon has an even less restrictive electoral climate than Minnesota (average rank of 4.14), with only fifteen cases over twenty years.

Nonetheless, moving forward, we imagine that a state's political culture and/or level of legislative professionalism might influence the frequency of fraud. In the first instance, we use Daniel Elazar's three categories of state culture, which he identifies as either individualistic, moralistic, or traditionalistic. Elazar argues that in moralistic state cultures, there is little toleration for corruption (Elazar 1966).[15] Hence, we leave out the moralistic states from the multivariate regression to test whether there is more fraud in either the individualistic or the traditionalistic states. We also look for a relationship between fraud and the Squire Index, our measure of legislative professionalism. Higher values indicate a more full-time state legislature. We imagine that full-time legislators would be especially keen to keep an eye on fraud and, perhaps, fund enforcement efforts more completely. Consequently, we expect less fraud or a negative relationship when the state legislature is better resourced.

We also control for the Gini Index of income inequality in the American states. Here, higher numbers indicate more inequality, which might frustrate some state citizens who feel left out. This inequality may cause them to seek redress through illegal channels such as voter or election fraud. Again, we anticipate a positive association. Next, we control for state education. Specifically, we use the percentage of state residents with a high school diploma. Better-educated state citizens may lead to more rational behavior, and, in the aggregate, less fraud occurs in states with a higher-educated citizenry. Again, we anticipate a negative association. We use 2010 values of both the Gini Index and the education consideration because the year falls near the middle of the timeframe the fraud cases occur. Lastly, we control for the competitiveness of each state's electoral climate. Here, we use the presidential election margin or the absolute value of the difference in the percentage of the votes earned by the two major political party candidates in 2012. We use the results of the 2012 election because the year falls near the middle of the timeframe studied. In this instance, a bigger number indicates a less competitive state electoral environment, and we anticipate less fraud and a negative coefficient in the regression run. The model's key test variable is each state's average COVI rank from 1996 to 2020.

Considering the results reported in table 7.6, the seeming randomness of fraud instances is striking. Not only does the cost of voting not relate to the frequency of fraud but reported fraud does not relate to state culture, legislative professionalism, state income inequality, or average educational attainment. The expectation was that state culture considerations would produce positive coefficients because these states are less "moralistic," but that did not happen. The one instance when we find some explanatory power is the consideration of state electoral competition. In the total fraud model, if we use a one-tailed test, we can be somewhat confident there is less fraud when the margin of victory in a presidential race is larger. More specifically, the coefficient derived from the test suggests that a 10 percent increase in the election margin is associated with about 1.5 fewer known fraud cases, on average, all else equal. Loosening the standard acceptable definition of statistical significance and considering voter fraud and total fraud, we get some sense that fraud occurs more commonly in competitive electoral environments. This finding is consistent with the rationality thesis explained earlier. When there is a greater chance that deceitful voting makes a difference, people may be more inclined to engage in fraud.

The test of the average COVI rank, which was supposed to be negatively

Table 7.6. Association between Voting Restrictions and the Frequency of Known Fraud Cases in the US States: Contemporary Era
Ordinary Least Squares Regression

Predictor variables	Voter fraud Coefficient (s.e.)	Election fraud Coefficient (s.e.)	Total fraud Coefficient (s.e.)
Average cost of voting rank	−.07 (.11)	.01 (.04)	−.06 (.11)
Individualistic state culture	−.88 (2.10)	−.17 (.73)	−1.05 (2.22)
Traditionalistic state culture	−.86 (3.31)	.88 (1.15)	−1.12 (3.51)
Squire Index of professionalism	−3.80 (7.97)	−.57 (2.76)	−4.37 (8.42)
Gini Index of income inequality	−22.35 (56.81)	.02 (19.66)	−22.33 (60.03)
% w/high school diploma	.08 (.14)	.02 (.05)	.10 (.14)
Presidential election margin	−.139 (.084)[t]	−.014 (.029)	−.153 (.089)*
Constant	13.83 (29.42)	−.51 (10.18)	13.32 (31.09)
F-Statistic	1.15	.68	1.12
Adjusted R^2	.02	−.05	.02
n	50	50	50

* $P < .05$; [t] $P < .10$ (one-tailed tests)

Source: Michael Pomante, Scot Schraufnagel, and Quan Li

associated with fraud, does produce negative signs in two of the three models, but these relationships are not even close to being statistically significant. Moreover, we uncover another positive relationship in the election fraud model. Consistent with the bivariate test, restricted voting associates, on average, with more election fraud. Importantly, in all the different tests, there is no evidence that more restrictions are associated with less fraud.

Unfortunately, our testing does not directly assess the possibility that some states keep a closer eye on fraud than others. If more restrictive states do this, it could explain the lack of a statistical association. However, it is relevant to remember that restrictions are supposed to prevent fraud and reduce the need for aggressive policing. Restrictions should allow state election administrators to worry less about monitoring fraudsters. In any event, to check on the possibility that more restrictive states police fraud more closely, we now turn to single-state qualitative tests. Specifically, we look closely at the states where the relative COVI rank moved the most from 1996 to 2020 (Colorado, Maryland, New Hampshire, and Wyoming).

First up, however, we must figure out what was going on in Minnesota from 2009 to 2011, and it makes sense to examine North Carolina more closely, as well. The Tar Heel State experienced a case of election fraud in 2018, which affected the results of a race for the US House of Representatives. We need to check if the state made voting a lot easier and whether this is part of the explanation for why the fraud occurred.

A Six-State Qualitative Examination of Restricted Voting and Fraud

Minnesota

Taking a deeper dive into Minnesota, we learn something about how cases of fraud surface. Considering Minnesota's 131 cases (130 voter fraud and 1 election fraud), 112 of them occurred between 2009 and 2011. This period marks the aftermath of a very hotly contested US Senate race in 2008 between Norm Coleman (R) and Al Franken (D), which Franken won by 225 votes, and the 2010 governor's race between Mark Dayton (D) and Tom Emmer (R), which Dayton won by less than 9000 votes. With these very close elections, there were multiple recounts, and election administrators went to great lengths to check each vote cast to ensure that the person voting was eligible to vote in the state. The officials took extraordinary steps to find any evidence of fraud. In the aftermath of these two elections, and after multiple recounts and checking, officials found 112 ineligible voters cast a ballot in one or the other election cycle. The other eighteen cases of voter fraud in Minnesota occurred in other years, and the one case of election fraud occurred in 2015. The ineligible voters from 2009 to 2011 were unqualified for various reasons, including having a felony conviction in the past, being undocumented, or failing to keep their voter registration current.

Minnesota election officials reported 5,044,867 votes cast, in the state, in the 2008 and 2010 elections combined (2,921,498 in 2008 and 2,123,369 in 2010).[16] After considerable cost and many recounts, state election administrators uncovered 112 ineligible voters, suggesting that 0.0022 percent of the votes cast were fraudulent. As noted, Al Franken won the 2008 race by only 225 votes. If all 112 ineligible votes cast in the 2008 election were in support of Franken, and they were not, this would still have not affected the outcome.[17]

As best we can tell, the fraudsters split their partisan preferences in roughly the same proportion as eligible voters. In all, we must accept that recounts, in close races, cause a larger number of fraud cases to surface. It is possible to imagine some ineligible voters cast a ballot because they knew these would be close races.

NORTH CAROLINA

In recent years, we know one instance of election fraud influencing a US House race. In 2018, in North Carolina, a campaign worker for the Republican Party candidate, and his coconspirators, falsified absentee voter applications causing their candidate to win by nine hundred votes. It is important to note that law enforcement caught the perpetrators, and the state overturned the election result. Yet, this kind of fraud is a real concern. Arguably, election fraud warrants scrutiny. Importantly, the North Carolina case was not voter fraud. It involved a campaign worker and not a single individual voting for a dead relative or someone failing to update their voter registration. These details bear mentioning because many contemporary state efforts to restrict registration and voting increase the cost of voting for individual citizens, without doing anything about the more serious threat of election fraud.

In 2012, North Carolina was the fourteenth easiest state to vote in. Yet by 2016, the election cycle before the fraud took place, North Carolina ranked twenty-fourth on the COVI. In other words, the state was in the middle of the pack regarding the restrictiveness of voting processes. The drop in ranking occurred partly because the state did not adopt an automatic voter registration system, a reform that could potentially make voter fraud less likely. Most relevantly, it is not the case that North Carolina had just made voting easier. In fact, the state held on to a restriction other states were eliminating. Overall, ranked twenty-fourth, North Carolina did not have a particularly inclusive electoral-institutional environment during the 2018 midterms when the fraud occurred. At the time, there were twenty-three other states where voting was more accessible, and there was no parallel instance of fraud to report in any of these states.

Presumably, the closeness of the House race motivated the criminals in the Tar Heel State.[18] In the equation discussed earlier, the "P" was greater. In other words, there was a heightened probability that their efforts could determine the election outcome. Correspondingly, committing election fraud was more rational. In all, the North Carolina case provides another piece of evidence that fraud is more likely to occur when elections are close. However, it is also the case that inconvenient voting does not explain fraud.

Colorado, Maryland, New Hampshire, and Wyoming

Concerning the results of the statistical tests, we note that states with a more restrictive electoral-institutional climate may be the same states that are more aggressive in their fraud enforcement efforts. Conversely, states with low COVI values might have lax enforcement. If this is the case, the results from the statistical tests may be spurious. In other words, the bivariate and multivariate tests have failed to uncover the true relationship between COVI ranks and incidents of fraud. Again, it bears mentioning that stricter enforcement seems to defeat the purpose of restrictions if this were the case. Nevertheless, because of the possibility of a spurious relationship, we take a closer look and check if different levels of enforcement across states affect the results obtained thus far. We can do this by testing changes to the relative cost of voting, over time, within a single state. There is much less likely to be an appreciable change in fraud enforcement from one election cycle to the next in a single state.

To ensure that we are not missing something, we look at the four states that traded their rank the most from 1996 to 2020. States with the largest changes provide the best opportunity to find voting restrictions that can effectively reduce fraud. Specifically, we examine two states that moved toward greater restriction (New Hampshire and Wyoming) from 1996 to 2020 and two that moved toward a more inclusive electoral-institutional climate (Colorado and Maryland). If the argument that voting restrictions prevent voter fraud has merit, the first two states should witness a decrease in fraud, and the latter two should see an increase.

Taking the states in alphabetical order, we consider Colorado first. One can note a substantial increase in COVI ranks in the Centennial State. In 2012, the state was ranked thirty-third and then moved up to the tenth easiest state to vote in by 2016, principally by adopting an all-mail voting process. The Heritage Foundation website listed seven fraud cases in the state after 2016. However, in two of the seven cases, the voter fraud occurred in 2013, before voting got easier in the state, and in another two, the fraud came in the form of false signatures on a petition, which is a form of election fraud, not voter fraud. There have been three cases of voter fraud since 2016 or in the five years since the state adopted mail-in voting. In the five years before 2016, there were also three instances of voter fraud. The analysis shows a net gain of zero voter fraud cases after the state made voting easier by adopting a vote-by-mail process.

Next, consider Maryland; the state went from forty-fourth in 1996 to nineteenth, four years later in 2000. The chief change was that the state reduced its voter registration deadline. Using 2000 as the cutoff point, there were no fraud cases before or after the state made it easier to register to vote. Then, the state adopted early voting and online voter registration before the 2012 election cycle and experienced another climb up the rankings. Between 2008 and 2012, the state goes from the twenty-seventh to the tenth easiest state. From 2012 forward, there are eight cases of fraud listed on the Heritage Foundation website, and there were no cases before 2012. Yet, when we scrutinize the eight cases, we learn that four fraud incidents occurred before 2012, when the state was more restrictive, with one case involving an individual who had been voting fraudulently since 1976. Therefore, there are four cases before 2012, when the state was more restrictive, and four cases after 2012, when the state made voting easier. Importantly, none of the four cases that happened after 2012 had anything to do with the state's early voting process.

Next, consider New Hampshire. Here we witness a significant climb down the rankings from the tenth easiest state to vote in during the 2008 election cycle to twenty-fifth in 2012, and then to fiftieth, or the most restrictive state by 2016. The primary cause of the Granite State's fall was the adoption of a voter identification requirement, a registration drive restriction, and the state's failure to adopt any of the more inclusive voting practices other states had been passing. One might imagine a steep decrease in fraud cases after the state became, relatively speaking, more restrictive. Looking at the 2008 election cycle and earlier, there are only two reported fraud cases, a time when the state made voting relatively easy. There are two additional cases when considering the 2012 election cycle. One uncovered a voter who participated fraudulently in both the 2008 and 2012 elections. Then, there are two cases from the 2014 midterm elections. By the time the state was ranked fiftieth, the fraud incidents actually increased. One sees eleven new cases reported from 2016 through the 2020 election cycle. Of course, this move is in the wrong direction for those who propose that more restricted voting prevents fraud. More limited voting in New Hampshire should associate with less fraud, but there is an actual increase in fraud.

Lastly, consider Wyoming. The state went from the sixteenth easiest state to vote in for the 2012 election cycle and moved down to thirty-ninth by 2016. The drop occurred because the state failed to adopt early voting, online voter registration, or a permanent option to vote absentee when other states were making moves to reduce the cost of voting. Presumably, the state was keeping these restrictions in place to thwart potential fraud. In 2021 and 2022, many Republican state legislators considered reducing early voting and removing the option of permanent absentee voter status to prevent voter fraud.

In Wyoming, we get the first confirming case. There were three reported fraud cases in the Equality State before 2012, when voting was relatively easier. Since 2016, there have been no new fraud cases after the state made voting harder. So, did more restricted voting in Wyoming reduce voter fraud? Perhaps. However, it is challenging to imagine a causal argument. Only three cases were spread out over fourteen years when it was relatively easier to vote in the state. One occurred in 1998, one in 2000, and a third person voted fraudulently in 2010 and 2012. There have not been fourteen years since 2016 to make a meaningful check for the difference. Three cases of fraud, over fourteen years, and zero cases in the six years since the state has been more restricting by itself is not much evidence that restrictions reduce fraud. Based on evidence from Wyoming, it would be challenging to sell any reasonable audience that one can expect a reduction in fraud cases when states strictly regulate voting. This is especially the case given that two other states show no change and a third state shows a shift in the wrong direction.

Conclusion

By looking at the four states with considerable change in rank, we use best-case scenarios to prove that easier voting is associated with an increase in voter fraud. If this were the case, the level of fraud change would most likely occur in states making the biggest moves. However, we find nothing going on. With the data provided by the Heritage Foundation and based on quantitative and qualitative testing, we must conclude that there is no relationship between the cost of voting and incidents of voter fraud or election fraud. Overall, with the minimal number of verifiable voter fraud cases, the argument that voting needs to be more challenging to prevent individual voting misbehavior seems to be a solution to a made-up problem. One must add to this consideration the possible disenfranchisement of voters, which occurs when voting is more difficult. Researchers estimate that making voting sufficiently more restrictive to catch one double voter, on average, would cause approximately three hundred people not to vote because voting would be costlier in terms of the increased time and effort required (Goel et al. 2020, 456).

Notably, all the statistical tests are somewhat problematic because we use average COVI values and fraud instances spread over a considerable period. However, a positive bivariate relationship between voting restrictions and total fraud cases appears when we exclude Minnesota from the analysis. This correlation should be troubling for advocates of more restrictions. As it stands, the United States, with our decentralized election administration and two-stage voting process (registering to vote and casting a ballot), makes the voting cost quite high relative to other countries. In addition, there is lower voter turnout, on average, in the United States to show for it (Powell 1986). If there was a trade-off and increased restrictions produced less fraud, it might be worth it. However, that is not the case.

This research has made use of interstate variation in voting restrictions and rather exhaustively went looking for a meaningful negative relationship between restricted voting and cases of fraud and cannot find one. Instead, we learn that the volume of known fraud cases is very difficult to predict. One might imagine uneven interstate enforcement of fraud would explain variance in reported fraud, but single-state analyses suggest this is not the case. Moreover, in table 7.3, which reports known cases from 2021 to 2022, we learn that when fraud occurs, especially election fraud, it is most likely in local races when committing fraud is more rational because of smaller constituencies or pools of voters. We uncover that a close election may prompt a greater likelihood of fraud. This finding is expected and evidence that fraudsters are "rational." Indeed, most people are rational, which is why so little fraud occurs. Importantly, we also learn that throughout all the different analyses, there is no partisan bias regarding fraud. It is not the case that members of one major party are more likely to commit fraud.

Some contemporary reformers who argue for more restrictions or getting rid of some of the recent changes that made voting more convenient focus their contention on the perception of fraud and how that potentially delegitimizes elections. Of course, perceptions of fraud and the damage it can cause in terms of public efficacy and lower voter turnout are of paramount importance. However, our research suggests that more voting restrictions do not address the problem. Instead, reformers concerned with public perceptions of fraud ought to support public awareness campaigns that point out the extreme likelihood that when voter fraud does occur, it does very little to compromise election outcomes, on average. Moreover, making the public aware that our country's low level of fraud is bipartisan and that members of one political party are not more likely to commit fraud should also help with public misperceptions. We now test whether making voting easier, on average, is more likely to help the Democratic Party.

8: The Second Big Lie: More Convenient Voting Helps Democrats

In an article in the *American Political Science Review* in 1980, cited earlier, James DeNardo (1980) argued, "The joke's on the Democrats." Specifically, DeNardo looked for evidence that greater voter turnout benefits the Democratic Party. He does not find anything like a consistent electoral advantage for either one or the other major political parties. However, he provides a sound theoretical argument and some empirical confirmation that greater voter turnout helps the "out party" or the minority party in Congress. In the end, he concludes, "it depends." In follow-up research, Jack Nagel and John McNulty (1996) find regional and temporal distinctions in partisan benefit. In other words, the Democratic Party has benefited from greater voter turnout in specific instances in certain states. However, in other instances, the Republican Party profited from higher turnout. In the end, their study reveals "complex patterns" that are "impressively consistent with DeNardo" (Nagel and McNulty 1996, 780).

Still more, scholars find that voters represent the preferences of nonvoters quite well (Highton and Wolfinger 2001, 179). In other words, there is no big difference in the partisan preference of nonvoters and voters. The two groups are dissimilar in socioeconomic status but not partisan allegiance. Using sophisticated statistical tests, others conclude that if there had been universal voter turnout, this might have tipped the scale in favor of the Democrat Party candidate in some very close presidential elections (Sides, Schickler, and Citrin 2008). Yet, the evidence still needed to be more conclusive. Moreover, the basis of Sides et al.'s (2008) conclusion is an extrapolation to "universal" or 100 percent voter turnout, which is not a realistic real-world scenario. We know from our analysis that making voting easier will increase voter turnout. However, no truly open society ever reaches 100 percent voter participation. Indeed, when a country reports 100 percent voter turnout, it is most likely that there is misreporting and dishonesty at play.

Did More Accessible Voting Hurt Trump in 2020?

With the 2020 election in the rearview mirror, we have an excellent opportunity to test how the cost of voting affected President Donald Trump's electoral performance. Importantly, it was not the case that the 2020 election was particularly close. President Biden wins the popular vote (51.3 percent to 46.9 percent) and a majority of the Electoral College vote (306 to 232). Yet, we can compare former president Trump's performance in 2020 to 2016, when he obtained 46.1 percent of the nationwide vote. Most specifically, we compare how Trump does, state by state, in 2020 versus 2016. Notably, because of the global pandemic, many states made voting easier in 2020, and the state-by-state comparison provides an opportunity to see if easier voting caused Trump to fail in his reelection bid.

As noted previously, four states adopted vote-by-mail for the 2020 elections. Many other states relaxed absentee voting processes. For instance, many states dropped the requirement that voters needed a state-sanctioned excuse to vote absentee. These changes in 2020 undoubtedly are partly responsible for the increase in voter turnout in this election cycle. The voter turnout of eligible voters climbed to 66.2 percent in 2020, up from 55.7 percent in 2016. For testing purposes, in this chapter, we recalculated and created a new COVI, labeled 2020c. The "c" is our abbreviation for COVID-19. This version of the COVI includes the temporary changes states made in reaction to the global pandemic, which the original COVI for 2020 does not include. Because of the different measurement approaches, we see some change in state values and rankings between the original 2020 and the 2020c measure.

Figure 8.1 displays the 2020c COVI values by state. Chapter 3 explains the original 2020 COVI, and one can use figure 3.7 to identify all the changes in state rankings that occur when one considers the 2020c COVI. For instance, New Jersey and Vermont, two states that adopted vote-by-mail in response to the pandemic, move up from eighth to third and from twenty-third to fifteenth easiest states to vote, respectively. California, another state that made voting easier in response to the pandemic, moved up one space in the ranking, from sixth to fifth.

Our testing focuses on whether President Trump did worse in 2020, where voting was made easier. We conduct three tests using 2016 and 2020 data on Trump's performance against his Democratic Party opponents (Hillary

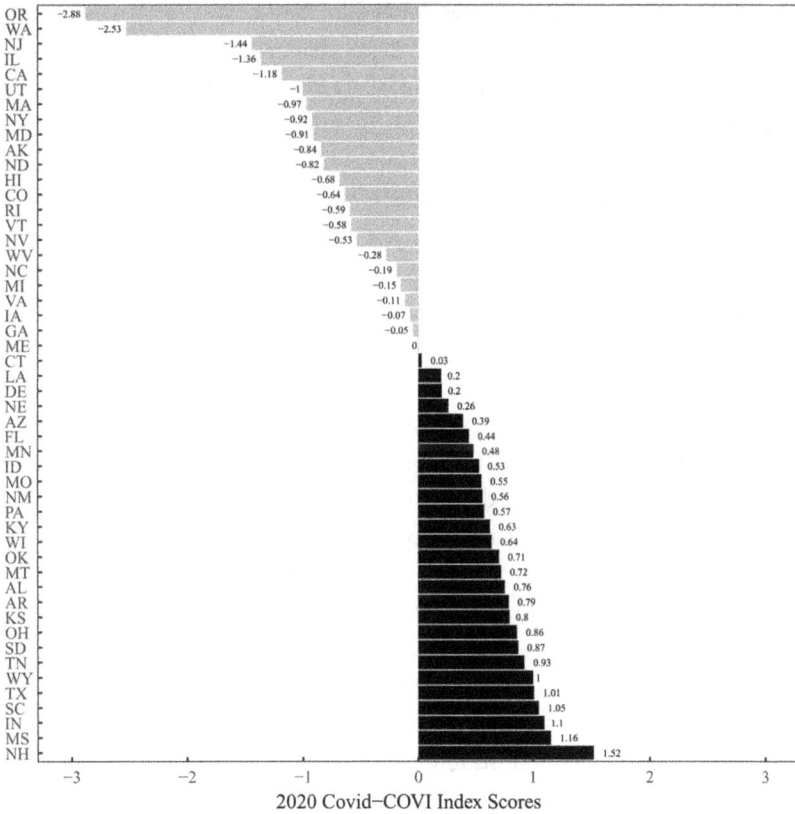

Figure 8.1. State 2020c COVI ranks

Source: Michael Pomante, Scot Schraufnagel, and Quan Li

Clinton and Joe Biden). First, we look at Trump's 2016 versus 2020 performance in states that used an exclusive vote-by-mail process. We know this is one of the most convenient ways for people to vote. By 2020, five states had permanently established a vote-by-mail process, and another four adopted the practice amid the pandemic. If easier voting hurt President Trump, this should be the case in these nine states. Second, using the 2020c values displayed in figure 8.1, we test whether easy voting in 2020 is associated broadly with a drop in support for Trump. Do lower COVI values, or easier voting, explain President Trump losing the 2020 election? Third, we test the effect of the increase in voter turnout in 2020 on President Trump's electoral fortunes.

In all three tests, we use what we label the Democratic Party two-party vote differential, calculated by state, as the dependent variable. Specifically, we calculate the percentage of the two major party vote received by the Democratic candidates in 2016 and 2020. We do this by finding the difference between the percentage of the two-party vote received by Secretary of State Hillary Clinton in 2016 and Vice President Joe Biden in 2020. We learn that Biden outperforms Clinton in forty-four of the fifty states, and the Democratic two party vote differential is positive. With this measure in hand, we can test if Biden's relatively better performance than Clinton against Trump occurs in (1) vote-by-mail states, (2) when COVI values were lower, and (3) when voter turnout was higher.

Table 8.1 displays our first test results relating to the vote-by-mail states. A positive value indicates that Biden outperformed Clinton in the state, and a negative value means Clinton did better in 2016 than Biden did in 2020. In both election cycles, the Democratic Party candidate faced the same opponent—Donald Trump. The size of the differential is also important; a bigger number suggests that Biden did much better than Clinton did, and so forth. On average, or across all fifty states, Biden receives 1.77 percent more votes than Clinton. If vote-by-mail hurt President Trump, we should expect values over 1.77 percent in those states that made voting easier through postal balloting. In other words, vote-by-mail should cause Biden to outperform Clinton more than average (1.77 percent).

The table shows that 67 percent of the time, six out of nine times, Trump did better in 2020 than he did in 2016 in the vote-by-mail states. On the other hand, Biden outperformed Clinton in three of the nine states where the franchise was very easy in 2020. In three out of four states that adopted all mail-in voting for the 2020 election, California, Nevada, New Jersey, and Vermont, Trump outperformed in three out of four states. The only exception is Vermont. In other words, 75 percent of the time, when states eased voting restrictions in response to the global pandemic, the change helped Trump.[1]

Besides Vermont, Trump underperformed in the vote-by-mail states of Oregon and Colorado. Both states had vote-by-mail processes before the 2020 election cycle. Conversely, 2020 was the first time Hawaii had a firmly established vote-by-mail process. As a result, the Aloha State saw a dramatic increase in voter turnout in 2020, an increase of more than 14 percent of the state's voting-eligible population. Notably, the increase in turnout in Hawaii

Table 8.1. The Democratic Two-Party Vote Differential between 2016 and 2020 in Vote-by-Mail States: Average for All 50 States Equals 1.77 Percent

State	Clinton's share of the two-party vote	Biden's share of the two party vote	Democratic Party two-party differential
			2020
Permanent vote-by-mail states	2016	2020	minus 2016
Colorado	52.68	56.94	4.26
Hawaii	67.44	65.03	–2.41
Oregon	56.16	58.31	2.15
Utah	37.62	39.31	1.69
Washington	58.79	59.93	1.14
Pandemic vote-by-mail states			
California	66.13	64.91	–1.22
Nevada	51.29	51.22	–.07
New Jersey	57.28	58.07	.79
Vermont	65.19	68.30	3.11

Source: The United States Election Project, accessed July 30, 2022, http://www.electproject.org.

Source: Michael Pomante, Scot Schraufnagel, and Quan Li

causes Trump to perform better in the state. He received 2.41 percent more of the votes cast in Hawaii in 2020 than he did in 2016. In other words, the two-party vote differential decreased by 2.41 percent. The new Hawaiian voters, made possible, in part, by less costly voting, went decidedly for Trump. Considering our findings, if vote-by-mail created a partisan advantage, in 2020, the benefit went to the Republican Party candidate. However, we also test the effect of the overall cost of voting in 2020 on Trump's performance using the 2020c COVI values.

Figure 8.2 is a scatterplot showing 2020c values on the x-axis. Here, we are using the cost of voting values to predict the Democratic Party two-party vote differential found on the y-axis. Note the positive trend line indicating that when the cost of voting was greater, in 2020, the Democratic two-party vote differential was larger. Put differently, on average, Trump did better in 2020 than in 2016 in states where voting was easier. Of course, we already know about Hawaii and can see the state at the bottom of the figure (the state has a negative COVI value, and Clinton outperformed Biden). However, this is also true in California, Illinois, Nevada, New York, and many other states. For example, in Illinois, where the cost of voting is relatively easy, ranked the fourth easiest state using the 2020c COVI, Trump did better in 2020, and the Democratic Party's two-party vote differential was negative.

In neighboring Iowa (ranked twenty-first), Biden improves only .88 percent over Clinton. Recall that the average gain over Clinton across all fifty states was 1.77 percent. This finding suggests Biden underperforms, or Trump outperforms, in Iowa, in 2020. Ranked twenty-first, voting was easier than average in Iowa in 2020, and the Republican Party picked up two seats in US House races during this election cycle. Moreover, incumbent US senator Joni Ernst (R), from Iowa, believed to be in serious trouble in her reelection effort in 2020, won handily. The Hawkeye State saw an increase in voting-eligible turnout from 69.1 percent to 73.3 percent. As a result, the Republican Party did very well in the state. Trump did better, Republicans picked up two House seats, and the incumbent Republican senator easily won reelection. The irony of this story is that the Republican-led state legislature in Iowa passed new voting restrictions after the 2020 elections, a move that, could benefit the Democratic Party.[2]

Does Higher Voter Turnout Help Democrats?

In all, our first two tests suggest that if making voting easier creates a partisan advantage, it is the Republican Party that does better. However, we have the third test. We have been talking quite a bit about voter turnout. So, what does a systematic look at voter turnout turn up? We report the results in figure 8.3. In the figure, the x-axis shows the increase in voter turnout by state between 2016 and 2020. Note that there are no negative values on the horizontal axis. That is, voter turnout increased in all fifty states between the two election cycles. The y-axis is the Democratic two-party vote differential. Where voter turnout went up the most, did it advantage Biden? Put differently, does Trump underperform where voter turnout increased the most? The answer is an emphatic "no."

Recall that the Democratic two-party vote differential depicts the difference between Joe Biden's vote percentage in each state in 2020 and Hillary Clinton's vote percentage in 2016. When we run a correlation between Biden's performance and the increase in voter turnout by state, we get a statistically significant negative relationship ($r = -.30$ $P < .04$, n = 50, two-tailed test). In

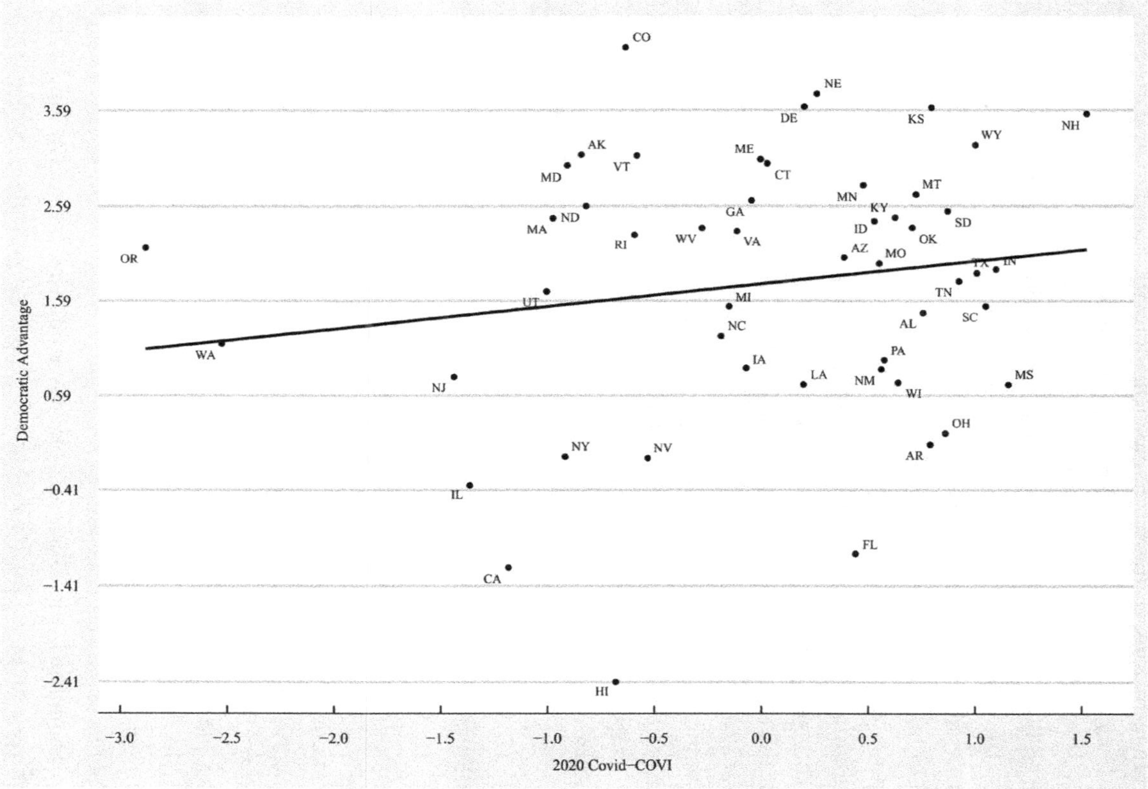

Figure 8.2. The COVID COVI and the difference in support for Joe Biden in 2020 versus Hillary Clinton in 2016

Source: Michael Pomante, Scot Schraufnagel, and Quan Li

other words, Biden's vote share declined, compared to Clinton, as voter turn-out increased. Again, where voter turnout went up the most, Trump did better in 2020 than in 2016. In the figure, note the dramatic increase in voter turn-out in Hawaii, which worked to President Trump's advantage. Also, note the location of New Hampshire in the top left-hand quadrant of the figure. Voter turnout in the Granite State went up less than 3 percent (2.97 percent). This turnout is much lower than the national average increase (6.35 percent).[3] If more accessible voting is supposed to help Democrats, we expect President Trump to improve or do much better in New Hampshire in 2020. However, that is not what happens. Instead, Joe Biden does 3.55 percent better in the state than Clinton. Biden's performance in New Hampshire exceeds his average in-crease (1.77 percent) over Clinton. In addition, consider Oklahoma; the state rests on the trend line in the upper left quadrant. The state makes voting rel-atively challenging (ranked thirty-seventh on the 2020c COVI). Correspond-ingly, the increase in voter turnout (2.69 percent) was considerably below the national average, but Biden did better in the state than Clinton (2.36 percent). If Democrats benefit when there is greater voter turnout, this should be the other way around.

Conclusion

It is interesting to speculate about the percentage increase in voter turnout in 2020, resulting from states making voting easier amid the pandemic. In addi-tion, we know that 2020 experienced a particularly competitive electoral envi-ronment with a polarizing incumbent presidential candidate who was either loathed or adored. These circumstances speak to the "benefits" of voting be-cause people perceive their vote as more critical in such scenarios. Increasing the benefits of voting can undoubtedly explain some of the rises in voter turn-out (6.35 percent increase overall). Arguably, a reduction in the cost of voting also explains some of the increase.

New Hampshire and Oklahoma may be somewhat instructive in this re-gard. The two states saw an increase in voter turnout by around 3 percent com-pared to over 6 percent nationwide. These two states did not adopt any more inclusive policies intended to make voting more accessible during the pan-demic. We, therefore, imagine the increased "benefits" of voting can explain

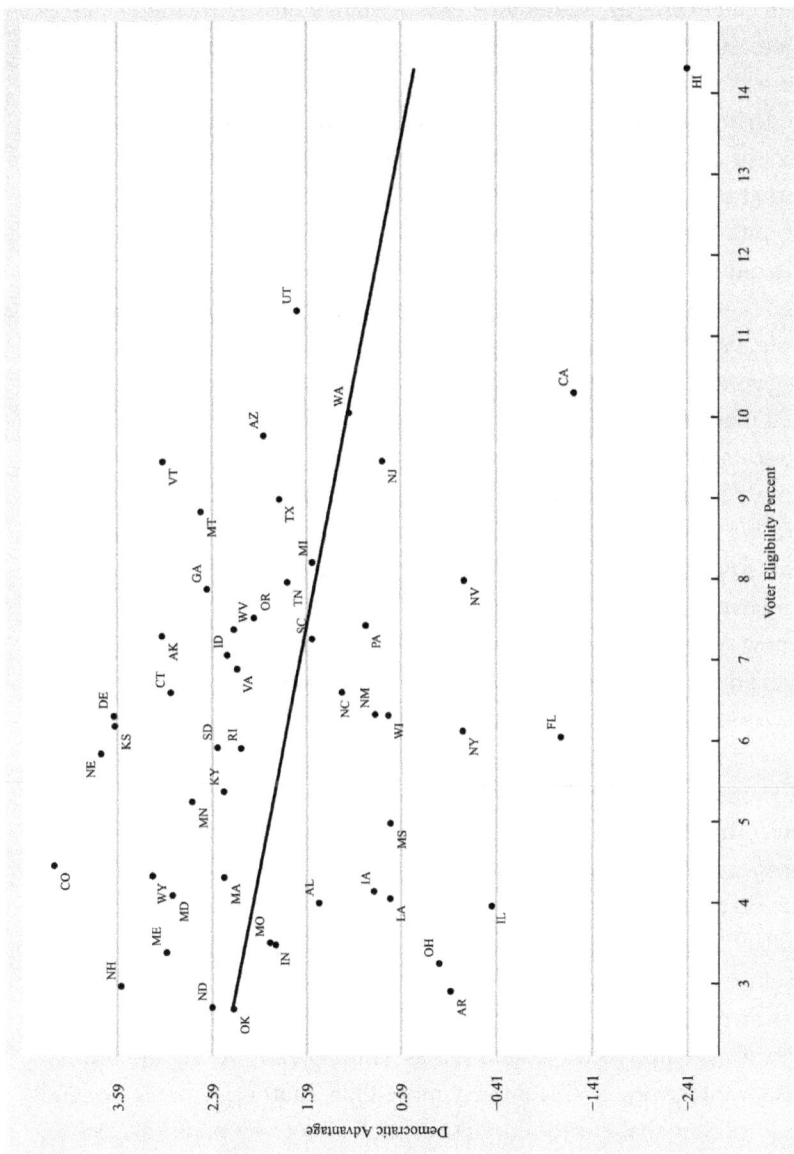

Figure 8.3. The percent increase in voter turnout and the difference in support for Joe Biden in 2020 versus Hillary Clinton in 2016

Source: Michael Pomante, Scot Schraufnagel, and Quan Li

the increase in voter turnout in these states. Subtracting the 3 percent increase due to the increase in the benefits of voting from the over 6 percent overall increase in voter turnout, we imagine that perhaps a little more than 3 percent of the increase in voter turnout in 2020 can be explained by states making voting easier.

Considering the 2020 election witnessed a spike in voter turnout and a few dozen, or perhaps a few hundred, fraudulent voters, it would be difficult to claim that easier voting or fraud propelled President Biden to victory. Remember, not all fraudulent voters favor the same candidate! Where voting is accessible, and voter turnout was higher, on average, President Trump did better in 2020 than in 2016. Moreover, his Republican Party brethren running for state legislative seats, in the US House, and the US Senate also benefited from increasing voter turnout in 2020. Before the election, many commentators had speculated that the 2020 election would result in the Democratic Party gaining more seats in the House of Representatives and flipping majority control of some state legislatures. The increase in Democratic seats did not happen. Therefore, we must accept that the Republican Party outperformed expectations in 2020 when many states made voting more accessible in response to the COVID-19 pandemic.

We know state legislators can design electoral policies to create a partisan advantage. For example, the Jim Crow–era laws discussed in chapter 1 benefited the Democratic Party in an earlier era. These policies helped keep white Democrats in power in the "Solid South"—a reference to the electoral dominance of Democrats in the former Confederate states from the last decades of the nineteenth century to at least the first fifty years of the twentieth century (Webster 1992). Moreover, when Republican legislators in Wisconsin tried to fashion a voter ID law in 2012, it was clear the state's legislature was trying to write the law to gain a partisan advantage. Specifically, the law would have required eligible voters to pay for a state-issued identification card and student identification cards would not be accepted. Moreover, we can imagine creative ways to write absentee voting laws, such as banning early voting on Sundays, which disadvantage one political party more than another. However, overall, evidence is missing that electoral practices such as vote-by-mail, early voting, or automatic voter registration create a decidedly Democratic Party advantage. Equally important, considering the research reported in chapter 7, rather than causing more voter fraud, each of these reforms can potentially decrease voter mischief.

Conclusion

In both the 116th and 117th Congresses, Democratic Party majorities in the House of Representatives passed legislation to modernize voter registration and balloting and standardize these practices across the fifty states (H.R. 117–1). After the passage of the National Voter Registration Act of 1993, the For the People Act was the first national government effort to suggest national standards that would reduce the cost of voting throughout the American states. Title I of H.R. 117–1 would require states to adopt online voter registration, automatic voter registration, same-day voter registration, preregistration of individuals sixteen and older in secondary schools, and two weeks of early in-person voting for national elections. Unfortunately, the proposed legislation included many other provisions that do not directly address the cost of voting. These other concerns relate to campaign financing, lobbying, and ethics reforms and their inclusion in this omnibus legislation arguably made the passage of the cost of voting provisions less likely.

Positive reforms intended to reduce the cost of voting have a tough uphill climb. Fueling the difficulty is misinformation. Unfortunately, former president Trump and other Republicans spread false claims about election integrity during and in the aftermath of the 2016 and 2020 election campaigns. Moreover, and more broadly, the Trump presidency exposed the underbelly of hateful rhetoric that defines much contemporary political discourse in the United States as "us versus them." More troubling, racial and xenophobic implications lie near the surface of the rhetoric used to oppose easier voting. Further, it is not difficult to imagine that efforts by Democrats in the national legislature to reduce the cost of voting have spurred additional restrictions in Republican-controlled state governments in recent years. This is somewhat ironic, given that the extension of the preclearance formula present in the Voting Rights Act of 1965 received broad bipartisan support as recently as 2006.

Preclearance: The Need for a New Formula

The 2008 election of Barack Obama broke the glass ceiling and was a tremendous win for Black Americans and other supporters of the forty-fourth president. Finally, a Black man occupied the White House and one of the most influential political offices in the world. The Obama win made many in the white political class and their followers uncomfortable because they feared losing their country, culture, or political power. Many white officeholders were not only concerned that a Black man won the presidency in 2008 but that Black Americans showed up to vote at a high rate.[1] After the 2008 election, many Republican state legislators began efforts to change their state's electioneering practices to make them more restrictive, presumably discouraging minority voter turnout. The adoption of restrictive policies significantly increased after the *Shelby County v. Holder* (2013) ruling. This ruling meant states with a history of discriminatory election policies would no longer need preclearance to change state election laws.

When Barack Obama's vice president, Joe Biden, won the presidency in 2020, the racial threat felt by white Republicans, stoked by outgoing president Trump, was again palatable. Fueling the dissent, early in 2021 Joe Biden pledged to make his cabinet the most diverse in US history.[2] Commentators have noted that white males have played a smaller role in the Biden administration than in any previous presidential administration in the history of the United States.[3] This executive branch diversity, accompanied by Democratic Party success in Georgia early in 2021, has undoubtedly caused many Republican-controlled states to increase the cost of voting. Specifically, within months of the Trump loss, Republican state lawmakers introduced hundreds of bills to restrict voting. The Brennan Center for Justice estimates that between November 2020 and May 14, 2021, legislators in forty-eight states introduced 389 bills to restrict voting access.[4]

Two states where Republican legislators have advocated for more restrictions are Georgia and Pennsylvania. In 2022, restrictions passed in Georgia, but Pennsylvania's Democratic Governor Tom Wolf refused to sign similar laws. Notably, in 2022, both states had Republican majorities in the state legislature, and Joe Biden flipped both states to the Democratic Party column in the 2020 presidential contest. The loss in Georgia was particularly disconcerting to Republican Party stalwarts, as the state had traditionally been a Republican stronghold. However, a review of recent statewide elections does note the state had been trending toward the Democratic Party in recent election cycles. Then, early in 2021, individuals representing the Democratic Party won both Georgia's US Senate seats. In the aftermath of the Democratic gains, Republican state legislators introduced sweeping changes to limit absentee voting, purge voter rolls, and make voter registration more difficult. In the end, the state passed more minor modifications related to election administration. Meanwhile, Republican legislators in Pennsylvania have advocated for a new voter identification law and a repeal of no-excuse absentee voting, arguably as ways to turn the state back around and make it more solidly Republican. However, we have just learned in chapter 8 that these types of efforts can backfire. At best, the academic consensus regarding the partisan advantages of more restrictive voting is inconclusive.

Georgia is important because the state needed preclearance for election law changes before the *Shelby v. Holder* decision in 2013. Georgia has a long history of racial discrimination in voting practices dating back to the post–Civil War era. The recent changes in the state, at first blush, seem like another attempt to suppress the votes of Black Americans in a manner like early Jim Crow–era attempts. One Georgia Republican publicly admitted the rationale for change. A white female member of the Gwinnett County Elections Board told a local newspaper, "They don't have to change all of them [election policies], but they've got to change the major parts of them so that we at least have a shot at winning."[5] In January 2021, these comments arguably reveal a blatant attempt to use election laws to create a Republican Party advantage. Moreover, the racial undertone is very thinly veiled. It is reasonable to assume that the "we" the election board official refers to is the white community. Presumably, Republicans (at least in Georgia) seek to disenfranchise Black citizens because the group disproportionately supports Democratic Party candidates.

Recall that the 2013 Supreme Court opinion rebuked Congress for holding on to an outdated preclearance formula. Importantly, though, the high court, in the majority opinion, held that discrimination in voting was "an insidious and pervasive evil which had been perpetuated in certain parts of our country through unremitting and ingenious defiance of the Constitution."[6] The court continued by suggesting that any amount of racially motivated voting restriction was too much. We would add that any amount of voting restrictions hamper the functioning of a healthy democracy. This is the case because excluding people from participating in elections can compromise citizen efficacy or the feeling that one can change things for the better. Moreover, in the introduction, we made the case that political stability and economic prosperity depend on an active and engaged citizenry that fundamentally supports governing arrangements. We suggest that the United States is not so different from other countries in this regard and that if citizens feel left out, at some point, they protest. We hold that those who care about the quality of democracy in the United States must remain vigilant. Accordingly, we wish to introduce a systematic way to identify states that should still receive preclearance from federal judges before changing their election laws. We hope this effort might serve as a starting point for meaningful debate on a new preclearance formula.

Specifically, we suggest using two criteria to identify states where law changes should receive additional scrutiny. In the first instance, we borrow from the original method. The first formula identified nine states with a history of discriminatory electioneering practices. We begin by looking at these states. Specifically, with new COVI values in hand, dating back to 1996, we can learn whether any of the original nine states have mended their ways over the past twenty-five years. If so, we could rightfully argue that preclearance is no longer necessary in these states. If not, these state's election law changes should continue to receive scrutiny.

Second, we use the COVI to identify states that have fallen off or fallen behind appreciably when it comes to making it easier for state citizens to participate in elections. Once we can identify these laggards—or states that seemingly have gone out of the way to make voting more difficult—since 1996, election law changes in these states also need oversight. Specifically, in this vein, we can identify three states that have systematically refused to stay current by adopting less restrictive voting practices when neighboring states are doing so and/or have instituted unnecessary restrictions in recent years.

The Original Preclearance States

Since the original nine preclearance states have a history of racist election policy, it only seems fitting to start here. Figures 9.1 and 9.2 display the COVI rankings for the former preclearance states for each presidential election since 1996. Figure 9.1 displays values for the four states that we argue still need oversight: Alabama, Mississippi, South Carolina, and Texas. In each state, the cost

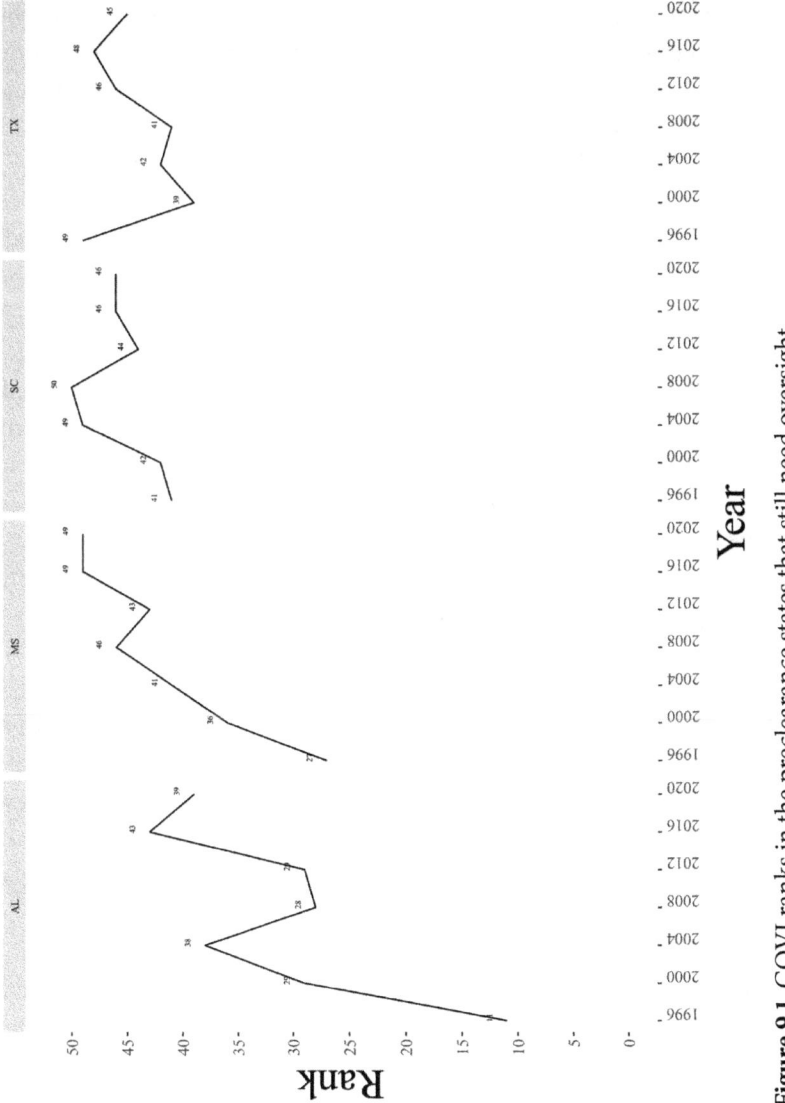

Figure 9.1. COVI ranks in the preclearance states that still need oversight

Source: Michael Pomante, Scot Schraufnagel, and Quan Li

of voting has stayed relatively high compared to other states, and in many ways, voting has become relatively more restricted in the past twenty-five years.

Ironically, Alabama started as the eleventh most accessible state to vote in 1996, perhaps because of the need for the preclearance of changes to state voting laws. However, the state has done little to make voting easier over the past quarter-century. In 2020, Alabama still had an unnecessary registration deadline, or no same-day voter registration. Notably, after the Supreme Court ruling in *Shelby v. Holder*, which dropped the need for preclearance, the state quickly adopted a photo ID law. Additionally, following President Trump's defeat at the polls in 2020, the Republican-controlled legislature introduced six new policies to make voting more restrictive. These legislative proposals signal that this former preclearance state still needs oversight of its election policymaking.

In 1996, Mississippi started out ranked twenty-seventh. However, with each passing election, the relative difficulty of voting in the state increased, leading it to become the second most restrictive state by 2016, and the ranking was the same in 2020. Following President Trump's claims of voter fraud in the aftermath of the 2020 election, members of the state legislature introduced thirteen new bills intended to restrict voting. Over the last twenty-five years, the trend and the most recent actions demonstrate that Mississippi would still benefit from federal oversight of its election law changes.

Unlike the trends toward more restriction seen in Alabama and Mississippi, South Carolina has consistently been one of the ten most difficult states for citizens to exercise the right to vote. In 1996, South Carolina ranked forty-first and had remained in the bottom ten states over the seven presidential election cycles, including 2020. The Palmetto State has introduced seven new restricting policies since the 2020 election. Considering ranks for South Carolina as presented in figure 9.1, it is doubtful the state has moved beyond the behavior that would benefit from preclearance or oversight.

Lastly, Texas has consistently been among the most challenging states for citizens to vote. In 1996, the state ranked forty-ninth, and seven presidential election cycles later, in 2020, the state ranked forty-fifth. There has been no movement in the inclusiveness of the electoral-institutional climate in the state of Texas. Consistent with other conservative states, Texas has introduced multiple bills to increase the difficulty of voting since the 2020 election. One major overhaul of state elections passed in the fall of 2021. Given past racist electioneering practices, we suggest the state of Texas still needs federal oversight of changes to the state's election laws.

On the other hand, the other five states that initially needed preclearance have improved, and the relative cost of voting has decreased dramatically in a couple of instances. We present ranks, over time, for these five states in figure 9.2. In 1996, Alaska was the forty-second most difficult state to vote in when we began tracking state election laws. However, the state climbed to ninth place by 2020. Moreover, Alaska is one of the early adopters of an inclusive automatic voter registration law, and the Last Frontier State has consistently moved forward since 1996. Conspicuously, Alaska has maintained Republican Party control of the state legislative process during our study, indicating that not all Republican-led legislatures are pro-restriction. However, we should note that Alaska does not have a large Black population or a fast-growing Hispanic population, both factors that correspond with Republican-led states moving in more restrictive directions.

Arizona, Georgia, Louisiana, and Virginia have improved since 1996. Virginia is notable because it initially made voting relatively more difficult and then did a serious about-face. By 2020, Virginia was ranked eighteenth, up from forty-ninth in 2008. In each of the states, outlined in figure 9.2, movement in rank suggests these states no longer require scrutiny or oversight of state election law changes. Importantly, Georgia passed fewer restricting laws in 2021 than were first proposed; furthermore the Peach State, like Alaska, was an early adopter of an automatic voter registration process. We have outlined in chapter 3 the changes made in Virginia between the 2016 and 2020 presidential elections. The state appears to have become a voting rights bastion as the state legislature continued to find ways to make voting easier, early in 2021. The Arizona and Louisiana storylines are complex, but neither has staked a spot at the bottom of the rankings. Recall that Arizona was the first state to adopt voter registration via the internet. Louisiana adopted civics education and preregistration of sixteen-year-olds by the 2016 election cycle, and the state has never strictly enforced its photo ID law.

OTHER STATES THAT SHOULD BE CONSIDERED FOR PRECLEARANCE

While the former preclearance states provide a good starting point to identify states that may make voting more difficult for discriminatory reasons, we should not limit our focus to the previously problematic states. When

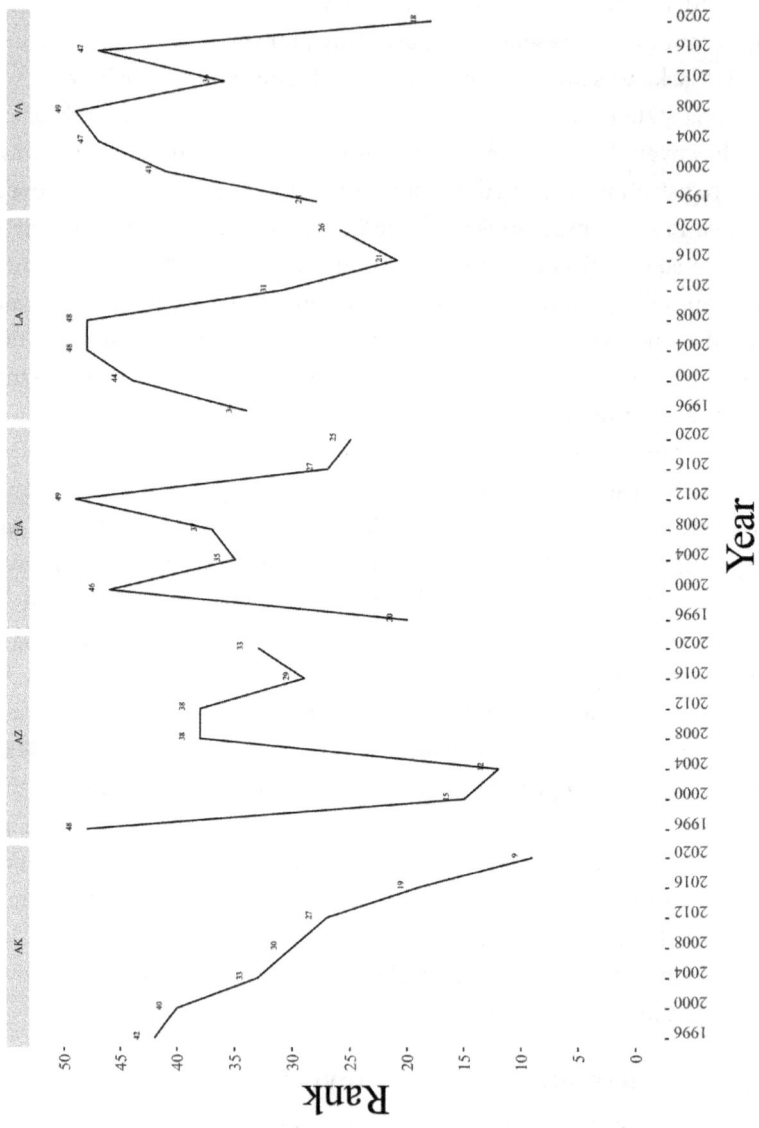

Figure 9.2. COVI ranks in the preclearance states that have mended their ways

Source: Michael Pomante, Scot Schraufnagel, and Quan Li

examining the change in state ranks from 1996 to 2020, we learn a one standard deviation in the change in rank is a little more than twenty places. We suggest that if a state drops its ranking by more than 1.5 standard deviations over the past seven presidential election cycles, this signals that the state needs oversight of its election law changes. Specifically, we mean a drop of thirty places in about twenty-five years. Three states meet this criterion: New Hampshire, Wisconsin, and Wyoming. Between 1996 and 2020, New Hampshire dropped forty-four spots, Wisconsin dropped thirty-four places, and Wyoming dropped thirty-five spots.

We have noted that some states drop in ranking because they fail to keep pace and adopt policies to reduce the burden of voting, which is the case in each of the three states we have identified. However, these three states all also passed new restrictive voting policies following the election of Barack Obama in 2008. When Obama won office, the states were ranked eighth, eleventh, and ninth. Yet, by the end of Obama's presidency, each state had made voting significantly more difficult by adopting policies such as registration drive restrictions and voter identification laws. Moreover, as of 2023, none of the three states has the option to register online, and none of them has adopted a preregistration law establishing a public high school curriculum focused on voting or civic involvement. In legislative matters, it is challenging to pin motives for inaction or action. However, the precipitous drop in ranking coinciding with the election of the country's first Black president deserves scrutiny.

We indicated that our reconsideration of a preclearance policy represents a starting point for legislative debate. Importantly, a new national law, such as the one the 116th and 117th House of Representatives proposed, would standardize voting practices considerably and potentially undo the need for oversight of legislative changes at the state level. However, congressional failure to pass national standards suggests a new preclearance formula may still be in order. Judiciously, any new preclearance law should contain remedial provisions. In other words, states ought to have an opportunity to modernize and adopt new secure technologies that reduce voting costs to avoid the preclearance requirement. Unfortunately, the overabundance of recently proposed changes in Republican state legislatures in the aftermath of the 2020 election suggests that those in power in these states persist in gaming the system anew. Moreover, by default, many attempts to create a partisan advantage may suppress the turnout of minority voters, the undereducated, and renters.

Final Thoughts

While this text has discussed minority group exclusion and the role the Republican Party has played in recent years in adopting or maintaining a restrictive electoral climate, the book has not been solely about either race or party politics. As we noted earlier, both major political parties have played a role, historically, in repressing the civic engagement of populations less likely to support them (Epperly et al. 2020). Often the efforts focus on minority populations. Unfortunately, as of 2022 the Republican Party continued to advocate for restrictive voting policies in the name of "election security." Yet, we know this does not add up. Specifically, we learned about voter and election fraud from the Heritage Foundation. The group tracks fraud cases, and one must conclude that both broad categories of fraud are infrequent, and when they do occur, it is nearly at random. The only exception is some evidence that close elections encourage fraudsters. Still more, using the group's data, we uncover no partisan context to fraud, and there is no noticeable increase or decrease in fraud associated with the restrictiveness of a state's election posture.

This book has first and foremost been about citizen participation, quality democracy, and good governance. We write this book using the premise that all citizens have equal rights to participate in the political process in a competent political system (Bühlmann, Merkel, and Weßels 2012). Moreover, we believe inclusive voting rights allow citizens to have their voices heard and that the ability for all citizens to vote legitimizes the governing apparatus and, by extension, creates political stability. Still more, we know politicians are more responsive to groups who vote (Griffin and Newman 2005). Therefore, if state governments pass policies that directly or indirectly exclude segments of the voting population from participating in elections, politicians are less responsive to these groups and their needs (Avery and Peffley 2005; Hajnal and Trounstine 2005; Hill and Leighley 1992). When those who are excluded are from underrepresented minority groups, there is an additional cause for concern, especially concerning the potential for violating citizens' civil rights.

We are far from the "postracial" world some have hoped for and others have claimed exists. Since the Civil Rights Act of 1964 and the Voting Rights Act of 1965, states have passed many laws that do not mention race, arguably to avoid suspect classifications, but still demobilize minority voters. Unfortunately, the racial motive seems alive and well, even if the push for restrictions on voting is more directly an effort to gain partisan advantage. Particularly concerning, the results reported in chapter 4 demonstrate that either sizable or growing minority populations lead to more voting restrictions. Whites, particularly white males, are still overrepresented in positions of political influence in the twenty-first-century United States. Moreover, we learned in chapter 6 that the Black, Hispanic, and female representation gap in state legislatures is larger in states with a more restrictive electoral-institutional climate.

The problem of citizen anomie, or lack of efficacy, and the underrepresentation of minorities is a powder keg for unrest. Still more, we now know with certainty that the undereducated are less likely to participate in the political process when the cost of voting is greater. It is easy to imagine a firebrand political figure mobilizing these citizens to participate in civil disorder. Put simply, when people do not have a voice in political decision-making, or even if they perceive they do not have a voice, a charismatic leader can use their angst to stoke unrest. When combined with an economic downturn, or a health crisis, restrictive election laws are a prescription for political strife. The riotous crowds in the summer of 2020 and January of 2021 represent different ends of the ideological spectrum in the United States. However, the two subpopulations were alike in some ways. Both groups felt cheated and felt that justice would not prevail, which motivated some in each group to provoke violence. This type of unrest occurs worldwide and in every century of recorded history. Our position is that the United States is not immune.

We began writing this book before the unrest in 2020 and 2021, and these events are a stark reminder for us of what motivates our work. One might imagine there is currently a lull in these types of disturbances as we write the final chapter of this volume in the summer of 2022. However, we are not convinced. Gun violence, mental health concerns, and societal troubles of every ilk are omnipresent. It is safe to say there is individual and group alienation around every corner in the contemporary United States. We are social animals. These social problems intensify when election laws discriminate and exclude eligible voters from democratic decision-making. There are implications for individuals, groups, and the broader community. With the surplus of potential social ills besetting a mass society, we do not need to heap voting restrictions on the pile of citizen despair.

To be clear, we are not suggesting that making voting more accessible remedies many of society's woes. However, we suggest it is senseless to contribute to this distress by making voting more restrictive with the potential to delegitimize government and create a more unstable political future. Despite some recent arguments by Republican Party operatives, we uncover no harm derived from a more inclusive electoral climate. Election laws that make voting easier may result in different people in power, but these laws do nothing to delegitimize our governing system. In fact, inclusive voting has great potential to enhance righteousness, lawfulness, and social justice.

Appendix A
Measurement Challenges and Omitted Variables

One of the challenges we faced in creating an index is the complexity of state election law. The level of familiarity with state election practice required to develop a comprehensive index is far-reaching. Moreover, the assumptions we needed to make in constructing a usable index were a considerable hurdle. Nevertheless, challenges acknowledged, we forged forward because the potential value is significant, especially if one can use the values to elucidate variance in state socioeconomic or policy outcomes. Moreover, a composite index can expose potential civil rights violations if state lawmakers purposefully make it more difficult for minorities, the aged, or citizens with disabilities to participate in elections.

During the deliberation regarding criteria for inclusion in the index, we ultimately dropped several policies that we considered at one time or another. For instance, we dropped considerations such as mail-in voter registration and purges for nonvoting in national elections because the 1993 National Voter Registration Act created a national standard. In addition, we left out other considerations because of data limitations. For example, the Brennan Center for Justice attempts to chronicle how often each American state purges voter registration roles for reasons other than nonvoting.[1] However, inconsistent state reporting hampers the group's efforts. Moreover, it is likely impossible to decipher if a purge is a legitimate elimination of ineligible registrants or a purposeful ploy intended to reduce voter turnout. Finally, even when data are available, it would require speculative judgment to derive a value for a state in any given year.

We found the effective use of other considerations compromised by intra-state variations. For example, one might imagine that when states draw jury pools from registered voters, they may opt for a policy that raises the cost of voting for some. The problem with this consideration is variation at the sub-state level. Most states do not have a consistent practice regarding how each judicial district fashions a pool of potential jurists, which confounds any effort to assign a state-specific value. In this case, we are reasonably confident that within and across-state variation is considerable and sufficiently random and that index validity is not compromised. These policies do not create a systematic bias in the COVI.

Another problematic consideration is the location of precinct polling stations. Convenient polling stations reduce the cost of voting (Brady and McNulty 2011; Haspel and Knotts 2005). However, local election administrators have considerable discretion in this regard. Consequently, polling stations are more convenient in some parts of a state than in other parts. Moreover, any across-state comparison is prickly because proximity likely interacts with other inter- and intrastate considerations, such as the ease of travel. Most critically, one might imagine that rural parts of a state are more disadvantaged by the distance to the polls than urban or suburban areas. Hence, we might use population density as a surrogate for the convenience of polling locations. Yet, the most common means of transportation in rural versus urban areas are often different, and the level of convenience might be challenging to determine.[2] Again, we must assume inter- and intrastate variation on this consideration is sufficiently random not to cause bias in index values.

Appendix B
More Specifics on Constructing the Cost of Voting Index[3]

Each election year, the assortment of relevant state policies is subject to Principal Component Analysis (PCA). Scholars commonly use PCA "to reduce the dimensionality of a data set consisting of a large number of interrelated variables" (Jolliffe 2002, 1). As a statistical procedure, PCA uses an orthogonal transformation that converts a set of observations of potentially correlated variables into a set of values of linearly uncorrelated items called principal components. The method measures the extent to which a single basic continuum underlies a set of theoretically linked considerations. Political scientists have used PCA to calculate everything from mass belief systems (Carmines and Stimson 1982), central bank independence (Banaian, Burdekin, and Willett 1998), to groups of like-minded senators (Jakulin, Buntine, La Pira, and Brasher 2009).

Using PCA, the number of principal components extracted is always less than or equal to the number of original variables included in the analysis. In our case, the "variables" are the different issue areas. We use between six and nine issue areas, depending on the year considered. With PCA, the first principal component accounts for as much of the variability in the data as possible. Then, each succeeding component explains the topmost variance, considering that the component is orthogonal to the previous component(s). The first "*few*" (Jolliffe 2002, ix; *emphasis in the original*) components are then weighted and combined to illuminate the internal structure of the data in a way that best clarifies variance in the data. The process produces a score for each unit of analysis, in our case, each US state. The score represents the state's relationship to the other units of analysis, or states. We hold that the underlying continuum we capture is the cost of voting. Because we score our data so that higher numbers always mean a greater cost, a larger score suggests the state is more restrictive than other states. Conversely, a negative PCA index value indicates a more inclusive state electoral-institutional climate, or a lower cost of voting.

With each COVI update, we found it necessary to add considerations to index construction. We do this to keep pace with the dynamic nature of state election law and, perhaps someday, national election law. This dynamic process results in a different number of components possibly being included in index construction each election year. The possible variation in the number of components included will continue with future iterations of the COVI. W. John Braun writes, "Remember that the objective is to use only the first few components. The usual technique is to look for where there is a sharp drop in the component variance."[4] We follow these directions precisely and use three components for the election years 1996, 2000, 2004, and 2008 and four components for 2012, 2016, and 2020 indices, including the COVID-19 COVI (2020c).[5]

Appendix C
Sensitivity Analysis

Before settling on a particular mode of index construction, we consider many possible approaches to combining the available data in a meaningful manner. Each approach requires making a set of assumptions; hence, we assemble a series of cost of voting indices. The index reported in this book is the one that is most like all the other versions. Importantly, we base the chosen index on suppositions with considerable face validity. Most specifically, we test alternative weighting schemes, aggregation methods, and the use of correspondence scores for each issue area not captured by a ratio variable instead of the ordered scales and additive subindices. Finally, we settle on the proportion of variance explained by each included principal component as our weighting strategy, a linear aggregation, and the ordered scales and additive subindices.

Weighting is a prominent concern for index construction. Our intuition is that the "proportion of variance explained" by each principal component, representing different issue areas, would be the soundest strategy. This approach privileges the issue areas most useful in extracting an underlying dimension. However, we also test equal and random weights for the included principal components. Concerning aggregation methods, we consider geometric aggregation to test the suitability of our initial choice of a linear or additive approach. We prefer the simpler linear aggregation because the range of numbers representing each issue area is quite similar. Moreover, because each issue area is theoretically related, the "normalization" of the data achieved by a geometric or nonlinear aggregation is unnecessary.[6]

Using the index values from our preferred approach as our benchmark, we conduct pairwise comparisons of indices and test the absolute value of the average change in state rank given different tallying approaches. Because we construct each index for each presidential election year, independent of one another, with a unique set of variables organized by issue area, the actual COVI values are not comparable from one election cycle to the next. However, state rank, or how states compare to one another, is comparable across time.

Charles Stewart III and the MIT Election Data Science Lab, in conjunction with the PEW Charitable Trust, also use "change in state rank" when calculating over time change in the Election Performance Index, which measures the competent administration of state elections.[7]

In an appendix to our 2018 article (Li, Pomante, & Schraufnagel 2018), we provide the results of this sensitivity analysis, which tests different weighting and aggregation methods. Using a geometric combination with random weights, in 2016 we obtained an index most distinct from the baseline COVI. The pairwise correlation for the remaining twenty-three indices is always greater than or equal to .80. Additionally, fifteen of the twenty-four indices correlated with our baseline index at .90 or greater. In the one instance where the correlation drops below .80 ($r = .79$), the pairwise correlation to the baseline index is still easily statistically significant using the most conservative criteria ($P < .001$).

Weighting and aggregation methods aside, we put our measurement strategies to another test. Some might be skeptical of our use of ordered scales and additive subindices to tap concepts such as "registration restriction" or "voting inconvenience." To address this, we check ourselves by conducting correspondence analyses for each issue area that uses subindices. In this instance, issue areas captured by ratio variables are unchanged, but we use correspondence scores instead of subindex values to capture issue area assessments.[8] The correspondence scores, along with the ratio variables, create another possible cost of voting index.

Notably, the two indices' pairwise correlation is .74 ($P < .001$), and the Kendall rank correlation coefficient is 0.56, demonstrating that the two indices are strongly related. Nevertheless, we learn that specific rankings, for some states, change rather dramatically when using the correspondence scores in certain election cycles. For example, considering our 2016 index and using the ordered scales and additive subindices, the process ranks Florida as one of the more costly states to vote in. However, when using the correspondence scores in the PCA, the Sunshine State is ranked seventh. In 2016, Florida still required voters to register to vote a full twenty-eight days out from Election Day, and the state had seven of the eight registration restrictions used at that time. It seems the use of correspondence scores is in some way confounding the analysis.[9] Based on our judgment, the more parsimonious and intuitive ordered scales and additive subindices is the better of the two approaches. Moreover, using the correspondence scores, North Dakota dropped to twelfth in 2016, which is problematic. Recall that North Dakota is the only state that does not require voter registration.

Appendix D
Construct Validity Check, the COVI, and State Voter Turnout

To test the construct validity of the COVI, we put our measurement strategy to task. To do this, we check the relationship between index values and state voter turnout in each of the seven election cycles studied. It is important to consider that "the cost of voting" is only a part of what explains voter turnout (Stevens 2006). Yet, it should be the case that costly voting is associated negatively with aggregate voter turnout. We expect a negative relationship between index values and state voter turnout because we constructed the COVI so that larger numbers indicate greater cost. Each test's sample size is fifty, representing the fifty US states. Figure D1 displays the results.

We learn that there is a negative and statistically significant correlation between COVI values and voter turnout. Considering the line labeled "2020c," this is a test of a second version of the COVI that we assembled in 2020 after states changed voting policies in response to the COVID-19 pandemic. In 2020, many states relaxed absentee voting processes, dropping the voter's requirement to have a state-sanctioned excuse. Moreover, as noted previously, four additional states moved to a universal vote-by-mail process. Note that the COVI and voter turnout correlation is nearly identical for both versions of the 2020 COVI. Yet, the 2020c COVI does perform very slightly better.

Considering all eight tests (1996–2020c), the relationship between COVI values and voter turnout is statistically significant seven times, using the standard 95 percent confidence criteria. The only exception is COVI values and voter turnout in 2016. However, that year, the relationship was still negative, as anticipated, and nearly statistically significant. These correlations suggest that COVI values comport with expectations. One might imagine that the correlations would be higher. However, it is essential to remember that the cost of voting does not capture the benefits of voting in each state. The decline in correlation values after 2004 might result from more polarized politics in more recent election cycles, driving up the perceived benefits of voting.

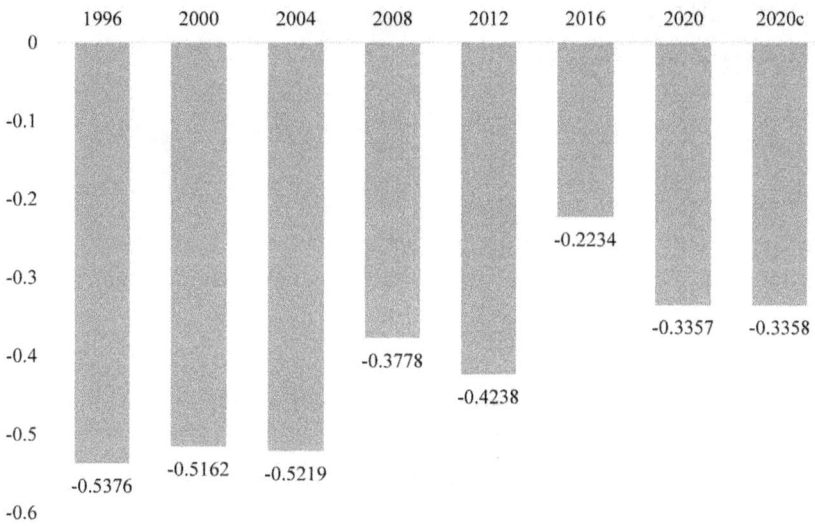

Figure D1. Testing the relationship between COVI values and voter turnout: 1996–2020c

Source: Michael Pomante, Scot Schraufnagel, and Quan Li

Appendix E
Chapter 4 Tables

The two tables here report the regression results for the model runs discussed in chapter 4. Moreover, these are the results used to produce figures 4.1 and 4.2 in the same chapter.

Table E4.1 for Figure 4.1. The Effect of Larger Black Populations and Republican Control of State Legislatures: The Cost of Voting in 49 States, 1996–2020
Between Regression (regression on group means)

Variable	Coefficient (Standard error)
Percent Black population	–.051 (.038)
Percent GOP state legislators	–.008 (.007)
Percent Black population*	
Percent GOP state legislators	.0017 (.0008)*
Electoral competition	–.0006 (.010)
Squire Index (legislative professionalism)	.003 (.006)
Constant	–.007 (.379)
F-Statistic	4.49*
Between R-squared	.34
n	343

Note: We follow the lead of other researchers who omit Nebraska's nonpartisan state legislature from analyses of variation in interstate outcomes (Gary and Lowery 1995; Emmert and Traut 2003; Sanbonmatsu 2003). When we assign Nebraska the same partisan value as neighboring Kansas, we obtain no appreciable difference in the results reported in the table.

*$P < .05$; $^{t} P < .10$ (two-tailed tests)

Source: Michael Pomante, Scot Schraufnagel, and Quan Li

Table E4.2 for Figure 4.2. The Effect of a Growing Hispanic Population and GOP State Legislators: The Cost of Voting in 49 States, 1996–2020

Fixed-Effects (within) Regression

Variable	Coefficient (Standard error)
Percent Hispanic population	−.102 (.020)*
Percent GOP atate legislators	.001 (.004)
Percent Hispanic population* Percent GOP state legislators	.0015 (.0004)*
Electoral competition	.0007 (.004)
Squire Index (legislative professionalism)	.022 (.008)*
Constant	−.359 (.305)
F-Statistic	9.73*
Within R-squared	.14
n	343

Note: We follow the lead of other researchers who omit Nebraska's nonpartisan state legislature from analyses of variation in interstate outcomes (Gary and Lowery 1995; Emmert and Traut 2003; Sanbonmatsu 2003). When we assign Nebraska the same partisan value as neighboring Kansas, we obtain no appreciable difference in the results reported in the table.

*$P < .05$; $^t P < .10$ (two-tailed tests)

Source: Michael Pomante, Scot Schraufnagel, and Quan Li

Appendix F
State COVI Values by Presidential Election

Table F1 reports the COVI values for each state, in each presidential election cycle, from 1996 through 2020. We list the states alphabetically for presentation and ease of reader access. All our data is available on our website (cost ofvotingindex.com). We hope other scholars, think tanks, and other interested parties use the data to help ensure the representation of all citizen voices. We also report these values in order of "cost" in chapter 3.

Table F1. COVI Values for the Fifty US States: Presidential Elections 1996 through 2020

State	1996	2000	2004	2008	2012	2016	2020	2020c*
AL	−0.399	0.000	0.577	0.247	0.222	0.616	0.776	0.756
AK	0.664	0.572	0.361	0.291	0.181	−0.152	−0.826	−0.842
AZ	0.821	−0.256	−0.263	0.506	0.453	0.256	0.446	0.388
AR	0.346	1.377	0.639	0.825	0.818	0.555	0.798	0.790
CA	0.530	0.023	0.006	0.013	−0.548	−1.262	−1.024	−1.184
CO	0.749	−0.118	0.014	0.180	0.395	−0.721	−0.678	−0.636
CT	0.084	0.204	−0.034	0.080	−0.718	−0.227	0.033	0.028
DE	0.359	0.341	0.437	0.540	0.193	0.126	0.091	0.203
FL	−0.057	1.771	0.723	−0.003	0.640	0.458	0.355	0.440
GA	0.007	1.129	0.469	0.445	0.997	0.211	0.093	−0.046
HI	0.312	1.653	0.707	−0.486	0.299	−0.727	−0.721	−0.683
ID	−1.180	−1.247	−1.484	−1.236	−0.444	−0.053	0.533	0.528
IL	0.254	−0.381	−0.477	−0.297	−0.177	−0.650	−1.356	−1.365
IN	0.458	0.162	0.162	0.775	0.839	0.686	1.175	1.098
IA	−0.037	−0.555	−0.251	−0.943	−1.127	−0.757	−0.154	−0.072
KS	0.317	−0.603	0.007	0.123	0.720	0.382	0.906	0.797
KY	0.484	0.735	0.573	0.772	0.671	0.688	0.526	0.625
LA	0.434	0.914	0.872	0.830	0.355	−0.142	0.115	0.198
ME	−2.170	−1.567	−1.907	−1.636	−1.219	−0.867	−0.152	−0.004
MD	0.676	−0.209	0.013	0.243	−0.536	−0.777	−0.983	−0.908
MA	−0.762	−0.574	−0.051	0.090	−0.187	−0.697	−1.032	−0.974
MI	−0.004	0.974	0.474	0.250	0.449	0.594	−0.073	−0.151
MN	−1.544	−0.829	−0.722	−0.894	−0.493	−0.261	0.373	0.478
MS	0.346	0.325	0.674	0.777	0.684	1.086	1.212	1.155

State	1996	2000	2004	2008	2012	2016	2020	2020c*
MO	−0.134	0.558	0.738	0.238	0.419	0.320	0.439	0.552
MT	0.384	0.113	0.715	−0.502	−0.185	−0.149	0.662	0.723
NE	−0.114	−0.231	0.054	−0.021	−0.218	−0.294	0.162	0.261
NV	0.783	−0.095	−0.111	0.158	−0.018	0.320	−0.523	−0.532
NH	−1.230	−0.357	−0.532	−0.788	0.081	1.218	1.437	1.523
NJ	0.676	−0.116	−0.240	0.299	−0.309	−0.670	−0.921	−1.439
NM	0.716	−0.141	0.174	0.444	0.481	0.575	0.422	0.560
NY	0.431	−0.241	0.127	0.516	−0.456	0.010	−0.753	−0.919
NC	0.396	−0.069	−0.368	−0.943	−0.987	−0.052	−0.490	−0.189
ND	−2.592	−0.606	−2.039	−2.727	−1.034	−0.896	−0.651	−0.819
OH	0.142	−0.218	0.062	0.645	0.660	0.605	0.878	0.861
OK	0.435	−0.094	0.244	0.411	0.383	0.371	0.601	0.705
OR	−0.195	−1.838	−1.992	−0.887	−1.674	−2.016	−2.917	−2.881
PA	−0.004	−0.078	−0.126	0.092	0.113	0.417	0.424	0.575
RI	0.600	−0.023	0.272	0.383	−0.103	−0.107	−0.593	−0.594
SC	0.624	0.711	0.974	0.883	0.693	0.821	0.981	1.050
SD	−0.013	−0.162	0.583	0.334	0.428	0.464	0.823	0.872
TN	1.011	1.166	1.038	0.714	1.088	0.598	1.026	0.925
TX	0.915	0.571	0.675	0.608	0.761	0.900	0.933	1.008
UT	−1.267	−0.587	−0.051	−0.130	−0.398	−1.090	−1.033	−1.004
VT	−1.007	−0.786	−0.851	−1.058	−0.080	−0.249	0.042	−0.583
VA	0.351	0.666	0.822	0.857	0.433	0.900	−0.164	−0.114
WA	0.418	0.186	0.155	0.377	−1.396	−0.915	−2.513	−2.526
WV	0.564	0.046	−0.162	0.159	−0.131	−0.287	−0.307	−0.277
WI	−1.362	−1.038	−0.934	−0.893	−0.771	0.250	0.771	0.639
WY	−1.216	−1.178	−0.747	−0.659	−0.243	0.591	0.830	1.002

* These COVI values consider some states' temporary policies to provide safe and convenient voting for their citizens during the 2020 COVID-19 pandemic. In previous COVI iterations, we included only enshrined laws in the index calculation.

Source: Michael Pomante, Scot Schraufnagel, and Quan Li

Appendix G
Chapter 5 Tables

The tables here provide the results of all model runs used to produce figures 5.1 through 5.8 in chapter 5.

Table G5.1. The Effect of the COVI on Black Reported Voting in the 2016 Election: States with the Fastest-Growing Black Populations
Model: Logistical Regression (Figures 5.1 & 5.2)

Independent variables	Model 5 Coef. (s.e.)
COVI values (Cost of voting)	−.051 (.038) [t]
Competitiveness (benefit of voting)	.010 (.002)*
Black	.175 (.156)
COVI* Black	−.689 (.313)*
Education	.451 (.018)*
Income	−.053 (.026)*
Income squared	.006 (.001)*
Married	.294 (.052)*
Homeowner	.621 (.056)*
Female	.188 (.046)*
Age	.010 (.008) [t]
Age squared	.000 (.000)
Unemployed	.115 (.149)
Constant	−2.44 (.20)*
F-Statistic	130.45*
No. of observations	38,083

* $P < .05$ (two-tailed tests); [t] $P < .10$ (one-tailed test)

Source: Michael Pomante, Scot Schraufnagel, and Quan Li

Table G5.2. The Effect of the COVI on Hispanic Reported Voting in the 2016 Election

Model: Logistical Regression (Figures 5.3 & 5.4)

Independent variables	Model 6 Coef. (s.e.)
COVI values (cost of voting)	−.068 (.015)*
Competitiveness (benefit of voting)	.015 (.001)*
Hispanic	−.337 (.031)*
COVI* Hispanic	−.232 (.037)*
Education	.408 (.008)*
Income	.004 (.011)
Income squared	.003 (.001)*
Married	.233 (.022)*
Homeowner	.407 (.023)*
Female	.193 (.020)*
Age	.026 (.003)*
Age squared	−.000 (.000) ᵗ
Unemployed	−.112 (.056)*
Constant	−2.65 (.09)*
F-Statistic	588.90*
No. of observations	150,673

* $P < .05$ (two-tailed tests); ᵗ $p < .10$ (one-tailed test)

Source: Michael Pomante, Scot Schraufnagel, and Quan Li

Table G5.3. The Effect of the COVI on Asian American Reported Voting in the 2016 Election

Model: Logistical Regression (Figures 5.5 & 5.6)

Independent variables	Model 7 Coef. (s.e.)
COVI values (Cost of voting)	−.121 (.015)*
Competitiveness (benefit of voting)	.014 (.001)*
Asian	−1.061 (.057)*
COVI* Asian	−.128 (.063)*
Education	.425 (.008)*
Income	−.003 (.011)
Income squared	.003 (.001)*
Married	.246 (.022)*
Homeowner	.416 (.023)*
Female	.196 (.020)*
Age	.027 (.003)*
Age squared	−.000 (.000)
Unemployed	−.122 (.057)*
Constant	−2.72 (.089)*
F-Statistic	607.94*
No. of observations	150,673

* $P < .05$ (two-tailed tests)

Source: Michael Pomante, Scot Schraufnagel, and Quan Li

Table G5.4. Reported Voter Turnout: The Effect of the COVI on the Undereducated in the 2016 Election

Model: Logistical Regression (Figures 5.7 & 5.8)

Independent variables	Model 8 Coef. (s.e.)
COVI values (Cost of voting)	−.151 (.015)*
Competitiveness (benefit of voting)	.013 (.001)*
No high school diploma	−1.166 (.033)*
COVI* No high school diploma	−.145 (.043)*
Income	−.050 (.011)*
Income squared	.008 (.001)*
Married	.299 (.022)*
Homeowner	.385 (.023)*
Female	.250 (.020)*
Age	.034 (.003)*
Age squared	−.0001 (.000)*
Unemployed	−.192 (.056)*
Constant	−1.59 (.09)*
F-Statistic	484.86*
No. of observations	150,673

* $P < .05$; ' $P < .07$ (two-tailed tests)

Source: Michael Pomante, Scot Schraufnagel, and Quan Li

Notes

1. The language minority stipulation was not in the original 1965 VRA. However, in 1975 Congress amended the act to protect non-English speaking citizens with the addition of section 203.

2. Joyce White Vance, "Ruth Bader Ginsburg Lost Her Battle to Save Voting Rights. Here's How We Can Take up the Fight to Honor Her Legacy," *Time*, September 21, 2020, https://time.com/5890983/ruth-bader-ginsburg-voting-rights/.

3. Brennan Center for Justice, "The Effects of *Shelby County v. Holder*," August 6, 2018, https://www.brennancenter.org/our-work/policy-solutions/effects-shelby -county-v-holder.

4. Aaron Blake, "Republicans Keep Admitting That Voter ID Helps Them Win, for Some Reason," *Washington Post*, April 7, 2016, https://www.washingtonpost.com /news/the-fix/wp/2016/04/07/republicans-should-really-stop-admitting-that-voter -id-helps-them-win/.

5. In the aftermath of the 2020 presidential election, state legislators have been hard at work shifting election laws seemingly without any other motive than gaining a partisan advantage.

6. William Riker was a transformative political scientist who introduced formal modeling to the discipline of political science and worked tirelessly to produce only empirically verifiable political proclamations or findings.

CHAPTER 1: A BRIEF HISTORY OF VOTING RESTRICTIONS IN THE UNITED STATES

1. For a summary of African American electoral success during the Reconstruction era, see "Black Leaders during Reconstruction," History.com, accessed July 18, 2022, https://www.history.com/topics/american-civil-war/black-leaders-during-re construction.

2. After Reconstruction, no African Americans would serve in Congress until 1929 even though Black citizens were a majority in many congressional districts.

3. In the post-Reconstruction era, many states still required some minimum of

property ownership. In Virginia, white males could only vote if they owned one hundred or more acres of land or had twenty-five acres of "well-maintained" land. These laws often prevented poor whites from voting, even though southern white populations often received reassurances from state legislators that they would not be adversely affected by the restrictions (Feldman 2004, 135–136).

4. See question no. 4, Alabama 1965 Literacy Test, accessed July 18, 2022, https://www.ferris.edu/HTMLS/news/jimcrow/pdfs-docs/origins/al_literacy.pdf.

5. While we believe that the Constitution is clear about the role Congress may play in establishing federal guidelines pertaining to election laws, on June 30, 2022, the US Supreme Court agreed to hear the *Moore v. Harper* case from North Carolina. This case focuses on the "independent state legislature" theory, which argues that state legislatures have complete power to regulate federal elections, without interference from the courts. The court's ruling was not published at the time of this book's printing.

6. The national government has also passed laws limiting the amount of money that people may contribute to candidates for national office and has required that individuals and interest groups publicly disclose hard money or direct contributions to election campaigns.

7. In recent years, the Democratic Party majorities in the 116th and 117th Congresses have passed legislation to address the issue of national standards in voting practice. Unfortunately, the legislation was very broad in scope. The proposed bills included changes to campaign finance law (Division B) and government ethics (Division C). The far-reaching aspects of the proposals, arguably, made it more difficult for the legislation to gain traction.

8. Douglass R. Hess, *Washington Post*, July 4, 2015, "States Are Ignoring Federal Law about Voter Registration. Here's Why," https://www.washingtonpost.com/news/monkey-cage/wp/2015/07/04/states-are-ignoring-federal-law-about-voter-registration-heres-why/.

9. Despite evidence that the NVRA increased registration (Cocker 2013), research has shown that it failed to increase actual turnout appreciably (Martinez and Hill 1999; Brown and Wedeking 2006).

10. See United States Department of Justice, "Cases Raising Claims under the National Voter Registration Act," accessed July 18, 2022, https://www.justice.gov/crt/cases-raising-claims-under-national-voter-registration-act. With all the pending litigation and the inability to know whether a purge is illegal until well after the state has completed the task, we do not, yet, consider variation in registration purge policies in our attempts to tap the relative cost of voting in each American state.

11. Robert Barnes and Anna Marimow, "Appeals Court Strikes Down North

Carolina's Voter ID Law," *Washington Post*, July 29, 2016, https://www.washingtonpost
.com/local/public-safety/appeals-court-strikes-down-north-carolinas-voter-id
-law/2016/07/29/810b5844-4f72-11e6-aa14-e0c1087f7583_story.html?utm_term=
.5821274ead36.

12. "Photo ID," Wisconsin Election Commission, https://elections.wi.gov/pho
toid.

13. Reuters staff, "Wisconsin Official Told DMV Not to Push Free Voter ID Cards,"
September 7, 2011, https://www.reuters.com/article/us-wisconsin-voter-id/wiscon
sin-official-told-dmv-not-to-push-free-voter-id-cards-idUSTRE78713P20110908.

14. Emily Schultheis, *Politico*, "Voter ID Laws to Have Smaller Impact," October
25, 2012, https://www.politico.com/story/2012/10/voter-id-laws-to-have-smaller-im
pact-on-election-082893.

15. Todd Richmond, "Wisconsin AG Suggests Voter ID Helped Trump Win the
State," Associated Press, April 13, 2018, https://apnews.com/article/87fabc13bf724009
ae68972dce79d189; Ari Berman, "Rigged: How Voter Suppression Threw Wisconsin
to Trump," *Mother Jones*, November/December 2017, https://www.motherjones.com
/politics/2017/10/voter-suppression-wisconsin-election-2016/.

16. German Lopez, "Southern States Have Closed Down at Least 868 Polling
Places for the 2016 Election," *Vox*, November 4, 2016, https://www.vox.com/policy
-and-politics/2016/11/4/13501120/vote-polling-places-election-2016.

CHAPTER 2: THE CHANGING NATURE OF STATE ELECTION LAW

1. In addition to the variables covered in this chapter, we deliberated on several
other considerations to be included in the index. We declined to include them for
various reasons, which we outline in appendix A.

2. See "Voting Laws Roundup: December 2021," Brennan Center for Justice, December 21, 2021, https://www.brennancenter.org/our-work/research-reports/voting
-laws-roundup-december-2021.

3. With the 1996 index, we use the first three components obtained and weigh
each component by the proportion of variance explained before using a linear aggregation or summation. The codebook available at costofvotingindex.com provides
the weights used and all coding details, which allow for replication of our approach.

4. In the 2022 COVI update (Schraufnagel, Pomante, & Li 2022), we present an
alternative version of the COVI that utilizes the insights of item response theory
(IRT). Some recent scholarship has identified IRT as an appropriate method for
measuring state variance in the difficulty of registering to vote (Jansa, Motta, and

Herrick 2021). We find the two approaches produce index values that are very highly correlated. For the sake of consistency, we recommend the PCA values to scholars who wish to make use of the COVI to study other state-level phenomena. One can find additional information on variable measurement strategies in appendix B and the results of sensitivity analyses in appendix C.

5. Specifically, research has shown that an easing of registration policies can increase voter turnout somewhere between 5 and 10 percentage points (Highton 1997; Rhine 1996; Knack 1995; 2001; Wolfinger and Rosenstone 1980; Rosenstone and Wolfinger 1978; Rosenstone and Hansen 1993; Mitchell and Wlezien 1995). Scholars have long identified registration requirements as one of the greatest barriers to voting in the United States (Rosenstone and Wolfinger 1978).

6. By 2020 it was safe to say that the United States no longer has a specific "Election Day." Instead, the country has an election period, with Election Day serving as the last official day of voting.

7. Before the passage of the NVRA in 1993, the range of state registration policies was vast. For example, in 1960, several states required voters to register every year (Rosenstone and Wolfinger 1978, 24). This changed by 1972 when all states, except two, had policies enacted to keep voters permanently registered. Moreover, prior to the passage of the 1970 VRAA, there was no limit on the number of days before an election that a state could require voters to be registered. The 1970 VRAA limited the registration deadline to no more than thirty days for presidential elections (Rosenstone and Wolfinger 1978, 24). Notably, a Supreme Court ruling struck down the federal law in *Marston v. Lewis* and *Burns v. Fortson*, which allowed Arizona and Georgia to retain their fifty-day registration deadline until the NVRA passed in 1993 and reestablished a thirty-day maximum.

8. The table also distinguishes the measurement strategies used for each issue area. For instance, we measure the registration deadline in days. We simply preserve the number of days as a stand-alone ratio variable or consideration. Next, we measure registration restrictions using an additive index. Currently a state receives a score from "0" (no restrictive policy) to "4," indicating the state has each of the four more restrictive policies. We measure the preregistration category (Issue Area No. 3) using an ordered scale that ranges from "0" to "5." States that have gone out of their way to write a law that allows sixteen-year-olds to preregister score "0" and states without a law addressing preregistration score "5." Again, it is always the case that a larger number indicates greater cost.

9. Still more, research shows that registration deadlines disproportionately affect the turnout of younger eligible voters and others who have recently moved (Knack and White 2000).

10. As mentioned, North Dakota does not require voter registration; as such the

Peace Garden State receives a score of "0" on this consideration, indicating the least costly option.

11. Maine was the first state to implement EDR, in 1973. Minnesota and Wisconsin quickly followed suit in 1974 and 1975. Until the passage of the NVRA, no other states passed this specific provision. The NVRA mandated states either adopt EDR or accept mail-in voter registration. To comply with the new national government law, Idaho, Wyoming, and New Hampshire adopted EDR, while all other states began to allow voter registration by mail.

12. If a state does not have EDR, we score the state "1"; states with the policy score "0."

13. From 1996 to 2004, the number of states that allowed EDR at polling locations stayed the same (seven states). However, one state (New Hampshire) required citizens to go elsewhere to register on Election Day. In 2008 two additional states (Montana and North Carolina) adopted EDR, but individuals had to go to a different location to register. However, North Carolina's law is slightly different from others because it only allows individuals to register through its early voting period. Every presidential election since 2008 has seen a considerable increase in states adopting EDR. In 2020 twenty-two states allowed some form of same-day voter registration.

14. Michelle Alexander (2010) argues that although states have been required to drop most Jim Crow voting laws, this law has persisted and has created a citizen underclass that has no say in how they are ruled.

15. Vermont's allowance for felons to vote dates to a 1799 legal decision. VTDigger, "Fact-Check: Sanders Set Off a Firestorm over Prisoners Voting, but His Facts Are Straight," April 24, 2019, https://vtdigger.org/2019/04/24/fact-check-sanders-set -off-firestorm-prisoners-voting-facts-straight.

16. We develop an ordered scale and give states that allow sixteen-year-olds to preregister a score of "0," representing the most inclusive policy. We also score North Dakota "0" on this consideration because the state does not require voter registration. States without preregistration law score "5" on the ordered scale.

17. We should note there is a national standard in this regard. States are required to allow all individuals who will be eighteen by the next election to register to vote ahead of the election.

18. Our 1996 measure of voting inconveniences, uses a five-point additive index, which ranges from zero to four. We reserve the value of "0" for states that have none of the policies. A "4" indicates the state has all four of the more burdensome practices.

19. Again, we consider in-person absentee voting to be distinct from early voting. With early voting, state electoral jurisdictions establish unique locations and advertise the hours of operation, often with allowances for after-hours or weekend voting. In-person absentee voting requires traveling to a specific government office.

20. We make coding exceptions for Kentucky, which closes state offices only in presidential elections (not for midterm elections), and New York, where state offices do not close but state workers are given the option of taking a different day off with pay if they work on Election Day. In our coding, we score the states that do not have a state holiday "1," Kentucky is scored ".5," New York is scored ".75." We score the states where state buildings do close and state employees do get the day off "0."

21. When the data becomes available, in 2008, we add to the inconvenience scale a consideration related to private businesses giving employees time off from work to vote and whether the time off is paid.

22. Specifically, we use NCSL's research into enforcement and establish a five-item ordered scale with "0" indicating only a signature is required and "4" indicating the state strictly enforces a photo ID policy. Please see table 2.1 for the other values.

23. In close races, some states will contact those who voted provisionally and allow them to return to a government office with the ID after Election Day. If the voter does not provide the identification in the state-mandated period, the ballot is not counted. A federal law labeled the Help American Vote Act of 2002 mandates that states have a provisional ballot option if they pass an identification law. With passage of the act, Arizona became the first state to take advantage of the provisional ballot option and passed a strict non-photo identification policy, with implementation in place for the 2004 presidential election. By 2008, Ohio had joined with its own strict non-photo ID policy. No other state adopted this type of policy until 2020, when North Dakota changed from a non-strict photo ID to a non-photo ID with strict enforcement.

24. In 2016 Virginia ranked as the state with the forty-seventh most restrictive electoral institutional climate, or the state with the forty-seventh highest COVI value. Changes in state law in 2020 move the state in the direction of inclusion, and for the 2020 election cycle, the state had only the eighteenth most restrictive set of policies. Chapter 3 will discuss state ranks and change in state ranks in more detail.

25. This time distinction is relevant because we subtract each state's average number of poll hours from the maximum poll hours. The manipulation reverses the values and creates a variable where higher values indicate greater cost. For example, in 2000, Oregon received a "0" (20–20). On the other hand, New Hampshire, in 2000, specified that polling locations must be open a minimum of eight hours and a maximum of twelve hours for an average of ten hours. Therefore, in 2000, Vermont received a score of "10" (20–10), representing the most restrictive state policy that year.

26. Some local electoral districts in these states conducted elections via the mail before Oregon's statewide policy in 1998. However, since local election administrators made these decisions and there was no statewide policy, we do not include vote-by-mail until the 2000 COVI.

27. Because vote-by-mail precludes the need to vote early, states adopting this policy also score "0" on the early voting consideration.

28. One can note the success of registration drives in the 2004 election cycle, when four million more individuals registered to vote than during the 2000 election cycle (Kasdan 2012, 3). Yet, the academic record as it relates to voter turnout and registration drives has produced mixed results. Some research finds an increase in voter turnout for Black citizens (Vedlitz 1985), Hispanics (Kasdan 2012, 2), and younger voters (Ulbig and Waggener 2011), while others find these efforts only assist in the mobilization of a nontrivial portion of citizens. They argue there is no appreciable change in the demographic composition of the electorate (Nickerson 2015).

29. Confounding matters, Appelbaum, Bonnie, and Karlawish (2005) find that those with mild cases of Alzheimer's still maintain the mental competency needed to cast a ballot, while those who have severe cases are not likely to have the capacity needed. To help identify legislation that meets these criteria, we use information gathered by the Bazelon Center for Mental Health Law. See Bazelon Center, *Vote. It's Your Right: A Guide to the Voting Rights of People with Mental Disabilities,* last accessed June 9, 2022, http://www.bazelon.org/wp-content/uploads/2020/10/Bazelon -2020-Voter-Guide-Full.pdf.

30. We scored Oregon "0" on this consideration in 2008 because the state's vote-by-mail process precludes the need to vote absentee. We score other states with vote-by-mail "0" on this consideration in subsequent versions of the COVI.

31. In our analysis, we code only those states that allow *all* citizens this opportunity "0."

32. In 2012 we also score Washington "0" because it adopted vote-by-mail that year.

33. The vote-by-mail states score "0" on this consideration because voting by mail precludes the need to travel to a polling location on Election Day, whether in one's neighborhood or at a more convenient voting center.

34. Scholars consider voter turnout in the United States low when compared to other advanced democracies (Powell 1986). Moreover, scholars argue that having elections take place in the middle of the workweek, on a Tuesday, is part of the reason this is so (Farber 2009).

35. Given the relative complexity of these state laws, we opt for a simple binary consideration. This binary coding decision identifies any state law that mandates employers give their hourly employees time off to vote. We also score the states with vote-by-mail "0." Voting by mail suggests that a potential voter will not need time off from work to vote on Election Day.

36. See Diana Kasdan, "State Registrations on Voter Registration Drives," Brennan Center for Justice, November 30, 2012, http://www.brennancenter.org/publication /state-restrictions-voter-registration-drives.

37. By 2020 Texas drops the reporting provision, and the state receives a score of "3" that year.

38. We score states without any registration drives restriction "0."

39. Additionally, we score New Hampshire and Wyoming "5" in Issue Area No. 7, assuming that an outright ban is more restrictive than any other combination of the four policies.

40. On this consideration, we score Rhode Island "0" in 2012, suggesting it does not have the more restrictive policy. Moreover, in 2012, and with each COVI reiteration, we score all states that have EDR "0" on this consideration.

41. We score states adopting automatic voter registration "0" and those that do not we score "1."

42. In many other countries, voter registration is more akin to obtaining a social security card in the United States. The process is routine and not duplicated once complete.

43. Because of decentralized election administration, state implementation of AVR processes varies, which we account for when this becomes a stand-alone issue area.

44. Jackie Borchardt, "Automatic Voter Registration Has Bipartisan Support in Ohio," *Cincinnati Enquirer*, April 24, 2019, https://www.cincinnati.com/story/news /politics/2019/04/24/automatic-voter-registration-has-bipartisan-support-in-ohio /3562581002/.

45. See "Democracy Diverted: Polling Place Closures and the Right to Vote," CivilRights.org, last accessed July 19, 2022, https://civilrights.org/democracy-diverted/.

46. Nevada is a good example. In 2020 the state had a deadline of twenty-eight days prior to an election for registration by mail but allowed in-person registration on Election Day and required those who register online to complete the process five days before the election.

47. In 2020 Vermont had the shortest online voter registration deadline, allowing voters to register via the internet on Election Day. On the other end of the spectrum, six states required citizens to register online thirty days before the election. We find that the median online voter registration deadline is twenty-one days, indicating that half of the states have deadlines shorter than twenty-one days. We arrange the online deadlines numerically to determine the median number of days. We rank states that do not allow for registration via the internet last.

48. We score states with these other types of absentee restrictions "1" in Issue Area No. 4.

49. The twenty-three states that have yet to adopt early voting are initially scored "0." However, like poll hours, we needed to reverse these values so that a larger

number indicates a greater cost. Specifically, we subtract each state's value from forty-two to reverse the values, and the twenty-three states without early voting in 2020 receive a score of "42" (42–0).

50. These five states, along with Virginia, all scored "0" in 2020.

51. See "What Methods Did People Use to Vote in the 2020 Election?" United States Census Bureau, last accessed July 19, 2022, https://www.census.gov/library /stories/2021/04/what-methods-did-people-use-to-vote-in-2020-election.html.

52. In our 2022 update, we explore the option of using Item Response Theory to calculate COVI values. With the two approaches producing values that are highly correlated (Pearson-R = .93; P <.001; n = 50), we opt for the use of PCA for the sake of consistency in measurement strategy (Schraufnagel, Pomante, and Li 2022).

53. One can also find directions and explanations of our measurement strategies in the 2018 *Election Law Journal* publication, Quan Li, Michael J. Pomante II, and Scot Schraufnagel, "The Cost of Voting in the American States," *Election Law Journal: Rules, Politics, and Policy* 17, no. 3 (2018): 234–247 and at costofvotingindex.com.

54. See "Data Details," Cost of Voting Index, last accessed July 19, 2022, costo-fvotingindex.com/data.

CHAPTER 3: FALLING BEHIND OR JUMPING AHEAD: MOVEMENT IN THE STATE COST OF VOTING RANK

1. Importantly, Heather Gerken (2009) has advocated for the reform of state election laws by suggesting a Democracy Index for the American states, and Charles Stewart III and the MIT Election Data Science Lab have worked with the PEW Charitable Trust to construct an Elections Performance Index, which measures the effectiveness state election administration. The Election Performance Index focuses on things that occur during or after the election—indicators such as voter turnout, voter registration rates, and the average length of time people spend at polling locations. Our effort differs appreciably in that our concern is state law and the electoral-institutional climate those laws create versus the actual administration of elections. See also Burden and Gaines (2015) for an effort to measure the relative convenience of "early voting" versus "absentee voting," paying special attention to the administration of these laws.

2. Besides the seven presidential election cycles (1996–2020), we also have a COVI that captures state changes in response to the 2020 COVID-19 pandemic. We label this index "2020c" in the replication database, which can be found at costo-fvotingindex.com. This provides another iteration to consider as we test the soundness of our measurement strategy. In this instance, we predicted that the states that

adopted a universal vote-by-mail process for the 2020 election would see a reduced cost of voting, relative to other states, and this is precisely what occurred.

3. However, state rank change does not occur as readily when a state is already at one or the other extreme. There simply is not as much room to change in rank.

4. Arizona and North Dakota scored "o" on this consideration in 2004. North Dakota receives a "o" because the state does not require voter registration.

5. Data for this consideration are obtained through the Council of State Governments, *Book of the States*, vol. 4 (Lexington, KY: Council of State Governments, 2004), 278, for earliest years (available at https://issuu.com/csg.publications/docs /bos2004), with more contemporary data being collected from the Office of Legislative Research. See Kristin Sullivan, *State Voter Competence Laws*, Office of Legislative Research, January 27, 2020, https://www.cga.ct.gov/2020/rpt/pdf/2020-R-0018.pdf.

6. Although Colorado was the first state to adopt this change, we also score Oregon "o," assuming that vote-by-mail precludes the need to go anywhere other than the mailbox to cast one's vote.

7. In 2004 the Florida legislature amended state law and introduced a standardized and mandatory process for in-person early voting in Florida elections. See Florida Senate Committee on Ethics and Elections, "The Effect of Early Voting on Voter Turnout in Florida Elections; 2010 Update," October 2010, https://www.flsenate.gov /UserContent/Session/2011/Publications/InterimReports/pdf/2011-118ee.pdf.

8. Wyoming's drop in rank over time is particularly ironic given that it was the first to grant women the right to vote, which is the justification for the state's nickname, "The Equality State."

9. We also score Oregon "o" on this new consideration because vote-by-mail precludes the need to vote absentee.

10. The group Fair Vote provided an in-depth discussion of how preregistration was intended to make Rhode Island a more inclusive state. Unfortunately, the story is no longer available on their website. However, see https://archive3.fairvote.org/ (last accessed July 20, 2022).

11. By 2016, two states, Montana and North Carolina, had joined New Hampshire.

12. See "Colorado Law Allowing 16-Year-Olds to Pre-Register to Vote May Become Model for U.S.," CBS News Colorado, February 22, 2019, https://denver .cbslocal.com/2019/02/22/colorado-register-vote-drivers-license/.

13. Despite Oregon's deadline, the state has largely removed the burden of reregistering when citizen's change addresses in the state. There is an automatic registration of state residents when they visit a state agency, such as a drivers licensing facility. Subsequently, the state sends the potential voter a postcard, which gives them an option to drop their registration. If the residents do nothing, they remain registered to vote.

14. Since 2012 New Hampshire has reduced the number of polling locations throughout the state. We assume a reduction in polling locations increases the cost of voting; this is especially the case in New Hampshire because the state requires citizens to vote in person on Election Day.

15. See "North Dakota Agrees to Court-Ordered Relief Easing Voter ID Laws for Native Americans on Reservations," Native Americans Rights Fund, April 24, 2020, https://www.narf.org/nd-voting-rights/.

16. See Associated Press, "Gov. Kemp: MLB 'Caved to Fear' over Voting Bill," You-Tube Video, accessed July 20, 2022, https://www.youtube.com/watch?v=ojEDectn-FM.

17. See "Data Details," Cost of Voting Index, accessed July 20, 2022, http://costofvotingindex.com/data.

CHAPTER 4: MINORITY POPULATIONS, REPUBLICANS, AND THE COVI

1. See "Democracy Index 2016," *Economist*, last accessed July 21, 2022, https://www.eiu.com/public/topical_report.aspx?campaignid=DemocracyIndex2016.

2. Ian Gray, "Jim Greer, Ex-Florida GOP Chair, Claims Republican Voting Laws Focused on Suppression, Racism," *Huffington Post*, November 26, 2012.

3. Stephen Stromberg, "Someone Is Trying to Rig the Election. It's Just Not Who Donald Trump Claims," *Washington Post*, August 2, 2016, https://www.washingtonpost.com/blogs/post-partisan/wp/2016/08/02/someone-is-trying-to-rig-the-election-its-just-not-who-donald-trump-claims/.

4. WTMJ-TV Milwaukee, April 5, 2016. Comment made during a television interview. Additionally, Circuit Court Judge Richard Posner stated in his 2013 book *Reflections on Judging* (Cambridge, MA: Harvard University Press), "Indiana voter photo ID law is a not-too-thinly-veiled attempt to discourage election-day turnout by certain folks believed to skew Democratic" (46).

5. As quoted in Scott Bauer, "Trump Adviser Caught on Tape: Voter Suppression Key to GOP Battleground Efforts," *Huffington Post*, December 20, 2019, https://www.huffpost.com/entry/trump-adviser-gop-voter-suppression-poll-watching-2020_n_5dfd46c5e4b0843d35fc2322.

6. Between 2013 and 2016, numerous courts concluded there was evidence of concerted efforts to disenfranchise subpopulations of voters, striking down or greatly weakening strict voter identification laws in Kansas, North Carolina, North Dakota, Texas, and Wisconsin.

7. We already note Wyoming drops down the COVI rankings precipitously during the period studied, and it is not necessarily the case that state legislators went out of

their way to make voting more difficult. Initially, the state simply did not keep pace with innovations such as online voter registration and preregistration of those under eighteen years of age. Then, the state adopted a series of new laws after the 2008 election cycle. In Kansas, after the 2008 election, the state legislature changed the law so that a citizen had to register to vote twenty-one days before Election Day instead of fifteen days at a time when other states were adopting EDR policies. Moreover, just before the 2012 presidential election, Kansas adopted a strict photo ID policy.

8. This modeling will correct for potential autocorrelation of the error term and allows us to combine 343 elections into a single regression run ((50 states * 7 elections = 350)—7 for Nebraska). Because there is so little variation within each state (i.e., states with low Black populations stayed that way throughout the period studied), we are most interested in a Between Effects model that will illuminate interstate, or between state, variation in COVI values.

9. We do not round these values in the models and use the precise election percentage gap between the two major-party candidates as our predictor variable. For instance, in the example of Utah in 2012, we use the value 46.693 to predict the cost of voting that year.

10. We also measure electoral competition using the closeness of the presidential contest in the corresponding election cycle (2012 competition used to predict 2012 cost of voting values) and do not obtain results that are substantively or statistically distinct from our reported measurement strategy.

11. In a seminal work, Daniel Elazar (1966) provided theoretical arguments for why states and their governing institutions take on different personalities; his work demonstrates that there is a tie between state cultures and immigration patterns, namely of the European immigrants who settle in different parts of the country.

12. We conducted a similar test to the one we use when considering Black populations using the percentage of the state Hispanic population, in interaction with the percentage of GOP state legislatures. The interaction term is always positive. However, the relationship is not statistically significant. The t-values were always at or near "1."

13. To provide a more complete test of this finding, we run a form of Generalized Least Square model for data arrayed over time and across sections (the forty-nine partisan state legislatures). In this instance, however, the change over time in the size of the Hispanic population suggests that a Fixed-Effects model is most appropriate. This will test intrastate change in the Hispanic population alongside the change in the percentage of Republican state legislators. Specifically, the test will tell us if an intrastate shift in these two considerations, working together, will predict higher COVI values.

14. In 2019 the state legislature was more than 74 percent Republican.

15. Now, because there is both between-state variation in the size of the Black population and intrastate growth in state Hispanic populations, over time, we use a random-effects Generalized Least Squares regression model.

16. Using a one-tailed statistical significance test, we can claim that we are 95 percent confident that when there is a larger state Black population or a growing state Hispanic population, more GOP members in a state legislature associate with higher COVI values.

17. When one considers the %GOP State Legislators and a one-tailed test.

18. Specifically, nine states required preclearance to change election laws in at least some parts of the state prior to the 2013 ruling. They were Alabama, Alaska, Arizona, Georgia, Louisiana, Mississippi, South Carolina, Texas, and Virginia. Particularly interesting is that these nine states correlated with a higher cost of voting throughout the period studied (Pearson-r = .31; $P < .01$; n = 350), which suggests the need for preclearance, or that some sort of scrutiny of state election laws was justified.

19. For an alphabetical listing of state COVI values, for the seven presidential cycles, see appendix F.

CHAPTER 5: THE COVI AND REPORTED VOTER TURNOUT

1. For data supplied by the US Department of Education from 2018, see National Center for Education Statistics, "Fast Facts: Dropout Rates," accessed July 21, 2022, https://nces.ed.gov/fastfacts/display.asp?id=16.

2. For a notable exception see Ritter and Tolbert (2021) who, using the COVI (Li, Pomante, and Schraufnagel 2018), find selective evidence of demobilization.

3. For example, if a survey respondent is Hispanic, we score that case "1" in the database and all non-Hispanic cases we score "0." Then, we create a new variable equal to the Hispanic variable multiplied by the COVI value for the state the respondent resides in. We do this for all cases in the dataset and include all three variables in the modeling, the Hispanic marker, the state COVI value, and the product of their interaction.

4. Previous research informs our expectations. Scholars find greater distrust of government among some minority group members (de la Garza 1987) and that participatory norms taught in the US education system might be less embraced by minorities, especially if they started their education in a different country (Cho 1999).

5. This phenomenon can be especially worrisome if those who report voting, but did not vote, are systematically different from those who are honest about their

electoral participation (Holbrook and Krosnick 2010; Ansolabehere and Hersh 2012). We can note that previous scholarship has uncovered evidence that Black Americans are more likely to over-report voting than other groups (Bernstein, Chadha, and Montjoy 2001; Silver, Anderson, and Abramson 1986).

6. In all this, we measure voter turnout dichotomously. We score a case "1" if the respondent says they voted and "0" if they claim they did not vote. Because our dependent variable is binary, we use a Logistical Regression (LOGIT) for model runs.

7. It is important to note that we weigh the CPS Survey data to account for the relative size of each state's voting eligible population (VEP). Voting experts strongly recommended this modeling strategy (Holbrook and Heidbreder 2010), because of concerns over the differences between the VEP and the voting age population (McDonald 2002).

8. Importantly, the use of 1.5 percent for the Black populations and 5 percent for the Hispanic population are not arbitrary or random markers. We chose these numbers because there is a natural break in each subpopulation around these values. Importantly, choosing values smaller than either 1.5 percent or five percent, respectfully, tells the same story or that when states have smaller population levels the COVI values do not associate with less voting, on average. When we move to larger values, the hypothesized relationship appears, as expected.

9. As we mentioned in the introduction, some states passed grandfather clauses during the Jim Crow era to give voting rights to illiterate whites (Mabry 1936, 309).

10. We know that young Asian Americans graduate from high school at a higher rate than the general population. See National Center for Education Statistics, "Fast Facts: Dropout Rates,". However, this trend had not translated into a higher high school graduation rate for the general Asian American population as of 2016.

11. We weight the data to obtain a sample that best reflect each state's voting eligible population. Michael McDonald, a leading expert on voter turnout at the University of Florida, recommends this procedure and we use his weighting instructions. In 2016, the eligible voting population was nearly 191 million. The precise estimated target population size used for the weighting exercise is 190,947,267.

12. We can note that Black turnout in 2008, as a percentage of population size, nearly equaled the turnout of whites for the first time in United States history, irrespective of income or education. See "Voter Turnout Rates: Voter Participation by Race and Ethnicity," Pew Research Center, accessed July 26, 2022, https://www.pewresearch.org/hispanic/2009/04/30/voter-turnout-rates/.

13. To illustrate, we subtract the percent Black, in 1990, from the percent Black in 2019, divide by the percent Black in 1990, and multiple by 100. Imagining a state that

moves from 10 percent to 12.5 percent Black ((12.5-10.0)/10.0) * 100 = 25, we obtain a 25 percent increase in the state Black population.

14. Our research findings differ from Ritter and Tolbert's (2021, 106) regarding Asian Americans. They do not find obvious demobilization. However, our results are resoundingly robust. Specifically, we find that Asian Americans living in states with higher COVI values will report voting less often after controlling for other considerations.

CHAPTER 6: MINORITY CANDIDATE ELECTORAL SUCCESS AND THE UNDERREPRESENTATION OF MINORITIES AND WOMEN

1. See Katherine Schaeffer, "Racial, Ethnic Diversity Increases Yet Again with the 117th Congress," Pew Research Center, January 28, 2021, https://www.pewresearch.org/fact-tank/2021/01/28/racial-ethnic-diversity-increases-yet-again-with-the-117th-congress/.

2. In 2021 there were seven at-large House districts. The country elected a single representative for the US House of Representatives from Alaska, Delaware, Montana, North Dakota, South Dakota, Vermont, and Wyoming.

3. The gerrymandering strategy of packing, whereby like-minded constituents from the opposing party are drawn into a single district to create a partisan advantage in neighboring districts, has increased minority candidate electoral success in some states. This is especially true when gerrymandering has led to majority-minority districts (Engstrom 2013, 197–198). This is an interesting phenomenon that deserves scrutiny; however, because our COVI values distinguish states, and not legislative districts within a state, we are unable to wrestle directly with the role gerrymandering is playing in increasing or decreasing minority representation.

4. Importantly, we do not get appreciably different results if we run the analysis with either raw values or ranks.

5. In the first model, Logistical Regression (LOGIT) is most appropriate because the dependent variable is dichotomous or only takes on two unique values, "0" and "1." With LOGIT, the "0s" and "1s" are converted to odds ratios and then using the principles of calculus, and the constant "*e*," are converted again to create an interval-level measure that can be effectively used in regression models (Mehmetoglu and Jakobsen 2017, 163–65). In the second and third model runs, we use Ordinary Least Squares Regression because the dependent variable values are election margins, which already reasonably approximate an interval-level measure.

6. We know that members of the two largest minority groups in the United

States, on average, have lower education and income than other citizens do (Kao and Thompson 2003). In this chapter, the question becomes: when members of either of the two largest minority groups have overcome the lower socioeconomic class obstacles and run for public office, how do they fare?

7. We label this "Democrat" and score all candidates who ran for statewide office representing the Democratic Party "1" and Republican Party candidates "0."

8. We use the previous national election cycle value for odd-year races for statewide office. For instance, when Donald McEachin, a Black Democrat, ran for attorney general in Virginia in 2001, we used the competition at the top of the ticket in the 2000 Virginia presidential election cycle.

9. We label this variable "Female" and score female candidates "1" and male candidates "0."

10. One might imagine that lower educational attainment, or income, on average, can explain the lack of minority office seekers we just uncovered. This possibility, alone, speaks volumes about the potential disadvantages minorities experience in trying to gain equal political footing in a majority white country.

11. Because we are conducting tests using a single year, it is most appropriate to use the raw COVI values versus COVI ranks, which standardized COVI values when running tests over time or multiple election cycles.

12. Many know that professional sports teams, such as the New England Patriots and Boston Celtics, with fans in Massachusetts underrepresent Black players on their rosters. See Erin Haines Whack, "Boston Sports Struggle with Perception Built on Racist Past," Associated Press, May 3, 2017, https://apnews.com/article/c1cd5883 01c640fc9cdd58cd813f876a.

13. In 2019 the state with the largest female population is Alabama, with 51.7 percent of residents being women. The state with the lowest percentage of females was Alaska with 47.9 percent. We use these state percentages when calculating the female gaps displayed in figure 6.4 and in the modeling that follows.

14. In chapter 4, we used legislative professionalism as a proxy or surrogate for state culture. We learned that higher Squire Index ranks, indicating a more traditional state culture, helps explain variation in state COVI ranks. Therefore, we include this variable in these models to ensure the COVI is not picking up some of the explanatory power of legislative professionalism.

15. When we test a simple bivariate relationship between Squire Index values and the three dependent variables, we learn there are more minorities and women in state legislators that have above-average professionalism scores. In the case of females, the bivariate relationship between the professionalism of the state legislature and representation approaches statistical significance, and in the case of Hispanics

in state legislatures, the relationship is statistically significant (Pearson R = .28 *P* < .05, two-tailed, n = 50).

CHAPTER 7: THE FIRST BIG LIE: ACCESSIBLE VOTING LEADS TO WIDESPREAD VOTER FRAUD

1. "Some Republicans Acknowledge Leveraging State Voter ID Laws for Political Gain," *New York Times*, September 20, 2016.

2. S.v. "fraud," Merriam-Webster, accessed April 5, 2022, https://www.merriam-webster.com/dictionary/fraud.

3. "Cheney Tells Truth about Election, but G.O.P. Is Tired of Hearing It," *New York Times*, May 5, 2021.

4. There are some gray areas, and one can make an argument that the categories are neither exhaustive nor mutually exclusive. Nonetheless, in the coding of fraud cases, we placed each case in one and only one of the six categories. If the case involved people registering to vote at an address where they no longer live and casting a fraudulent ballot in that electoral jurisdiction, we classify these cases as "voter fraud 1." Under the same scenario, if the person votes twice, by using the two different addresses, we code these cases as "voter fraud 3," indicating double voting, under the assumption that this is the more serious offense. In all, even though there is some imprecision, we hold the categories provide a useful heuristic to understand fraud better and makes reasonably clear the important distinction between voter fraud and election fraud.

5. There are several instances of vote buying chronicled by the Heritage Foundation on their website: "Election Fraud Cases," Heritage Foundation, accessed March 24, 2022, https://www.heritage.org/voterfraud/search.

6. The benefits of voting fraudulently are minimal because the likelihood that one or two fraudulent votes will determine an election outcome is infinitesimal. However, this probability does increase in local elections, primary elections, and off-cycle elections when voter turnout is much lower. Now the "P" or probability that your vote will affect the outcome goes up. In the data culled from the Heritage Foundation website, one notices straightaway that known cases of election and voter fraud occur mainly in low information and low turnout elections. Most commonly, the election the fraudster is trying to influence is local (Heritage Foundation, "Election Fraud Cases").

7. A sampling of fraud cases presented on the Heritage Foundation website demonstrates that election fraud often leads to jail time: Heritage Foundation, "Election Fraud Cases."

8. The Heritage Foundation reports they have 1,349 proven instances of fraud, as of March 2022. The discrepancy occurs because some of their entries have multiple defendants. In other instances, the group creates an entry for each individual, even when the people are involved in the same corrupt scheme. Still more, the discrepancy occurs because the group lists cases from the US territories and Washington, DC, and these are not included in this analysis (Heritage Foundation, "Election Fraud Cases").

9. For a compelling story, see the video produced by the National Public Radio: Greg Myre and Shannon Bond, "Russia Doesn't Have to Make Fake News: The Biggest Election Threat Is Closer to Home," NPR, September 29, 2020, https://www.npr.org/2020/09/29/917725209/russia-doesn-t-have-to-make-fake-news-biggest-election-threat-is-closer-to-home.

10. One of the first to uncover convincing evidence that nonvoters split their party allegiance roughly the same as voters was James DeNardo (1980). In follow-up work, Jack Citrin, Eric Schickler, and John Sides (2003) determine the partisan advantage gained when nonvoters vote is sensitive to the election cycle and the state the nonvoters reside in.

11. Academics have used a variety of methods, many quite sophisticated, to try to measure the frequency of voter fraud (Fukumoto and Horiuchi 2011; Christensen and Schultz 2014; Cottrell, Herron, and Westwood 2018), election fraud (Pericchi and Torres 2011; Beber and Scacco 2012; Montgomery, Olivella, Potter, and Crisp 2015), or both (Hood III, and Gillespie 2012). Relevantly, these scholars, without exception, use of the terms "voter fraud" and "election fraud" interchangeably. Yet, it is quite easy to distinguish the type of fraud each set of authors is trying to quantify. We hold that disentangling the two fraud categories is imperative, if we wish to move forward in the direction toward remediation of the more egregious election fraud, something one can likely accomplish without adopting policies that increase the cost of voting for individuals.

12. We fully appreciate that these tests of known fraud paint an incomplete picture; however, it makes sense to check if there is anything going on in this regard that could justify great concern. If there is, and restrictive electoral institutional arrangements associate with less fraud, additional voting restrictions may be justified as a means of combatting fraud.

13. Moreover, using average COVI ranks and total incidents of fraud over a considerable period can lead to faulty inferences if the average, or total values, are masking interesting year-specific relationships. Qualitative single-state testing can help in this regard.

14. In auxiliary analyses, not reported here, we used other COVI values, repre-

senting other presidential election years, with no fundamental change in the results reported in table 7.5.

15. For an excellent summary of the three cultures, see the description by Professor John Rausch from West Texas A&M University: John Rausch, "Explaining Policy Differences Using Political Culture, accessed March 31, 2022, https://www.wtamu .edu/~jrausch/polcul.html.

16. Office of the Minnesota Secretary of State, "Historical Voter Turnout Statistics," accessed July 28, 2022, https://www.sos.state.mn.us/election-administration -campaigns/data-maps/historical-voter-turnout-statistics/.

17. Less than half of the 112 ineligible voters found in the recounts were from the 2008 election.

18. For an excellent description of the North Carolina case, see the story by the Brookings Institute: Molly E. Reynolds, "Understanding the Election Scandal in North Carolina's 9th District," Brookings Institution, December 7, 2018, https:// www.brookings.edu/blog/fixgov/2018/12/07/understanding-the-election-scandal -in-north-carolinas-9th-district/.

CHAPTER 8: THE SECOND BIG LIE: MORE CONVENIENT VOTING HELPS DEMOCRATS

1. One might imagine that the adoption of vote-by-mail energized conservatives to show up in larger numbers at the polls on Election Day. If this is the case, we applaud the increase in voter turnout.

2. The state shortens early and Election Day voting. See Stephen Gruber-Miller, "Gov. Kim Reynolds Signs Law Shortening Iowa's Early and Election Day Voting," *Des Moines Register*, March 8, 2021, https://www.desmoinesregister.com/story /news/politics/2021/03/08/iowa-governor-kim-reynolds-signs-law-shortening -early-voting-closing-polls-earlier-election-day/6869317002.

3. One must imagine that voter turnout increased much less in New Hampshire because the state did nothing to make voting easier during the global pandemic.

CONCLUSION

1. The Pew Research Center estimates that 65.2 percent of eligible Black voters showed up at the polls in 2008: "Dissecting the 2008 Electorate: Most Diverse in U.S. History," April 30, 2009, https://www.pewresearch.org/hispanic/2009/04/30 /dissecting-the-2008-electorate-most-diverse-in-us-history/.

2. Alana Wise, "Bid Pledged Historic Cabinet Diversity. Here's How His Nominees

Stack Up," NPR, February 5, 2021, https://www.npr.org/sections/president-biden
-takes-office/2021/02/05/963837953/biden-pledged-historic-cabinet-diversity-heres
-how-his-nominees-stack-up.

3. Richard L. Zweigenhaft, "Diversity in Presidential Cabinets: From the Least
Diverse in 30 Years to the Most Diverse Ever," 2021, https://whorulesamerica.ucsc
.edu/power/diversity_in_presidential_cabinets.html; last accessed July 7, 2022.

4. See the Brennan Center for Justice, "State Voting Bills Tracker 2021," accessed March 5, 2021, https://www.brennancenter.org/our-work/research-reports
/state-voting-bills-tracker-2021. See also States United Democracy Center, "New
Report Reveals State Legislative Election Subversion Trend Accelerating and Evolv-
ing," accessed July 7, 2022, https://statesuniteddemocracy.org/2022/05/19/dcitm
-2022update.

5. Zach Montellaro, "State Republicans Push New Voting Restrictions after
Trump's Loss," *Politico*, January 24, 2021, https://www.politico.com/news/2021/01
/24/republicans-voter-id-laws-461707.

6. See https://constitutioncenter.org/the-constitution/supreme-court-case-li
brary/shelby-county-v-holder; last accessed May 17, 2023.

APPENDICES

1. See Myrna Pérez, *Voter Purges*, Brennan Center for Justice, September 30,
2008, https://www.brennancenter.org/publication/voter-purges.

2. In the end, those who study the effect of polling location convenience have
opted for analysis of a single city or a single state. If one were interested in homing in
on this variable alone, an across state comparison might be possible; however, in the
context of the construction of a broader index the consideration of polling location
convenience is knotty.

3. As noted throughout the manuscript, we always code state policies so that
larger numbers indicate a greater cost in time, energy, planning, etc. For instance, if
a state does not have in-person absentee voting, the state receives a score of "1" on
this consideration, and states with the option receive a score of "0." In the case of poll
hours and the number of early voting days, we need to reverse the values so that a
lower number indicates a greater cost. Specifically, we subtract each state's value from
the maximum state value.

4. W. John Braun was professor in the Department of Statistical and Actuarial
Sciences at Western Ontario University when he provided his notes on Principal
Component Analysis via the World Wide Web. Unfortunately, his analysis no longer appears to be accessible (http://www.stats.uwo.ca/faculty/braun/ss3850/notes
/sas10.pdf, last accessed May 7, 2018).

5. Letting the data speak for itself and using the "proportion of variance explained" by each component, we employ the following weight for each version of the Cost of Voting Index:

Table B1.

	1st component	2nd component	3rd component	4th component	Total explained
1996	0.3454	0.2567	0.1368		0.739
2000	0.3251	0.2223	0.178		0.7254
2004	0.2993	0.2498	0.1999		0.7491
2008	0.309	0.2346	0.1942		0.7378
2012	0.2838	0.1943	0.1582	0.1346	0.7709
2016	0.3051	0.1917	0.1624	0.1375	0.7967
2020	0.3536	0.192	0.1229	0.1006	0.7691
2020c	0.3609	0.194	0.1206	0.0877	0.7632

We normalize component weights by the total variance explained so that total weights for each year sum up to "1." Once the included components are weighted, we simply add the component values. Most importantly, when we use other weighting and aggregation methods as a baseline index, subsequent sensitivity analyses do not produce any evidence that other schema are more appropriate than the COVI values reported in this manuscript.

6. For a discussion of the value of a nonlinear extension of Principal Component Analysis see Jolliffe (2002, 373–81).

7. See Pew, Election Performance Index, August 9, 2016, http://www.pewtrusts.org /en/multimedia/data-visualizations/2014/elections-performance-index#indicator. The MIT Election Data Science Lab produces the 2016 Election Performance Index.

8. Considering this type of correspondence analysis, some people refer to it as reciprocal averaging. The method extracts an underlining dimension from a series of nominal variables, which in our case represent different election laws in specific issue areas.

9. In particular, the two issue areas we capture with ordered scales might be problematic for the correspondence analysis, which looks for the relationship between nominal variables while simultaneously describing the relationships between the categories for each variable. Relevantly, there is no sound theoretical basis for the correspondence scores produced by the procedure. We hold both pre-registration and voter identification laws are more sensibly thought of as ordinal considerations where states make voting progressively more difficult relative to other states.

References

Introduction

Alvarez, R. Michael, Thad E. Hall, and Susan D. Hyde. 2008. *Election Fraud: Detecting and Deterring Electoral Manipulation*. Brookings Institution Press.

Arbatli, Ekim, and Dina Rosenberg. 2021. "United We Stand, Divided We Rule: How Political Polarization Erodes Democracy." *Democratization* 28 (2): 285–307.

Behrens, Angela, Christopher Uggen, and Jeff Manza. 2003. "Ballot Manipulation and the 'Menace of Negro Domination.' Racial Threat and Felon Disenfranchisement in the United States." *American Journal of Sociology* 109 (3): 559–605.

Bentele, Keith G., and Erin E. O'Brien. 2013. "Jim Crow 2.0? Why States Consider and Adopt Restrictive Voter Access Policies." *Perspectives on Politics* 11 (4): 1088–1116.

Bowler, Shaun, and Todd Donovan. 2002. "Democracy, Institutions and Attitudes about Citizen Influence on Government." *British Journal of Political Science* 32 (2): 371–390.

Chamberline, Adam. 2012. "A Time-Series Analysis of External Efficacy." *Public Opinion Quarterly* 76 (1): 117–130.

Dahl, Robert A. 1971. *Polyarchy: Participation and Opposition*. New Haven, CT: Yale University Press.

———. 2005. "What Political Institutions Does Large-Scale Democracy Require?" *Political Science Quarterly* 120 (2): 187–197.

Dollar, Cindy Brooks. 2014. "Racial Threat Theory: Assessing the Evidence, Requesting Redesign." *Journal of Criminology* 47 (1): 1–7.

Eitle, David, Stewart J. D'Alessio, and Lisa Stolzenberg. 2002. "Racial Threat and Social Control: A Test of the Political, Economic, and Threat of Black Crime Hypotheses." *Social Forces* 81 (2): 557–576.

Ekman, Joakim. 2009. "Political Participation and Regime Stability: A Framework for Analyzing Hybrid Regimes." *International Political Science Review/Revue Internationale de Science Politique* 30 (1): 7–31.

Fails, Mathew D., and Heather Nicole Pierce. 2010. "Changing Mass Attitudes and Democratic Deepening." *Political Research Quarterly* 63 (1): 174–187.

Giles, Michael W., and Kaenan Hertz. 1994. "Racial Threat and Partisan Identification." *American Political Science Review* 88 (2): 317–326.

Goldman, Seth K. 2017. "Explaining White Opposition to Black Political Leadership: The Role of Fear of Racial Favoritism." *Political Psychology* 38 (5): 721–739.

Hare, Christopher and Keith T. Poole. 2014. "The Polarization of Contemporary American Politics." *Polity* 46 (3): 411–429.

Henry, Laura A. 2012. "Complaint-Making as Political Participation in Contemporary Russia." *Communist and Post-Communist Studies* 45 (3/4): 243–254.

Lowenthal, Richard. 1976. "Social Transformation and Democratic Legitimacy." *Social Research* 43 (2): 246–275.

Powell, G. Bingham. 1982. *Contemporary Democracies: Participation, Stability and Violence*. Cambridge, MA: Harvard University Press.

Riker, William H. 1965. *Democracy in the United States*. 2nd ed. New York: Macmillan. Stillman, Peter G. 1974. "The Concept of Legitimacy." *Polity* 7 (1): 32–56.

Whitt, Sam, Alixandra B. Yanus, Brian McDonald, John Graeber, Mark Setzler, Gordon Ballingud and Martin Kifer. 2021. "Tribalism in American: Behavior Experiments on Affective Polarization in the Trump Era." *Journal of Experimental Political Science* 8: 247–259.

CHAPTER 1

Adamson, Christopher R. 1983. "Punishment after Slavery: Southern State Penal Systems, 1865–1890." *Social Problems* 30 (5): 555–569.

Bass, Sandra. 2001. "Policing Space, Policing Race: Social Control Imperatives and Police Discretionary Decisions." *Social Justice* 28 (1): 156–176.

Bentele, Keith G., and Erin E. O'Brien. 2013. "Jim Crow 2.0? Why States Consider and Adopt Restrictive Voter Access Policies." *Perspectives on Politics* 11 (4): 1088–1116.

Brooks, F. Erik, and Glenn L. Starks. 2019. *African Americans and the Presidents: Politics and Policies from Washington to Trump*. Santa Barbara, CA: Greenwood.

Brown, Robert D., and Justin Wedeking. 2006. "People Who Have Their Tickets but Do Not Use Them: 'Motor Voter,' Registration and Turnout Revisited." *American Politics Research* 34 (4): 479–504.

Browne, Jaron. 2007. "Rooted in Slavery: Prison Labor Exploitation." *Race, Poverty, & the Environment* 14 (1): 42–44.

Crocker, Royce. 2013. *The National Voter Registration Act of 1993: History, Implementation, and Effects*. Washington, DC: Congressional Research Service.

Enos, Ryan D. 2016. "What the Demolition of Public Housing Teaches Us about the Impact of Racial Threat on Political Behavior." *American Journal of Political Science* 60 (1): 123–142.

Feldman, Glenn. 2004. *The Disfranchisement Myth: Poor Whites and Suffrage Restrictions in Alabama*. Athens: University of Georgia Press.

Gilmore, Kim. 2000. "Slavery and Prison—Understanding the Connections." *Social Justices* 27 (3): 195–205.

King, Ryan D., and Darren Wheelock. 2007. "Group Threat and Social Control: Race, Perspectives of Minorities and the Desire to Punish." *Social Forces* 85 (3): 1255–1280.

Levitt, Justin. 2014. "A Comprehensive Investigation of Voter Impersonations Finds 31 Credible Incidents Out of One Billion Ballots Cast, *Washington Post* (Wonkblog), August 6, 2014, https://www.washingtonpost.com/news/wonk/wp /2014/08/06/a-comprehensive-investigation-of-voter-impersonation-finds-31 -credible-incidents-out-of-one-billion-ballots-cast/?utm_term=.9a71d5208464.

Lieske, Joel. 2012. "American State Cultures: Testing a New Measure and Theory." *Publius: The Journal of Federalism* 42 (1): 108–133.

Logan, Rayford W. 1997. *The Betrayal of the Negro: From Rutherford B. Hayes to Woodrow Wilson*. New York: Da Capo Press.

Lopez, Tomas. 2014. "Shelby County: One Year Later." Brennan Center for Justice. https://www.brennancenter.org/sites/default/files/analysis/Shelby_County _One_Year_Later.pdf.

Maluk, Holly, Myrna Pérez, and Lucy Zhou. *Voter Registration in a Digital Age: 2015 Update*. Brennan Center for Justice, 2015. https://www.brennancenter.org/sites /default/files/publications/Voter_Registration_Digital_Age_2015.pdf.

Martinez, Michael D., and David Hill. "Did Motor Voter Work?" *American Politics Quarterly* 27 (3): 1999: 296–315.

Minnite, Lorraine C. 2010. *The Myth of Voter Fraud*. Ithaca, NY: Cornell University Press.

Prince, K. Stephen. 2012. "Legitimacy and Interventionism: Northern Republicans, the 'Terrible Carpetbagger,' and the Retreat from Reconstruction." *Journal of the Civil War* 2 (4): 538–563.

Shepherd, Michael E., Adriane Fresh, Nick Eubank, and Joshua D. Clinton. 2021. "The Politics of Locating Polling Places: Race and Partisanship in North Carolina Election Administration, 2008–2016." *Election Law Journal: Rules, Politics, and Policy* 20 (2): 155–177.

Smith, Earl, and Angela J. Hattery. 2008. "Incarceration: A Tool for Racial Segregation and Labor Exploitation." *Race, Gender & Class* 15 (1/2): 79–97.

Springer, Melanie J. 2012. "State Electoral Institutions and Voter Turnout in Presidential Elections, 1920–2000." *State Politics & Policy Quarterly* 12 (3): 252–283.

Worger, William H. 2004. "Convict Labour, Industrialists and the State in the U.S. South and South Africa, 1870–1930." *Journal of Southern African Studies* 30 (1): 63–86.

CHAPTER 2

Alexander, Michelle. 2020. *The New Jim Crow: Mass Incarceration in the Age of Colorblindness*. New York: New Press.

Alvarez, R. Michael, Stephen Ansolabehere, and Catherine W. Wilson. 2002. "Election Day Voter Registration in the United States: How One-Step Voting Can Change the Composition of the American Electorate." Working Paper, Caltech/MIT Voting Technology Project.

Alvarez, R. Michael, Thad E. Hall, Ines Levin, and Charles Stewart III. 2011. "Voter Opinions about Election Reform: Do They Support Making Voting More Convenient?" *Election Law Journal* 10 (2): 73–87.

Andolina, Molly W., Krista Jenkins, Cliff Zukin, and Scott Keeter. 2003. "Habits from Home, Lessons from School: Influence on Youth Civic Engagement." *P.S.: Political Science & Politics* 36 (2): 275–280.

Ansolabehere, Stephen, and David M. Konisky. 2004. "The Introduction of Voter Registration and its Effect on Turnout." Working Paper, Caltech/MIT Voting Technology Project.

Appelbaum, Paul S. 2000. "Law & Psychiatry: 'I Vote. I Count': Mental Disability and the Right to Vote." *Psychiatric Services* 51 (7): 849–863.

Appelbaum, Paul S., Richard J. Bonnie, and Jason H. Karlawish. 2005. "The Capacity to Vote of Persons with Alzheimer's Disease." *American Journal of Psychiatry* 162 (11): 2094–2100.

Banaian, King, Richard C.K. Burdekin, and Thomas D. Willett. 1998. "Reconsidering the Principal Components of Central Bank Independence: The More the Merrier?" *Public Choice* 97 (1/2): 1–12.

Bazelon Center for Mental Health Law. 2016. "It's Your Right: A Guide to Voting Rights of People with Mental Disabilities." http://www.bazelon.org/wp-content/uploads/2017/01/voting-rights-guide-2016.pdf.

Behrens, Angela, Christopher Uggen, and Jeff Manza. 2003. "Ballot Manipulation and the 'Menace of Negro Domination': Racial Threat and Felon Disenfranchisement in the United States." *American Journal of Sociology* 109 (3): 559–605.

Biggers, Daniel R., and Michael J. Hanmer. 2015. "Who Makes Voting Convenient? Explaining the Adoption of Early and No-Excuse Absentee Voting in the American States." *Politics and Policy Quarterly* 15 (2): 192–210.

Bradfield, Caitlyn, and Paul Johnson. 2017. "The Effect of Making Election Day a Holiday: An Original Survey and a Case Study of French Presidential Elections Applied to the U.S. Voting System." *Sigma: Journal of Political and International Studies* 34 (1): 19–34.

Brians, Craig Leonard, and Bernard Grofman. 2001. "Election Day Registration's Effect on U.S. Voter Turnout." *Social Science Quarterly* 82 (1): 170–183.

Carmines, Edward G., and James A. Stimson. 1982. "Racial Issues and the Structure of Mass Belief Systems." *Journal of Politics* 44 (1): 2–20.

Cherry, Ceridwen. 2011. "Increasing Youth Participation: The Case for a National Voter Pre-registration Law." *University of Michigan Journal of Law Reform* 45 (1): 481–515.

Cunningham, Dayna L. 1991. "Who Are to Be the Electors? A Reflection on the History of Voter Registration in the United States." *Yale Law and Policy Review* 9 (1): 370–404.

Delli, Michael X., and Scott Keeter. 1991. "Stability and Change in the U.S. Public's Knowledge of Politics." *Public Opinion Quarterly* 55 (4): 583–612.

Eisner, Jane. 2004. *Taking Back the Vote: Getting American Youth Involved in Our Democracy.* Boston: Beacon Press.

Erikson, Robert S. 1981. "Why Do People Vote? Because They Are Registered." *American Politics Quarterly* 9 (3): 259–276.

Farber, Henry S. 2009. *Increasing Voter Turnout: Is Democracy Day the Answer?* Princeton, NJ: Princeton University Press.

Fortier, John C. 2006. *Absentee and Early Voting: Trends, Promises, and Perils.* Washington DC: AEI Press.

Fournier, Patrick, Richard Nadeau, Andre Blais, Elisabeth Gidengil, and Niel Nevitte. 2004. "Time-of-Voting Decision and Susceptibility to Campaign Effects." *Electoral Studies* 23 (4): 661–681.

Fillmer, Elliot. 2021. *Tuesday's Gone: America's Early Voting Revolution.* New York: Lexington Books.

Galston, William A. 2004. "Civic Education and Political Participation." *P.S.: Political Science & Politics* 37 (2): 263–266.

Garmann, Sebastian. 2017. "The Effect of a Reduction in the Opening Hours of Polling Stations on Turnout." *Public Choice* 17 (1): 99–117.

Giammo, Joseph D., and Brian J. Brox. 2010. "Reducing the Costs of Participation." *Political Research Quarterly* 63 (2): 295–303.

Gimpel, James G., Joshua J. Dyck, and Daron R. Shaw. 2004. "Registrants, Voters, and Turnout Variability across Neighborhoods." *Political Behavior* 26 (4): 343–375.

Gopoian, J. David, and Sissie Hadjiharalambous. 1994. "Late-Deciding Voters in Presidential Elections." *Political Behavior* 16 (1): 55–78.

Gradwohl, John M. 1951. "Constitutional Law-Elections-Statues Allowing Employees Time Off to Vote with Pay." *Nebraska Law Review* 31:97.

Griffin, Rob, Paul Gronke, Tova Wang, and Liz Kennedy. 2017. "Who Votes with

Automatic Voter Registration? Impact Analysis of Oregon's First in the Nation Program." Center for American Progress.

Grimmer, Justin, et al. 2018. "Obstacles to Estimating Voter ID Laws' Effect on Turnout." *Journal of Politics* 80, no. 3: 1045–1051.

Gronke, Paul, Eva Galanes-Rosenbaum, and Peter A. Miller. 2007. "Early Voting and Turnout." *P.S.: Political Science and Politics* 40 (4): 639–645.

Hajnal, Zoltan, John Kuk, and Nazita Lajevardi. 2018. "We All Agree: Strict Voter ID Laws Disproportionately Burden Minorities." *Journal of Politics* 80 (3): 1052–1059.

Hamer, Helen P., and Mary Finlayson. 2015. "The Rights and Responsibilities of Citizenship for Service Users: Some Terms and Conditions Apply." *Journal of Psychiatric and Mental Health Nursing* 22 (9): 698–705.

Herron, Michael C., and Daniel A. Smith. 2014. "Race, Party, and the Consequences of Restricting Early Voting in Florida in the 2012 General Election." *Political Research Quarterly* 67 (3): 646–665.

Hicks, William D., Seth C. McKee, and Daniel A. Smith. 2016. "A Bipartisan Election Reform? Explaining Support for Online Voter Registration in the American States." *American Politics Research* 44 (6): 1008–1036.

Highton, Benjamin. 1997. "Easy Registration and Voter Turnout." *Journal of Politics* 59 (2): 565–575.

———. 2000. "Residential Mobility, Community Mobility, and Electoral Participation." *Political Behavior* 22 (2): 109–120.

———. 2004. "Voter Registration and Turnout in the United States." *Perspectives on Politics* 2 (3): 507–515.

Holbein, John B., and D. Sunshine Hillygus. 2016. "Making Young Voters: The Impact of Preregistration on Youth Turnout." *American Journal of Political Science* 60 (2): 364–382.

Jakulin, Aleks, Wray Buntine, Timothy M. LaPira, and Holly Brasher. 2009. "Analyzing the U.S. Senate in 2003: Similarities, Clusters, and Blocs." *Political Analysis* 17 (3): 291–310.

Jolliffe, Ian. 2002. *Principal Component Analysis*. 2nd ed. New York: Springer. Juelich, Courtney L., and Joseph A. Coll. 2020. "Rock the Vote or Block the Vote? How the Cost of Voting Affects the Voting Behavior of American Youth: Part of Special Symposium on Election Sciences." *American Politics Research* 48 (6): 719–724.

Karp, Jeffrey A., and Susan A. Banducci. 2000. "Going Postal: How All-Mail Elections Influence Turnout." *Political Behavior* 22 (3): 223–239.

Kasdan, Diana. 2012. "State Restrictions on Voter Registration Drives." Brennan Center for Justice.

Knack, Stephen. 1995. "Does "Motor Voter" Work? Evidence from State-Level Data." *Journal of Politics* 57 (3): 796–811.

————. 2001. "Election-Day Registration: The Second Wave." *American Politics Quarterly* 29 (1): 65–78.

Knack, Stephen, and James White. 2000. "Election-Day Registration and Turnout Inequality." *Political Behavior* 22 (1): 29–44.

Kuk, John, Zoltan Hajnal, and Nazita Lajevardi. 2022. "A Disproportionate Burden: Strict Voter Identification Laws and Minority Turnout." *Politics, Groups, and Identities* 10 (1): 126–134.

Leighley, Jan E., and Jonathan Nagler. 2014. *Who Votes Now? Demographics, Issues, Inequality, and Turnout in the United States*. Princeton, NJ: Princeton University Press.

Mann, Christopher B., Paul Gronke, and Natalie Adona. 2020. "Framing Automatic Voter Registration: Partisanship and Public Understanding of Automatic Voter Registration." *American Politics Research* 48 (6): 1–7.

Manza, Jeff, and Christopher Uggen. 2004. "Punishment and Democracy: Disenfranchisement of Nonincarcerated Felons in the United States." *Perspectives on Politics* 2 (3): 491–505.

McDonald, Michael P. 2009. *Voter Pre-registration Programs*. Fairfax, VA: George Mason University.

McDonald, Michael P., and Matthew Thornburg. 2010. "Registering the Youth through Voter Pre-registration." *New York University Journal of Legislation and Public Policy* 13 (1): 551–572.

Mitchell, Glenn E., and Christopher Wlezien. 1995. "The Impact of Legal Constraints on Voter Registration, Turnout, and the Composition of the American Electorate." *Political Behavior* 17 (2): 179–202.

Nickerson, David W. 2015. "Do Voter Registration Drives Increase Participation? For Whom and When?" *Journal of Politics* 77 (1): 88–101.

Niemi, Richard G., and Jonathan D. Klingler. 2012. "The Development of Political Attitudes and Behavior among Young Adults." *Australian Journal of Political Science* 47 (1): 31–54.

Okwerekwu, Jennifer A., James B. McKenzie, Katherine A. Yates, Renee M. Sorrentino, and Susan Hatters Friedman. 2018. "Voting by People with Mental Illness." *Journal of the American Academy of Psychiatry and the Law* 46 (4): 513–520.

Oliver, J. Eric. 1996. "The Effects of Eligibility Restrictions and Party Activity on Absentee Voting and Overall Turnout." *American Journal of Political Science* 40 (2): 498–513.

Patterson, Thomas E. 2002. *The Vanishing Voter: Public Involvement in an Age of Uncertainty*. Perez, Vanessa M. 2015. "Americans with Photo ID: A Breakdown of Demographic Characteristics." Project Vote, February 2015. https://www.projectvote.org/wp-content/uploads/2015/06/AMERICANS-WITH-PHOTO-ID-Research-Memo-February-2015.pdf.

Pew Charitable Trust. 2014. "Understanding Online Voter Registration." https://www.pewtrusts.org/~/media/Assets/2014/01/28/Understanding_Online_Voter_Registration.pdf?ls=en.

Piven, Frances Fox, and Richard A. Cloward. 1989. "Government Statistics and Conflicting Explanations of Nonvoting." *P.S.: Political Science and Politics* 22 (3): 578–589.

Pomante II, Michael J., and Scot Schraufnagel. 2015. "Candidate Age and Youth Voter Turnout." *American Politics Research* 43 (3): 479–503.

Powell, G. Bingham. 1986. "American Voter Turnout in Comparative Perspective." *American Political Science Review* 80 (1): 17–43.

Rankin, David. 2013. *U.S. Politics and Generation Y: Engaging the Millennials.* New York: Lynn Rienner.

Rhine, Staci L. 1996. "An Analysis of the Impact of Registration Factors on Turnout in 1992." *Political Behavior* 18 (2): 171–185.

Rocha, Rene R., and Tetsuya Matsubayashi. 2014. "The Politics of Race and Voter ID Laws in the States: The Return of Jim Crow?" *Political Research Quarterly* 67 (3): 666–679.

Rosenstone, Steven, and John M. Hansen. 1993. "Mobilization, Participation, and Democracy in America: A Retrospective and Postscript." *Party Politics* 22 (2): 158–164.

Rosenstone, Steven J., and Raymond E. Wolfinger. 1978. "The Effect of Registration Laws on Voter Turnout." *American Political Science Review* 72 (1): 22–45.

Schraufnagel, Scot, Michael J. Pomante II, and Quan Li. 2022. "Cost of Voting in the American States: 2022." *Election Law Journal: Rules, Politics, and Policy* 21 (3): 220–228.

Sobel, Richard, and Robert Ellis Smith. 2009. "Voter-ID Laws Discourage Participation among Minorities, and Trigger a Constitutional Remedy in Lost Representation." *P.S.: Political Science and Politics* 42 (1): 107–110.

Springer, Melanie J. 2012. "State Electoral Institutions and Voter Turnout in Presidential Elections, 1920–2000." *State Politics & Policy Quarterly* 12 (3): 252–83.

Squire, Peverill, Raymond E. Wolfinger, and David Glass. 1987. "Residential Mobility and Voter Turnout." *American Political Science Review* 81 (1): 45–65.

Stevens, Daniel. 2006. "Mobilization, Demobilization and the Economy in American Elections." *British Journal of Political Science* 37 (1): 165–186.

Uggen, Christopher, Ryan Larson, Sarah Shannon, and Arleth Pulido-Nava. 2020. "Locked Out: Estimates of People Denied Voting Rights Due to a Felony Conviction. The Sentencing Project. https://www.sentencingproject.org/publications/locked-out-2020-estimates-of-people-denied-voting-rights-due-to-a-felony-conviction/.

Ulbig, Stacy G., and Tamara Waggener. 2011. "Getting Registered and Getting to the Polls: The Impact of Voter Registration Strategy and Information Provision on Turnout of College Students." *P.S.: Political Science & Politics* 44 (3): 544–551.

Valentino, Nicholas A., and Fabian G. Neuner. 2017. "Why the Sky Didn't Fall: Mobilizing Anger in Reaction to Voter ID Laws." *Political Psychology* 38 (2): 331–350.

Vedlitz, Arnold. 1985. "Voter Registration Drives and Black Voting in the South." *Journal of Politics* 47 (2): 643–651.

Vonnahme, Greg. 2011. "Registration Deadlines and Turnout in Context." *Political Behavior* 34 (4): 765–779.

Walker, Hannah. L., Michael C. Herron, & Daniel A. Smith. (2019). "Early Voting Changes and Voter Turnout: North Carolina in the 2016 General Election." *Political Behavior* 41 (4): 841–869.

Wattenberg, Martin. 2012. *Is Voting for Young People?* 3rd edition. New York: Pearson Longman.

Weiser, W. R. 2016. "Automatic Voter Registration Boosts Political Participation." *Stanford Social Innovation Review.* https://ssir.org/articles/entry/automatic_voter_registration_boosts_political_participation.

Wolfinger, Raymond E., and Steven J. Rosenstone. 1980. *Who Votes?* New Haven, CT: Yale University Press.

Wolfinger, Raymond E., Ben Highton, and Megan Mullin. 2005. "How Postregistration Laws Affect the Turnout of Citizens Registered to Vote." *State Politics & Policy Quarterly* 5 (1): 1–23.

Wolfinger, Raymond E., David P. Glass, and Peverill Squire. 1990. "Predictors of Electoral Turnout: An International Comparison." *Policy Studies Review* 9:551–571.

Yu, Jinhai. 2019. "Does State Online Voter Registration Increase Voter Turnout?" *Social Science Quarterly* 100 (3): 620–634.

CHAPTER 3

Ansolabehere, Stephen, and David M. Konisky. 2006. "The Introduction of Voter Registration and Its Effect on Turnout." *Political Analysis* 14: 83–100.

Bentele, Keith G., and Erin E. O'Brien. 2013. "Jim Crow 2.0? Why States Consider and Adopt Restrictive Voter Access Policies." *Perspectives on Politics* 11 (4): 1088–1116.

Biggers, Daniel R., and Michael J. Hanmer. 2015. "Who Makes Voting Convenient? Explaining the Adoption of Early and No-Excuse Absentee Voting in the American States." *Politics and Policy Quarterly* 15 (2): 192–210.

Bowler, Shaun, and Todd Donovan. 2002. "Democracy, Institutions and Attitudes about Citizen Influence on Government." *British Journal of Political Science* 32 (2): 371–390.

Burden, Barry C., and Brian J. Gaines. 2015. "Presidential Commission on Election Administration: Absentee and Early Voting: Weighing the Costs of Convenience." *Election Law Journal* 14 (1): 32–37.

Chamberlain, Alyssa Whitby. 2012. "Offender Rehabilitation: Examining Changes in Inmate Treatment Characteristics, Program Participation, and Institutional Behavior." *Justice Quarterly* 29 (2): 183–228.

Downs, Anthony. 1957. *An Economic Theory of Democracy*. New York: Harper and Row. Ekman, Joakim. 2009. "Political Participation and Regime Stability: A Framework for Analyzing Hybrid Regimes." *International Political Science Review/Revue Internationale de Science Politique* 30 (1): 7–31.

Gerken, Heather K. 2013. "Make it Easy: The Case for Automatic Registration." *Democracy Journal* 28 (1).

Henry, Laura A. 2012. "Complaint-Making as Political Participation in Contemporary Russia." *Communist and Post-Communist Studies* 45 (3/4): 243–254.

Hershey, Marjorie Randon. 2009. "What We Know about Voter-ID Laws, Registration, and Turnout." *PS: Political Science & Politics* 42 (1): 87–91.

Jenkins, J. Craig, Kevin T. Leicht, and Heather Wendt. 2006. "Class Forces, Political Institutions, and State Intervention: Subnational Economic Development Policy in the United States, 1971–1990." *American Journal of Sociology* 111 (4): 1122–1180.

King, James D. 1994. "Political Culture, Registration Laws, and Voter Turnout among the American States." *Publius* 24 (4): 115–127.

Knack, Stephen. 1995. "Does "Motor Voter" Work? Evidence from State-Level Data." *Journal of Politics* 57 (3): 796–811.

Petras, James, and Steve Vieux. 1996. "Shrinking Democracy and Expanding Trade: New Shape of the Imperial State." *Economic and Political Weekly* 31 (30): 2014–2018.

CHAPTER 4

Almond, Gabriel A., and Sidney Verba. 1963. *The Civic Culture: Political Attitudes and Democracy in Five Nations*. Boston: Little, Brown.

Avery, James M., and Mark Peffley. 2005. "Voter Registration Requirements, Voter Turnout, and Welfare Eligibility Policy: Class Bias Matters." *State Politics and Policy Quarterly* 5 (1): 47–67.

Barreto, Matt A., Stephen A. Nuño, and Gabriel R. Sanchez. 2009. "The Disproportionate Impact of Voter-ID Requirements on the Electorate: New Evidence from Indiana." *P.S.: Political Science and Politics* 42 (1): 111–116.

Bentele, Keith G., and Erin E. O'Brien. 2013. "Jim Crow 2.0? Why States Consider and Adopt Restrictive Voter Access Policies." *Perspectives on Politics* 11 (4): 1088–1116.

Berelson, Bernard. 1952. "Democratic Theory and Public Opinion." *Public Opinion* 16 (3): 313–330.

Bullock, Charles S., III. 1988. "Regional Realignment from an Officeholding Perspective." *Journal of Politics* 50 (3): 553–574.

Colomer, Josep M. 1991. "Benefits and Costs of Voting." *Electoral Studies* 10 (4): 313–325.

Cooney, Robert P. J., Jr. 2005. *Winning the Vote: The Triumph of the American Woman Suffrage Movement.* Santa Cruz, CA: American Graphic Press.

DeNardo, James. 1980. "Turnout and the Vote: The Joke's on the Democrats." *American Political Science Review* 74 (2): 406–420.

Elazar, Daniel Judah. 1966. *American Federalism: A View from the States.* Ann Arbor: University of Michigan Press.

Emmert, Craig F., and Carol Ann Traut. 2003. "Bans on Executing the Mentally Retarded: An Event History Analysis of State Policy Adoption." *State and Local Government Review* 35 (2): 112–122.

Engerman, Stanley L., and Kenneth L. Sokoloff. 2005. "The Evolution of Suffrage Institutions in the New World." *Journal of Economic History* 65 (4): 891–921.

Filer, John E., and Lawrence W. Kenny. 1980. "Voter Turnout and the Benefits of Voting." *Public Choice* 35 (5): 575–585.

Fraga, Bernard L. 2018. *The Turnout Gap: Race, Ethnicity, and Political Inequality in a Diversifying America.* New York: Cambridge University Press.

Gray, Virginia, and David Lowery. 1995. "Interest Representation and Democratic Gridlock." *Legislative Studies Quarterly* 20 (4): 531–552.

Griffin, John D., and Brian Newman. 2005. "Are Voters Better Represented?" *Journal of Politics* 67 (4): 1206–1227.

Hajnal, Zoltan, and Jessica Trounstine. 2005. "Where Turnout Matters: The Consequences of Uneven Turnout in City Politics." *Journal of Politics* 67 (2): 515–535.

Hajnal, Zoltan, Nazita Lajevardi, and Lindsay Nielson. 2017. "Voter Identification Laws and the Suppression of Minority Votes." *Journal of Politics* 79 (2): 363–379.

Hayes, Danny, and Seth C. McKee. 2008. "Toward a One-Party South?" *American Politics Research* 36 (1): 3–32.

Hicks, William D., Seth C. McKee, Mitchell D. Sellers, and Daniel A. Smith. 2014. "A Principle or Strategy? Voter Identification Laws and Partisan Competition in the American States." *Political Research Quarterly* 68 (1): 18–33.

Hill, Kim Quaile, and Jan E. Leighley. 1992. "The Policy Consequences of Class Bias in State Electorates." *American Journal of Political Science* 36 (2): 351–365.

Jacobs, David, and Jason T. Carmichael. 2002. "The Political Sociology of the Death Penalty: A Pooled Time-Series Analysis." *American Sociological Review* 67 (1): 109–131.

Levitsky, Steven, and Lucan A. Way. 2010. *Competitive Authoritarianism: Hybrid Regimes after the Cold War.* New York: Cambridge University Press.

Li, Quan, Michael J. Pomante II, and Scot Schraufnagel. 2018. "The Cost of Voting in the American States." *Election Law Journal: Rules, Politics, and Policy* 17 (3): 234–247.

Marquez, Timothy, and Scot Schraufnagel. 2013. "Hispanic Population Growth and State Immigration Policy: An Analysis of Restriction (2008–12)." *Publius: The Journal of Federalism* 43 (3): 1–21.

Rocha, Rene R., and Rodolfo Espino. 2009. "Racial Threat, Residential Segregation, and the Policy Attitudes of Anglos." *Political Research Quarterly* 62 (2): 415–426.

Rocha, Rene R., and Tetsuya Matsubayashi. 2014. "The Politics of Race and Voter ID Laws in the States: The Return of Jim Crow?" *Political Research Quarterly* 67 (3): 666–679.

Sanbonmatsu, Kira. 2002. "Political Parties and the Recruitment of Women to State Legislatures." *Journal of Politics* 64 (3): 791–809.

Schedler, Andreas. 2002. "The Nested Game of Democratization by Elections." *International Political Science* 23 (1): 103–22.

———. 2006. *Electoral Authoritarianism.* Boulder, CO: Lynne Rienner.

Schraufnagel, Scot, Michael J. Pomante II, and Quan Li. 2020. "Cost of Voting in the American States: 2020." *Election Law Journal* 19 (4): 503–509.

Squire, Peverill. 2007. "Measuring State Legislative Professionalism: The Squire Index Revisited." *State Politics & Policy Quarterly* 7 (2): 211–227.

———. 2017. "A Squire Index Update." *State Politics & Policy Quarterly* 17 (4): 361–71.

Stephanopoulos, Nicholas O. 2013. "Our Electoral Exceptionalism." *University of Chicago Law Review* 80 (2): 769–858.

United States Government Accountability Office. 2014. "Elections: Issues Related to State Voter Identification Laws." Report to Congressional Requesters. https://www.gao.gov/assets/gao-14-634.pdf.

CHAPTER 5

Alvarez, Michael R., Delia Bailey, and Jonathan N. Katz. 2011. "An Empirical Bayes Approach to Estimating Ordinal Treatment Effects." *Political Analysis* 19 (1): 721–727.

Ansolabehere, Stephen, and Eitan Hersh. 2012. "Validation: What Big Data Reveal about Survey Misreporting and the Real Electorate." *Political Analysis* 20 (4): 437–459.

Barreto, Matt A. 2005. "Latino Immigrants at the Polls: Foreign-Born Voter Turnout in the 2002 Election." *Political Research Quarterly* 58 (1): 79–86.

Bernstein, Robert, Anita Cahdha, and Robert Montjoy. 2001. "Overreporting Voting: Why It Happens and Why It Matters." *Public Opinion Quarterly* 65 (1): 22–44.

Blais, André, Elizabeth Gidengil, Neil Nevitte, and Richard Nadeau. 2004. "Where Does Turnout Decline Come From?" *European Journal of Political Research* 43 (2): 221–236.

Cahill, Meagan, and Rachel S. Franklin. 2013. "Homeownership, Home Foreclosure, and Nativity: Evidence from Miami-Dade County, Florida." *Journal of Regional Science* 53 (1): 91–117.

Cho, Wendy K. Tam. 1999. "Naturalization, Socialization, Participation: Immigrants and (Non-) Voting." *Journal of Politics* 61 (4): 1140–1155.

de la Garza, Rudolfo O. 1987. *Ignored Voices: Public Opinion Polls and the Latino Community*. Austin: University of Texas Press.

Deufel, Benjamin J., and Orit Kedar. 2010. "Race and Turnout in U.S. Elections: Exposing Hidden Effects." *Public Opinion Quarterly* 47 (2): 286–318.

Filer, John E., Lawrence W. Kenny, and Rebecca B. Morton. 1993. "Redistribution, Income, and Voting." *American Journal of Political Science* 37 (1): 63–87.

Guterbock, Thomas M., and Bruce London. 1983. "Race, Political Orientation, and Participation: An Empirical Test of Four Competing Theories." *American Sociological Review* 48 (4): 439–453.

Hershey, Marjorie Randon. 2009. "What We Know about Voter-ID Laws, Registration, and Turnout." *PS: Political Science & Politics* 42 (1): 87–91.

Highton, Benjamin, and Arthur L. Burris. 2002. "New Perspectives on Latino Voter Turnout in the United States." *American Politics Research* 30 (3): 285–306.

Highton, Benjamin, and Raymond E. Wolfinger. 1998. "Estimating the Effects of the National Voter Registration Act of 1993." *Political Behavior* 20 (2): 79–104.

———. 2001. "The First Seven Years of the Political Life Cycle." *American Journal of Political Science* 45 (1): 202–209.

Holbrook, Allyson L., and Jon A. Krosnick. 2010. "Social Desirability Bias in Voter Turnout Reports: Tests Using the Item Count Technique." *Public Opinion Quarterly* 74 (1): 37–67.

Holbrook, Thomas, and Brianne Heidbreder. 2010. "Does Measurement Matter? The Case of VAP and VEP in Models of Voter Turnout in the United States." *State Politics & Policy Quarterly* 10 (2): 157–179.

Hood, M. V., and Charles S. Bullock. 2012. "Much Ado about Nothing? An Empirical Assessment of the Georgia Voter Identification Statute." *State Politics and Policy Quarterly* 12 (4): 394–414.

Jackson, Robert A. 2003. "Differential Influences on Latino Electoral Participation." *Political Behavior* 25 (4): 339–366.

Juelich, Courtney L., and Joseph A. Coll. 2020. "Rock the Vote or Block the Vote? How the Cost of Voting Affects the Voting Behavior of American Youth." *American Politics Research* 48 (6): 719–724.

Leighley, Jan E., and Arnold Vedlitz. 1999. "Race, Ethnicity, and Political Participation: Competing Models and Contrasting Explanations." *Journal of Politics* 61 (4): 1092–1114.

Li, Quan, Michael J. Pomante II, and Scot Schraufnagel. 2018. "The Cost of Voting in the American States." *Election Law Journal: Rules, Politics, and Policy* 17 (3): 234–247.

Lopez, Mark Hugo, Emily Kirby, and Jared Sagoff. 2003. "Electoral Engagement among Latino Youth." Center for Information & Research on Civic Learning & Engagement. January. https://circle.tufts.edu/sites/default/files/2019-12/FS_Elec toralEngagementLatinoYouth_2003.pdf.

Lyons, William, and John M. Scheb. 1999. "Early Voting and the Timing of the Vote: Unanticipated Consequences of Electoral Reform." *State and Local Government Review* 31 (2): 147–152.

Mabry, William Alexander. 1936. "Louisiana Politics and the 'Grandfather Clause.'" *North Carolina Historical Review* 13 (4): 290–310.

Masuoka, Natalie, Hahrie Han, Vivien Leung, and Bang Quan Zheng. 2018. "Understanding the Asian American Vote in the 2016 Election." *Journal of Race, Ethnicity, and Politics* 3 (1): 189–215.

Masuoka, Natalie, Kumar Ramanathan, and Jane Junn. 2019. "New Asian American Voters: Political Incorporation and Participation in 2016." *Political Research Quarterly* 72 (4): 991–1003.

McCabe, Brian J. 2013. "Are Homeowners Better Citizens? Homeownership and Community Participation in the United States." *Social Forces* 91 (3): 929–954.

McDonald, Michael. 2002. "The Turnout Rate among Eligible Voters for U.S. States 1980–2000." *State Politics and Policy Quarterly* 2 (2): 199–212.

Olsen, Marvin E. 1970. "Social and Political Participation of Blacks." *American Sociological Review* 35 (4): 682–697.

Ricketts, Erol R., and Isabel V. Sawhill. 1988. "Defining and Measuring the Underclass." *Journal of Policy Analysis and Management* 7 (2): 316–325.

Ritter, Michael, and Caroline J. Tolbert. 2021. *Accessible Elections: How the States Can Help Americans Vote.* New York: Oxford University Press.

Rocha, Rene R., and Tetsuya Matsubayashi. 2014. "The Politics of Race and Voter ID Laws in the States: The Return of Jim Crow?" *Political Research Quarterly* 67 (3): 666–679.

Rosenstone, Steven J. 1982. "Economic Adversity and Voter Turnout." *American Journal of Political Science* 26 (1): 24–46.

Sigelman, Lee. 1982. "The Nonvoting Voter in Voting Research." *American Journal of Political Science* 26 (1): 47–56.

Silver, Brian D., Barbara A. Anderson, and Paul R. Abramson. 1986. "Who Overreports Voting?" *American Political Science Review* 80 (2): 613–624.

Springer, Melanie J. 2012. "State Electoral Institutions and Voter Turnout in Presidential Elections, 1920–2000." *State Politics & Policy Quarterly* 12 (3): 252–283.

Squire, Peverill, Raymond E. Wolfinger, and David Glass. 1987. "Residential Mobility and Voter Turnout." *American Political Science Review* 81 (1): 45–65.

Tate, Katherine. *From Protest to Politics: The New Black Voters in American Elections.* Cambridge, MA: Harvard University Press, 1994.

Timpone, Richard J. 1998. "Structure, Behavior, and Voter Turnout in the United States." *American Political Science Review* 92 (1): 145–185.

Tolbert, Caroline J., and Ramona S. McNeal. 2003. "Unraveling the Effects of the Internet on Political Participation." *Political Research Quarterly* 56 (2): 175–185.

Uhlaner, Carole J., Bruce E. Cain, and Roderick Kiewiet. 1989. "Political Participation of Ethnic Minorities in the 1980s." *Political Behavior* 11 (3): 195–231.

Verba, Sydney, and Norman H. Nie. 1972. *Participation in America: Political Democracy and Social Equality.* New York: Harper & Row.

Wolfinger, Nicholas H., and Raymond E. Wolfinger. 2008. "Family Structure and Voter Turnout." *Social Forces* 96 (4): 1513–1528.

Wong, Paul, Chienping Faith Lai, and Richard Nagasawa. 1998. "Asian Americans as a Model Minority: Self-Perceptions and Perceptions by Other Racial Groups." *Sociological Perspectives* 41 (1): 95–118.

Xu, Jun. 2005. "Why Do Minorities Participate Less? The Effects of Immigration, Education, and Electoral Process on Asian American Voter Registration and Turnout." *Social Science Research* 34 (4): 682–702.

CHAPTER 6

Abascal, Maria. 2015. "Us and Them: Black-White Relationships in the Wake of Hispanic Population Growth." *American Sociological Review* 80 (4): 78–813.

Dolan, Kathleen. 2014. *When Does Gender Matter?* Oxford: Oxford University Press.

Engstrom, Erik J. 2013. *Gerrymandering and the Construction of American Democracy.* Ann Arbor: University of Michigan Press.

Hicks, William D., Carl E. Klarner, Seth C. McKee, and Daniel A. Smith. 2017. "Revisiting Majority-Minority Districts and Black Representation." *Political Research Quarterly* 71 (2): 1–16.

Htun, Mala. 2004. "Is Gender Like Ethnicity? The Political Representation of Identity Groups." *Perspectives on Politics* 2 (3): 439–458.

Hummel, Patrick. 2014. "Pre-election Polling and Third Party Candidates." *Social Choice and Welfare* 42 (1): 77–98.

Johnson, Kenneth M., and Daniel T. Lichter. 2008. "Natural Increase: A New Source of Population Growth in Emerging Hispanic Destinations in the United States." *Population and Development Review* 34 (2): 327–346.

Kao, Grace, and Jennifer S. Thompson. 2003. "Racial and Ethnic Stratification in Educational Achievement and Attainment." *Annual Review of Sociology* 29 (1): 417–442.

Lijphart, Arend. 1997. "Unequal Participation: Democracy's Unresolved Dilemma." *American Political Science Review* 91 (1): 1–14.

Lowande, Kenneth, Melinda Ritchie, and Erinn Lauterback. 2019. "Descriptive and Substantive Representation in Congress: Evidence from 80,000 Congressional Inquiries." *American Journal of Political Science* 63 (3): 644–659.

Mangum, Maurice. 2013. "The Racial Underpinnings of Party Identification and Political Ideology." *Social Science Quarterly* 94 (5): 1222–1244.

Mehmetoglu, Mehmet, and Tor Georg Jakobsen. 2017. *Applied Statistics Using Stata.* London: Sage.

Michener, Jamila, and Margaret Teresa Brower. 2020. "What's Policy Got to Do with It? Race, Gender and Economic Inequality in the United States." *Daedalus* 149 (1): 100–118.

Schnieder, Monica C., Mirya R. Holman, Amanda B. Diekman, and Thomas McAndrew. 2016. "Power, Conflict, and Community: How Gendered Views of Political Power Influence Women's Political Ambition." *International Society of Political Psychology* 37 (4): 515–531.

Schraufnagel, Scot. 2011. *Third Party Blues.* London: Routledge.

Shah, Paru. 2014. "It Takes a Black Candidate: A Supply-Side Theory of Minority Representation." *Political Research Quarterly* 67 (2): 266–279.

Smith, Adrienne R., Beth Reingold, and Michael Leo Owens. 2012. "The Political Determinants of Women's Descriptive Representation in Cities." *Political Research Quarterly* 65 (2): 315–329.

Squire, Peverill. 2007. "Measuring State Legislative Professionalism: The Squire Index Revisited." *State Politics & Policy Quarterly* 7 (2): 211–227.

———. 2017. "A Squire Index Update." *State Politics & Policy Quarterly* 17 (4): 361–71.

Thomsen, Danielle M. 2015. "Why So Few (Republican) Women? Explaining the Partisan Imbalance of Women in U.S. Congress." *Legislative Studies Quarterly* 40 (2): 295–323.

CHAPTER 7

Ahlquist, John S., Kenneth R. Mayer, and Simon Jackman. 2014. "Alien Abduction and Voter Impersonation in the 2012 U.S. General Election: Evidence from a Survey List Experiment." *Election Law Journal* 13:460–475.

Beber, Bernd, and Alexandra Scacco. 2012. "What the Numbers Say: A Digit-Based Test for Election Fraud." *Political Analysis* 20: 211–234.

Benson, George C. S. 1978. *Political Corruption in America.* Lexington, MA: Lexington Books.

Burnham, Walter Dean. 1986. "Those Nineteenth Century American Voting Turnouts: Fact or Fiction?" *Journal of Interdisciplinary History* 16:613–644.

Christensen, Ray, and Thomas J. Schultz. 2014. "Identifying Election Fraud Using Orphan and Low Propensity Voters." *American Politics Research* 42 (2): 311–337.

Citrin, Jack, Eric Schickler, and John Sides. 2003. "What If Everyone Voted? Simulating the Impact of Increased Turnout in Senate Elections." *American Journal of Political Science* 47 (1): 75–90.

Cottrell, David, Michael C. Herron, and Sean J. Westwood. 2018. "An Exploration of Donald Trump's Allegations of Massive Voter Fraud in the 2016 General Election." *Electoral Studies* 51: 123–142.

DeNardo, James. 1980. "Turnout and the Vote: The Joke's on the Democrats." *American Political Science Review* 74 (2): 406–420.

Downs, Anthony. 1957. *An Economic Theory of Democracy.* New York: Harper and Row.

Elazar, Daniel J. 1966. *American Federalism: A View from the States.* New York: Thomas Y. Crowell.

Fukumoto, Kentaro, and Yusaku Horiuchi. 2011. "Making Outsiders Count: Detecting Electoral Fraud through a Natural Experiment." *American Political Science Review* 105 (3): 586–603.

Gienapp, William E. 1982. "'Politics Seem to Enter everything:' Political Culture in the North." In *Essays on American Antebellum Politics, 1840–60*, edited by Stephen E. Maizlish and John J. Kushma, 25–32. College Station: Texas A&M University Press.

Goel, Sharad, Marc Meredith, Michael Morse, David Rothschild, and Houshmand Shirani-Mehr. 2020. "One Person, One Vote: Estimating the Prevalence of Double Voting in U.S. Presidential Elections." *American Political Science Review* 114 (2): 456–469.

Holman, Mirya R., and J. Celeste Lay. 2019. "They See Dead People (Voting): Correcting Misperceptions about Voter Fraud in the 2016 US Presidential Election." *Journal of Political Marketing* 18 (1–2): 31–68.

Hood III, M. V., and William Gillespie. 2012. "They Just Do Not Vote Like They Used To: A Methodology to Empirically Assess Election Fraud." *Social Science Quarterly* 93 (1): 76–94.

Keyssar, Alexander. 2000. *The Right to Vote: The Contested History of Democracy in the United States.* New York: Basic Books.

Levitt, Justin. 2007. *The Truth about Voter Fraud.* New York: Brennan Center for Justice.

Li, Quan, Michael J. Pomante, and Scot Schraufnagel. 2018. "The Cost of Voting in the American States." *Election Law Journal* 17 (3): 234–247.

Lichtman, Allan J. 2018. *The Embattled Vote in America: From the Founding to the Present.* Cambridge, MA: Harvard University Press.

Malesky, Edmund, Paul Schuler, and Anh Tran. 2012. "The Adverse Effects of Sunshine: A Field Experiment on Legislative Transparency in an Authoritarian Assembly." *American Political Science Review* 106 (4): 762–786.

Minnite, Lorraine C. 2010. *The Myth of Voter Fraud.* Ithaca, NY: Cornell University Press.

Montgomery, Jacob M., Santiago Olivella, Joshua D. Potter, and Brian F. Crisp. 2015. "An Informed Forensics Approach to Detecting Vote Irregularities." *Political Analysis* 23: 488–505.

Pericchi, Luis, and David Torres. 2011. "Quick Anomaly Detection by the Newcomb-Bedford Law, with Applications to Electoral Processes Data from the USA, Puerto Rico, and Venezuela." *Statistical Science* 26 (4): 502–516.

Powell, G. Bingham. 1986. "American Voter Turnout in Comparative Perspective." *American Political Science Review* 80 (1): 17–43.

Riker, William H., and Peter C. Ordeshook. 1968. "A Theory of the Calculus of Voting." *American Political Science Review* 62 (1): 25–42.

Schraufnagel, Scot, Michael J. Pomante II, and Quan Li. 2020. "The Cost of Voting in the American States: 2020." *Election Law Journal* 19 (4): 503–509.

Summers, Mark W. 1987. *The Plundering Generation: Corruption and the Crisis of the Union, 1849–61.* New York: Oxford University Press.

Udani, Adriano, and David C. Kimball. 2018. "Immigrant Resentment and Voter Fraud Beliefs in the U.S. Electorate." *American Politics Research* 46 (3): 402–433.

van Ham, Carolien, and Staffan I. Lindberg. 2015. "From Sticks to Carrots: Electoral Manipulation in Africa, 1986–2012." *Government and Opposition* 50 (3): 521–448.

Wilner, Alex S. 2018. "Cybersecurity and Its Discontents: Artificial Intelligence, the Internet of Things, and Digital Misinformation." *International Journal* 73 (2): 308–316.

CHAPTER 8

DeNardo, James. 1980. "Turnout and the Vote: The Joke's on the Democrats." *American Political Science Review* 74 (2): 406–420.

Highton, Benjamin, and Raymond E. Wolfinger. 2001. "The First Seven Years of the Political Life Cycle." *American Journal of Political Science* 45 (1): 202–209.

Nagel, Jack H., and John E. McNulty. 1996. "Partisan Effects of Voter Turnout in Senatorial and Gubernatorial Elections." *American Political Science Review* 90 (4): 780–793.

Sides, John, Eric Schickler, and Jack Citrin. 2008. "If Everyone Had Voted, Would Bubba and Dubya Have Won?" *Presidential Studies Quarterly* 38 (3): 521–539.

Webster, Gerald R. 1992. "Demise of the Solid South." *Geographical Review* 82 (1): 43–55.

CONCLUSION

Avery, James M., and Mark Peffley. 2005. "Voter Registration Requirements, Voter Turnout, and Welfare Eligibility Policy: Class Bias Matters." *State Politics and Policy Quarterly* 5 (1): 47–67.

Bühlmann, Marc, Wolfgang Merkel, and Bernhard Weßels. 2012. "The Democracy Barometer: A New Instrument to Measure the Quality of Democracy and its Potential for Comparative Research." *European Political Science* 11 (4): 519–536.

Epperly, Brad, Christopher Witko, Ryan Strickler, and Paul White. 2020. "Rule by Violence, Rule by Law: Lynching, Jim Crow, and the Continuing Evolution of Voter Suppression in the US." *Perspectives on Politics* 18 (3): 756–769.

Griffin, John D., and Brian Newman. 2005. "Are Voters Better Represented?" *Journal of Politics* 67 (4): 1206–1227.

Hajnal, Zoltan, and Jessica Trounstine. 2005. "Where Turnout Matters: The Consequences of Uneven Turnout in City Politics." *Journal of Politics* 67 (2): 515–535.

Hill, Kim Quaile, and Jan E. Leighley. 1992. "The Policy Consequences of Class Bias in State Electorates." *American Journal of Political Science* 36 (2): 351–365.

APPENDIX A

Brady, Henry E., and John E. McNulty. 2011. "Turning Out to Vote: The Costs of Finding and Getting to the Polling Place." *American Political Science Review* 105 (1): 115–134.

Haspel, Moshe, and H. Gibbs Knotts. 2005. "Location, Location, Location: Precinct Placement and Costs of Voting." *Journal of Politics* 67 (2): 560–573.

Index

www.ingramcontent.com/pod-product-compliance
Lightning Source LLC
Chambersburg PA
CBHW030356270326
41926CB00009B/1127